Choosing Choice

SCHOOL CHOICE
IN INTERNATIONAL PERSPECTIVE

Choosing Choice

SCHOOL CHOICE IN INTERNATIONAL PERSPECTIVE

David N. Plank
Gary Sykes
EDITORS

Teachers College
Columbia University
New York and London

We dedicate this book to Susan Drabik,
who does the hard and noble work of teaching every day;
and to Jane Miller,
whose passion for education and generous support
serve as an example for us all.

Published by Teachers College Press, 1234 Amsterdam Avenue, New York, NY 10027

Library of Congress Cataloging-in-Publication Data

Choosing choice : school choice in international perspective / David N. Plank, Gary Sykes, ediors.
    p. cm.
  Includes bibliographical references and index.
  ISBN 0-8077-4291-0 (cloth)
    1. School choice—Cross-cultural studies. I. Title: School choice in international perspective. II. Plank, David Nathan, 1954– III. Sykes, Gary.
LB1027.9.C534 2003
379.1′11—dc21   2002038431

ISBN 0-8077-4291-0 (cloth)

Printed on acid-free paper

Manufactured in the United States of America

10   09   08   07   06   05   04   03   8   7   6   5   4   3   2   1

Contents

Why School Choice?

David N. Plank
Gary Sykes

School choice policies are sweeping the globe. In countries on every continent, governments have decided that giving parents more choices among schools is an appropriate policy response to local educational problems. Not surprisingly, the problems that school choice policies are expected to address vary widely across countries, and so do the details of policy design. Nevertheless, increasing reliance on markets is generally accepted as a plausible strategy for encouraging improvement in the educational opportunities that governments provide for their citizens.

Although widespread, the move to give parents more choices about their children's education is not universal. In some countries parents have always had choices about the schools their children attend. In Belgium and the Netherlands, for example, students have for a century been able to take state funding to the schools of their choice, including religious schools. In much of Latin America, schools do not have attendance zones, and parents' choices are limited only by their ability to pay the costs of tuition or transportation.

In other countries governments have shown little enthusiasm for school choice policies. Cuba's highly regarded public school system remains tightly regulated, with virtually no options for parents. In France and Germany, traditional norms of equity and standardized treatment continue to hold sway, and judgments about schooling remain the prerogative of the state and educational professionals. In Japan parents have few opportunities to choose schools within the regular school system, but there is a thriving market for *juku* ("cram schools") and other supplementary educational programs.

These are the exceptions, however, and even in these countries the pressure to give parents more choices is increasing (Organisation for Economic Cooperation and Development [OECD], 1994). In most parts of the world, governments are moving steadily and often boldly to increase choice and competition in the educational system. They are giving parents more freedom to choose the schools that their children attend, and they are introducing policies that make the funding—and ultimately the survival—of schools dependent on their success in attracting and retaining pupils. Some are moving away from standardized educational provision and encouraging diversity in the kinds of schools and curricula from which parents make their choices.

The obvious question is: Why? Why are polices that expand the educational options available to parents being adopted in such a diverse set of countries? Why have governments in widely varying circumstances come to view school choice policies as an apt response to the educational issues that they face? These are the questions that we seek to answer in this brief essay.

WHAT IS "SCHOOL CHOICE"?

Moves to expand school choice may encompass a wide variety of policy options, ranging from the creation of alternative programs within individual schools to the provision of fully portable vouchers. Governments in the countries discussed in the case studies that follow have created a remarkably diverse array of policies in their common effort to give parents more choices. The specific features of a country's policy differ not only from country to country but also across time within countries.

For our purposes here, school choice policies have two essential features. First, on the demand side of the emerging market for schooling, they give parents more choices about the schools their children attend. In an "ideal type" state-centered education system, attendance at school is compulsory, and children are assigned to schools strictly on the basis of some set of "objective" criteria. Children are often assigned to attend a particular school on the basis of residence in a clearly defined attendance zone, but assignments may also be based on gender, race, or measured aptitude. With the introduction of school choice policies, the power of the state to assign children to specific schools declines and parents' power to choose their children's school correspondingly increases.

On the supply side of the market, school choice policies produce an explicit or implicit competition among schools for students and revenues. In the traditional state-centered system, students and revenues "belong" to specific schools. Parents can change their child's school only with considerable difficulty, by changing residence or (in most countries, but not all) leaving the public school system and paying tuition for private schooling. With the advent of school choice policies, however, schools no longer "own" their students. Parents can leave schools they dislike for schools they prefer, taking some share of public funding with them, and schools must consequently make a more concerted effort to attract and retain students.

There is considerable variability across countries and across time in the implementation of these two essential features of school choice policies. For example, under some policies parents may be *required* to choose a school, while under others they retain an entitlement to a place in the local public school. Some policies restrict the competition among schools to schools in the public sector, while others expand the market to include private and religious schools as well. Countries also vary in the extent to which governments provide ancillary services to support parents' choices, including such things as student transportation and the production and distribution of information about schools. The extent to which these services are publicly subsidized has a powerful effect on how the emerging market for schooling operates. In all of the countries discussed in this book, though, and in many others besides, school choice policies based on these two essential features have become an increasingly central feature of the educational system.

WHY SCHOOL CHOICE?

Why are governments around the world moving to adopt school choice policies? This question is especially intriguing because experience with these policies has been relatively brief. The idea that school choice might have desirable consequences for both children and schools has been around for some time (West, 1965), but the first moves by governments to introduce market forces into state-centered education systems were made in the 1970s. The evidence that school choice policies "work" remains provisional and equivocal, even in countries where choice policies have been in place for some time, but the move toward choice and competition in national education systems appears inexorable. In virtually no country is there a serious effort to expand the role of the state in educational provision or to restrict the educational choices of parents. How can we explain this?

We argue that the convergence of four interrelated trends lies behind the growing enthusiasm of governments around the world for

school choice policies. Changes in the intellectual, institutional, political, and demographic environments of national education systems
are all pushing governments in the same direction, toward policies
that offer parents more choices about the schools their children attend
and encourage schools to compete for students and revenues.

INTELLECTUAL AND IDEOLOGICAL SHIFTS

Just as governments have moved to expand school choice in response
to a number of different policy problems, analysts and advocates have
based their claims for choice on a variety of diverse and sometimes
competing arguments. Even more important than the variety of arguments in favor of school choice, however, is the virtual absence of a
politically credible alternative. The decisive fact is not the power of
arguments for market-based policies but the collapse of a plausible
argument in favor of standardized, state-centered educational provision. Governments around the world have worked energetically and
often feverishly for most of a century to build public school systems
that would provide educational opportunities for all of the nation's
children. As the goal has come into sight, however, the idea that standardized public educational provision is a worthy or desirable objective has been challenged from four distinct points of view.

The Construction of Community

One critique of the traditional public school system indicts the
bureaucratization and standardization of state-centered systems as in-
imical to the construction of community in and around schools. The
desire to create or encourage communities of value in schools has
been an important feature of school choice policies in a number of
countries, including Australia, New Zealand, Sweden, and the United
States. The affirmation of "community" values in education can take
a number of different forms, but proponents share a central premise:
that schools able to call on the shared values and purposes of a community are richer in social capital and more likely to succeed than
schools relying exclusively on the bureaucratic authority of the state
(Bryk, Lee, & Holland, 1993; Coleman & Hoffer, 1987; B. Fuller, 2001).

Equity and the Right to Choose

A second argument on behalf of expanded school choice decries the
unequal distribution of educational resources and opportunities in the

state-centered school system. Parents must be permitted to "escape" from the inadequate and unsuccessful schools in which attendance zones and bureaucratic regulations have "trapped" them. This argument has been especially salient in countries characterized by deep inequalities, including South Africa and the United States. Proponents note that prosperous households have always had choices about the schools their children attend, and they demand that poor families be offered the same range of opportunities (Coons, Clune, & Sugarman, 1969; H. Fuller, 2000; Jencks, 1966).

"Reinventing Government" and the Quest for Efficiency

A third argument is premised on populist dissatisfaction with government, rooted on one hand in resistance to burdensome taxation and regulation, and on the other in widespread perceptions of inefficiency, waste, and sometimes corruption in the public sector. In some countries, including Sweden and the United Kingdom, public authorities responded to these pressures by reducing taxes, cutting back regulations, decentralizing administrative authority, and increasing reliance on private actors and incentives to accomplish public purposes.

Closely associated with efforts to "reinvent government" are apprehensions about maintaining or increasing international competitiveness. Much of the hand-wringing about keeping up in the global economy asserts or assumes that national economic success is dependent upon the education of the nation's work force (Marshall & Tucker, 1993; Reich, 1991). Faced with political pressure to dramatically improve the performance of the educational system, governments have responded with policies that seek to reduce costs, increase efficiency, and spur enhanced performance by encouraging choice and competition in the education system.

Neo-liberalism and Free Markets

A final set of arguments has featured strong claims about the intrinsic frailties and incapacities of states and governments, accompanied by claims for the virtues of markets as instruments for solving a host of public and private problems. The enthusiasm of economists and others for the "magic of the market" has produced recommendations for privatizing virtually all the activities of the public sector, from pensions to prisons. In education, these arguments have been deployed in support of vouchers and increased private-sector participation in educational provision. Arguments that urge governments to "unleash" market forces in the education system have been powerfully influential in a number of countries, including Chile, the Czech Republic, the United Kingdom, and the United States.

The power and influence of these four arguments for increased choice and competition in the education system has been greatly enhanced by the virtual absence of a strong, positive argument in favor of state-centered educational policies. The claims put forward by the opponents of school choice policies typically aim to protect schools and students against the damage that markets can cause, rather than to affirm the advantages of public provision and standardization in the education system. The more potent arguments traditionally deployed by supporters of public education, featuring claims about the equalization of opportunities or the affirmation of a common culture, seem increasingly threadbare.

This absence has had two kinds of consequences. First, in countries previously committed to central planning and strict public regulation of the education system, like China and the Czech Republic, the policy vacuum left by the collapse or abandonment of socialist policies was filled mainly by free-market ideas. Second, in countries that first moved to adopt school choice policies under conservative governments, as in Chile, Sweden, and the United Kingdom, the return to power of centrist or left-wing governments has produced adjustments to school choice policies that aim to make the market for schooling work more efficiently and more fairly rather than to reaffirm state-centered policies.

TRANSNATIONAL INSTITUTIONS

Education is an increasingly standardized social service. As John Meyer and his colleagues have argued, the provision of education is deeply institutionalized, governed by norms and practices that are widely diffused around the world (Meyer, Ramirez, Rubinson, & Boli-Bennett, 1977; Meyer, Kamens, & Benavot, 1992). For example, education is almost universally provided in age-graded classrooms under the direction of professionally certified teachers. Over time, there has been a dramatic decline in variation across countries in the structure and organization of national school systems, including curricula. Fourth-graders from Argentina to Zimbabwe study fractions and learn about weather. Under these circumstances, conformity to globally sanctioned organizational models and institutionalized practices is deemed "normal." Divergence from these practices comes to appear irrational.

The emergence of a world education system means that policy innovations adopted and approved in one part of the system diffuse quickly. Information about policy innovation spreads rapidly through the system, even when change originates on the periphery (e.g., in Chile or New Zealand). Policies legitimated by adoption in core countries are widely imitated—indeed, resistance to such policies comes to seem retrograde and irrational. The press to "keep up" with powerful trends in the world system may quickly become irresistible.

Closely associated with the emergence of a deeply institutionalized and increasingly global model of schooling is the emergence of transnational agencies and networks that are explicitly responsible for diffusing policy information and advice to governments around the world. The World Bank and the OECD are especially influential. The World Bank has been a strong advocate for decentralization and market-based education policies in developing countries (World Bank, 1989, 1990, 1992). Policy advocacy has been backed up with loans, the disbursement of which are often made conditional on the adoption of policies approved by the Bank.

The OECD has less power than the World Bank to prescribe policies to its member governments, but it has been active in the dissemination of information about choice policies and "best practices" (OECD, 1994). Private foundations and "think tanks" have also played a key role in the United States and elsewhere. These agencies—institutionally and sometimes ideologically committed to free markets—have encouraged governments to adopt market-based policies in a number of different sectors, including health care and transportation as well as education.

SHIFTING PARENTAL PREFERENCES

School choice policies have also emerged in response to changing preferences about education among parents. Families are having fewer children in many parts of the world, and parents are consequently more concerned about the schooling that individual children receive (Schultz, 1974, 1981). Their concern is enhanced by the increasingly powerful connection between educational attainment and occupational success in information-based economies. As access to elite positions has come to depend mainly and sometimes entirely on educational attainment and the acquisition of specialized credentials, parents are naturally preoccupied with ensuring that their children obtain the best possible schooling.

Second, as universal access to schooling has been achieved, pressures to differentiate educational services have also emerged. When all children go to school (and, in a growing number of countries, graduate), going to school and staying in school are no longer a sufficient guarantee of occupational success. Well-off parents consequently seek strategies to maintain their children's privileges, and upwardly aspiring parents seek strategies to escape from the schools to which their children are assigned. These strategies may include demands for new opportunities to choose among schools, for public subsidies for private schools, or for vouchers. In New Zealand and South Africa, for example, school choice policies have created new opportunities for knowledgeable but otherwise disadvantaged parents to enroll their children in the best or most prestigious schools.

In addition, as parents take a deeper interest in their children's education, some may wish to achieve a closer match between the character of a school and their own educational preferences or the specific aptitudes of their children. Some parents may prefer particular curricula or instructional strategies (e.g., Montessori, foreign-language immersion), while others may seek out schools that specialize in working with children with specific talents or disabilities.

Finally, the universalization of educational access and the standardization of educational programs have been accompanied by increasingly assertive demands from ethnic or linguistic minorities to sustain or affirm their communities and cultures by providing specialized schools or programs. In New Zealand some schools have adopted a curricular focus on Maori culture and language; in Sweden schools have opened that offer programs designed specifically for Muslim immigrants. Similar developments can be observed in the United States and the United Kingdom.

THE ECONOMICS AND POLITICS OF SCHOOL CHOICE

School choice policies are especially appealing in an environment in which governments find it difficult to increase their revenues because they seemingly offer something for nothing. In contrast to other possible approaches to improving the performance of the education system, choice calls upon the "magic of the market" to spur improvement. From the point of view of public finance, competition is nearly costless, whereas other strategies, including improved training or compensation for teachers or increased reliance on technology, can be quite expensive.

Better yet, school choice policies may offer an opportunity for governments to shift some of the costs of education to the private sector, either through the recruitment of private companies to offer educational services or through the imposition of school fees or other costs on parents. This is an explicit purpose of school choice policies in China and South Africa, but it may be an important, if veiled, element of policies in countries where the subsidies provided to students in private and religious schools are smaller than the subsidies provided to students in regular public schools.

The desire of governments to shift some of the cost of schooling off the public budget may be reinforced by the desire of private-sector actors to increase their role in providing and managing schools. Policies that permit for-profit enterprises to compete with traditional public schools have been especially influential in countries where the demand for more and more varied educational opportunities has been intense, including Chile, China, the Czech Republic, and South Africa. The participation of private companies in the education system has relieved the pressure for public provision, while allowing some educational entrepreneurs to prosper. Moves toward privatization have been less significant in wealthier countries, but there has been increased private-sector participation in some countries, including the United States.

CHOICE IS HERE TO STAY

From the middle of the 19th century to the end of the 20th, the expansion and institutionalization of schooling were closely associated with the growing power of the modern state. In the past decade, though, we have seen the emergence of increasingly powerful challenges to the state's dominant (and in some countries exclusive) role in the provision of education. These challenges have converged in policies that give parents more choices about the schools their children attend. It is not yet clear whether this will produce new kinds of schooling or simply variations on the current model, but the move to increase choice and competition in the education system is unlikely to be reversed.

This does not mean that the power of the state in the education system has been fully and finally eclipsed. The current enthusiasm for markets as the solution to a host of public and private problems will almost certainly wane over time, as the consequences of market failure begin to manifest themselves. By their nature, markets create both winners and losers. As the losses associated with the emerging market for schooling become more evident, the regulatory role of the state and educational professionals will once again increase.

New policies that strengthen the regulatory powers of the central state have already been implemented in several of the countries that were among the earliest and most enthusiastic adopters of school choice policies. In New Zealand and the United Kingdom, for example, central governments have increased the regulatory authority of school inspectors in an effort to ensure compliance with national rules and standards. In Chile resumption of democratic government was quickly followed by policies that provided additional resources to high-poverty, low-performing schools and that also imposed new regulations on the labor market for teachers. In the United States and several other countries, the move to decentralize authority and expand choice in the education system has been accompanied by simultaneous efforts to codify and strengthen centrally defined standards for student and school performance.

Lindblom (2001) characterizes the dialectic between market and state as a three-act play:

> In the theater of efficient social coordination, Act I belongs to the state, in which, half-blindly and not efficiently, it makes the prior determinations that set the course for the next act. Act II belongs to the transactions of the market system. A long act with much audience participation, it moves not to but in the direction of an efficient ending. It cannot achieve that ending because it is limited to playing out the consequences of the first act. Act III again belongs to the state, which tries in its often blundering way to bring everyone the rest of the way to an efficient ending, largely through the redistributions of the welfare state. The state is only half aware that the obstacles are not only the failures of Act II but its own performances in Act I. It is a long-running play in which Act III always becomes Act I of the next performance, for which a new Act III is then written. (pp. 176–177)

Market-oriented policy is thus not a replacement for, but rather an instrument of, state action in the education system. The current move toward market-based policies to address social problems, including education, will in time produce demands for state efforts to correct the inequities and inefficiencies of the emerging market for schooling. The challenge that faces policy makers is therefore to devise policies that harness the power of choice and competition to bring about improvement in the educational opportunities provided for all children. Reflection on the growing number of international experiences with school choice policies can make an important contribution to this goal. It gives policy makers the opportunity to learn from the successes and mistakes of others as they move to expand opportunities for choice in their own education systems.

PLAN OF THE BOOK

The chapters in this book were originally prepared for a conference at Michigan State University, in March 2000, on the issue of "School Choice and Educational Change." The opening sessions of the conference focused on the adoption and implementation of school choice policies in nine countries: Australia, Chile, China, the Czech Republic, Hungary, New Zealand, South Africa, Sweden, and the United Kingdom. Each of the authors addressed the question of how the introduction of choice and competition had changed the educational system in a particular country.

The countries represented at the conference were chosen to reflect the wide diversity of international experiences with school choice. To date, virtually all the available comparative literature on choice has focused on a handful of Anglophone countries, including Australia, Canada, New Zealand, and the United Kingdom (e.g., Glatter, Woods, & Bagley, 1997; Lauder & Hughes, 1999). Some work has examined school choice policies in a broader sample of European countries (OECD, 1994; Walford, 1996), and there have been excellent case studies of individual countries, including Chile (Gauri, 1998) and New Zealand (Fiske & Ladd, 2000). Until now, though, there has not been any systematic effort to look at school choice and its impacts in a genuinely global perspective. This is a major omission, which the chapters in this book begin to rectify.

In her introductory chapter, Helen Ladd provides a comparative analysis of the lessons learned from international experiences with school choice policies, based on a review of the country case studies. She argues that reflection on how choice and competition have affected other countries' education systems can make a valuable contribution to policy development in the United States and elsewhere. On the one hand, these international experiences can generate new ideas for policy makers charged with the design of school choice policies. On the other hand, the lessons learned in other countries can help to identify the kinds of policy safeguards that are necessary to minimize the damage that the emerging market for schooling can do to schools and students.

The first two case studies report on school choice policies in Chile and New Zealand, the two countries that have moved most aggressively to introduce choice and competition into their education systems. Martin Carnoy and Patrick McEwan analyze the impact of Chile's national voucher plan, which was adopted in 1980. Under Chile's plan, parents may send their children to public, private, or religious schools; public funding follows the child to whatever school the parents choose. Carnoy and McEwan analyze data on student mobility and achievement to address three main questions. First, they ask whether private schools provide more effective, less costly instruction than public schools. Second, they seek to determine whether the competition among schools produced by the introduction of vouchers has had a positive impact on Chile's education system. Finally, they ask which families have taken advantage of school choice policies and what characteristics of schools influence their choices.

Edward Fiske and Helen Ladd review New Zealand's experience with school choice policies in their chapter. In the late 1980s New Zealand transformed its public education system, moving from a highly centralized and heavily bureaucratized system to one in which all schools were required to become self-governing. In addition, parents were given new opportunities to choose the schools their children would attend. Fiske and Ladd assess the consequences of these policy changes for schools and students, with a particular focus on how the introduction of choice and competition affected education systems in the urban areas of Auckland, Christchurch, and Wellington.

The two chapters that follow review experiences with school choice in England and Sweden, where government policies have sought to encourage competition among schools. Since the mid-1980s, a series of Conservative and Labour governments in England have experimented with policies that shift administrative and financial control to the school level and encourage parents to make choices among schools. Geoffrey Walford provides a synthesis of the rich scholarly literature on how school choice policies have changed England's education system, giving particular attention to the criteria that parents use to choose schools for their children and to the consequences of choice for social outcomes and academic performance.

In his chapter on Sweden, Holger Daun explores the tensions that have accompanied the introduction of choice and competition into an education system traditionally dedicated to the principle of equivalent educational opportunities. Since the beginning of the 1990s, Swedish governments have moved to give parents more choices about the schools that their children attend and to increase the financial support that independent schools receive from the government. Daun asks whether these policies have been a spur to improvement in Sweden's education system, and how school choice policies have influenced the development of Swedish education at both the school and system levels.

Max Angus reviews Australia's experience with school choice in his chapter, focusing on the complex relationships between state and federal policies, and between public and private schools. As a consequence of a series of policy choices dating back to the 1970s, the share of enrollments in private and religious schools has increased steadily in Australia, to the point where nearly one-third of all students are enrolled in nonpublic schools. The dramatic growth of the private sector has lately been encouraged by state and federal policies that introduce choice, competition, and quasi-market mechanisms into the school system. Angus analyzes these developments and assesses their implications for the future of public education in Australia.

The authors of the three concluding chapters review experiences with school choice policies in countries that are now emerging from decades of authoritarian government, under which parents' opportunities to choose schools were tightly restricted. John Pampallis examines how the end of apartheid in South Africa has opened up opportunities for parents to move their children from schools reserved for members of their own "racial" classification to schools previously restricted to children from other groups. The government's policies have introduced new options for many families, while simultaneously reinforcing new inequalities in the education system.

The Chinese government's move to introduce market forces and private-sector participation into the economy has created new opportunities for a variety of public and private actors to open new schools. This has produced new choices for parents in some parts of China, especially in urban areas. In his chapter, Mun Tsang analyzes the emergence of the nonstate school sector in China and provides detailed descriptions of institutional innovations in schooling in the urban communities of Tianjan and Beijing.

In the final chapter, Randall Filer and Daniel Munich provide an account of the rise of the nonstate school sector in the Czech Republic and Hungary. Private and religious schools have assumed an increasingly important role in the education systems of both countries in the years since the collapse of communism in 1989. Filer and Munich address a number of questions, including where nonstate schools are located, what kinds of programs and services nonstate schools offer, and how public schools are beginning to respond to their new competitors.

REFERENCES

Bryk, A. S., Lee, V. E., & Holland, P. B. (1993). *Catholic schools and the common good*. Cambridge, MA: Harvard University Press.

Coleman, J. S., & Hoffer, T. (1987). *Public and private high schools: The impact of communities*. New York: Basic Books.

Coons, J., Clune, W., & Sugarman, S. (1969). *Private wealth and public education*. Cambridge, MA: Belknap Press of Harvard University Press.

Fiske, E. B., & Ladd, H. F. (2000). *When schools compete: A cautionary tale*. Washington, DC: Brookings Institution Press.

Fuller, B. (Ed.). (2001). *Inside charter schools: The paradox of radical decentralization*. Cambridge, MA: Harvard University Press.

Fuller, H. (2000). *The continuing struggle of African Americans for the power to make real educational choices*. Paper presented at the Second Annual Symposium on Educational Options for African Americans. Washington, DC: Center for Education Reform.

Glatter, R., Woods, P. A., & Bagley, C. (Eds.). (1997). *Choice & diversity in schooling: Perspectives and prospects*. New York: Routledge.

Gauri, V. (1998). *School choice in Chile: Two decades of educational reform*. Pittsburgh, PA: University of Pittsburgh Press.

Jencks, C. (1966, Winter). Is the public school obsolete? *Public Interest, 2*, 18–27.

Lauder, H., & Hughes, D., with Watson, S., Waslander, S., Thrupp, M., Strathdee, R., Simiyu, I., Dupuis, A., McGlinn, J., & Hamlin, J. (1999). *Trading in futures: Why markets in education don't work*. Buckingham, UK: Open University Press.

Lindblom, C. (2001). *The market system. What it is, how it works, and what to make of it*. New Haven, CT: Yale University Press.

Marshall, R., & Tucker, M. (1993). *Thinking for a living: Education and the wealth of nations*. New York: Basic Books.

Meyer, J. W., Ramirez, F. O., Rubinson, R., & Boli-Bennett, J. (1977). The world educational revolution, 1950–1970. *Sociology of Education, 50*(4), 242–258.

Meyer, J.W., Kamens, D., & Benavot, A. (1992). *School knowledge for the masses: World models and national primary curricular categories in the twentieth century*. Washington DC: Falmer.

Organisation for Economic Cooperation and Development (OECD). (1994). *School: A matter of choice*. Paris: Author.

Reich, R. B. (1991). *The work of nations: Preparing ourselves for 21st century capitalism*. New York: Knopf.

Schultz, T. W. (Ed.). (1974). *Economics of the family: Marriage, children, and human capital*. Chicago: University of Chicago Press.

Schultz, T. W. (1981). *Investing in people: The economics of population quality*. Berkeley: University of California Press.

Walford, G. (Ed.). (1996). *School choice and the quasi-market*. Oxford Studies in Comparative Education, Volume 6(1). Oxford, UK: Triangle Books.

West, E.G. (1965). *Education and the state*. London: Institute of Economic Affairs.

World Bank. (1989). *Education in sub-Saharan Africa*. Washington, DC: International Bank for Reconstruction and Development.

World Bank. (1990). *Argentina: Reallocating resources for the improvement of education*. Washington, DC: International Bank for Reconstruction and Development.

World Bank. (1992). *Adjusting educational policies: Conserving resources while raising school quality*. Washington, DC: International Bank for Reconstruction and Development.

Acknowledgments

The Spencer Foundation provided the financial resources that made Michigan State University's International Conference on School Choice and Educational Change possible, and we would like to express our gratitude to the foundation and its staff. We would also like to thank President Peter McPherson, Provost Lou Anna Simon, and Dean Carole Ames of Michigan State University for supporting the conference and for supporting policy research on school choice in Michigan and beyond. The thoughtful commentaries and observations provided by our colleague and collaborator David Arsen have deepened and enriched our understanding of school choice policies over many years, and we are grateful for his wisdom and friendship. Jeannie Patrick assumed lead administrative responsibility for the conference and for the preparation of this volume, and we are grateful to her as well.

Many others also contributed to the success of the conference. We would like to thank the deans of International Studies and Programs, the College of Social Science, Urban Affairs Programs, James Madison College, the Detroit College of Law, and the Eli Broad College of Business for financial and administrative support. We extend special thanks to our students and colleagues in the College of Education, including Courtney Bell, Joan Eadie, Gerhard Glomm, Bettie Landauer-Menchik, Barbara Markle, Michael Mintrom, Lisa Ray, Chris Reimann, and Sarah West. Brian Ellerbeck has overseen the publication of the book by Teachers College Press, and we are grateful for his help.

Introduction

Helen F. Ladd

Increasingly there is a global marketplace of ideas regarding the reform of education. Among the ideas with a demonstrable global reach are parental choice and market competition. Throughout the late 1980s and 1990s, countries as different as Chile under a military dictatorship and Sweden and New Zealand with their welfare state traditions introduced packages of governance changes based on these ideas. Common ideas, however, generally do not play out in the same way in each country. Instead, they interact with a country's historical, economic, and political pressures to emerge in somewhat different forms over different time frames. The variation in forms and in timing makes it possible for policy makers in one country to benefit from the experiences of other countries.

The chapters in this book focus on the experiences of nine countries that expanded parental choice during the 1980s and the 1990s. First are Chile and New Zealand, which introduced the most comprehensive and dramatic reforms. Chile did so by introducing the equivalent of a voucher system that provided funds to private as well as public schools on an equal basis. New Zealand changed from a centralized and bureaucratic system to one of self-governing schools, full choice among public schools, and a new culture of competition. Although their reforms were somewhat less bold, England and Sweden also decentralized authority and provided parents more choice, with England making a number of significant policy changes over a 20-year period. Australia provides an example of a country that relies heavily on private schools. That heavy reliance, however, is less the result of purposeful policy decisions than of various funding decisions made over the years. Other countries considered are South Africa, China, and the former Soviet bloc countries of Hungary and the Czech Republic. South Africa's foray into choice reflects its effort to refashion a system of gross inequities designed to support apartheid into a more equitable and efficient post-apartheid system. China, Hungary, and the Czech Republic are taking small steps away from their inflexible totalitarian systems in the direction of somewhat more choice and flexibility, especially for those with the means to pay.

In some countries, such as New Zealand, the additional choices were primarily within the public school system. In others, such as Chile and Australia, the reforms promoted the private school market by making public funding available to such schools. While in some countries, the purpose of expanding parental choice was to increase the options for disadvantaged students, in others—especially those in which choice had historically been highly restricted—the new options were made available primarily to higher-income families who were willing to pay for better schools.

Underlying this volume is the belief that policy makers and educational researchers in all countries, including those in the United States, have much to learn from the experiences of other countries. These experiences force one to challenge presuppositions about how choice and competition operate. In addition, they provide insights into the systemic effects of reform, generate new ideas for policy makers, and suggest the policy safeguards needed to minimize undesirable outcomes of choice policies.

RELEVANCE TO DEBATES IN THE UNITED STATES

Disagreements about school choice and the role of competition in elementary and secondary education feature prominently in education policy debates across the United States. Advocates of giving parents more opportunities to choose the schools their children attend—whether through greater choice among public schools, the introduction of charter schools, or the use of vouchers that can be used at private schools—argue that greater choice will improve the education system. More choice, they claim, will expand educational opportunities for poor children, promote innovation, and, through the discipline of competition, increase student achievement. Defenders of the traditional public school system challenge many of these arguments.

Unfortunately, the recent growth in charter schools and the few small experiments with school vouchers provide at best limited and, to date, not very complete evidence on the validity of competing claims. For example, well-designed studies of small-scale voucher programs can shed light on whether the children who use vouchers to attend private schools achieve at higher levels than those without the voucher option. Because the voucher experiments are small, however, such studies provide no information on whether competition from private schools will improve the quality of education in the traditional public schools.

As a result, much of the U.S. debate takes place at an ideological level. Proponents of choice and competition often rely on simplistic arguments about the putative power of markets to generate higher-quality education at lower costs. Opponents of expanding choice and competition often object to any move in that direction on the grounds that it will destroy the public education system. Almost completely missing from the debate in the United States is attention to the lessons from the growing international experience with parental choice. Indeed, at times the U.S. policy debate seems predicated on the myth that choice in education is a distinctly American intervention. As the chapters in this book illustrate, the reality is far different.

The international experience is useful for several reasons. First, the boldness of the reforms in countries such as Chile and New Zealand makes it easier to detect their effects, both positive and negative, than when reforms are introduced in small increments. When they are large scale, one can observe how the whole system responds and learn something about how the various parts interact. Moreover, when reforms are sustained over a long period of time, as they have been in those countries, the full range of effects—intended as well as unintended—have time to emerge. Thus the experiences of certain countries can substitute for the type of large-scale experiment that researchers and policy makers in the United States would need in order to answer some of the fundamental questions about the impact of choice and competition.

Second, additional insights can be gained from countries undergoing more modest reforms, such as England, Sweden, and Australia. During a long period of Conservative rule, England experimented with a large number of different policies related to choice and competition. Its experience with various components, such as the City Technology Colleges in the 1980s or supply-side strategies in the 1990s, provides insights into particular models that could be of interest in the United States or other countries. Australia is of interest not so much because of purposeful reform efforts, but rather because the various changes it made over a period of time in the funding of private schools induced such a large increase in the share of students in private schools that the country now faces a serious policy dilemma about the future of public education.

Third, even the experiences of countries that differ greatly from the United States, such as South Africa, China, or the Czech Republic, can be relevant to U.S. policymakers. With its focus on the equity and adequacy of education funding for a population that is largely Black and disadvantaged, South Africa is grappling on a huge scale with many of the same issues that face large cities in the United States. Moreover, several countries, including South Africa, China, and the former Soviet republics of Hungary and Czechoslovakia, can provide models of how to use choice as a way to mobilize additional resources for education.

Fourth, the international experience serves to enrich one's understanding of the nature of choice-based governance changes and the forces that generate them. As discussed in the next section, such governance changes come in different forms and respond to a variety of ideological currents. While an ideology of the market played a prominent role in the adoption of many of the reforms described in this book, it is not the only relevant ideology. Significantly, in some of the countries the reforms were initiated not by conservatives but rather by more progressive parties. By observing the development and evolution of policy in other countries, one can gain the perspective that is often missing in domestic policy discussions.

It will undoubtedly be tempting for some U.S. proponents of choice to discount the international experience on the grounds that the reforms enacted in other countries differ from the specific policy options proposed or advocated for this country. Such discounting would be a mistake. The emergence of similar behavior in multiple settings, such as the tendency for parents in a choice environment to move their children to schools with higher proportions of advantaged students, indicates that powerful forces are at work that are likely to emerge in the United States and in other countries unless strong and forceful policy measures are introduced to offset them. Ignoring the international evidence would also be a mistake because of the insights into policy design that such evidence can provide. For example, advocates of charter schools or vouchers in the United States might do well to pay attention to the inspectorate approach to accountability used in countries such as England and New Zealand, to the way that China has addressed the challenge of insufficient educational and managerial capacity in newly established schools, or to how various countries have dealt with the challenge of oversubscribed schools.

NATURE AND GENESIS OF THE REFORMS

To some choice advocates, the most compelling justification for giving parents more choice over the schools their children attend is to force schools to compete for students and thereby to improve the quality of education they offer. The starting point for this instrumental view of choice is the monopoly power of the traditional education system, which many people believe has allowed schools to become bureaucratic and wasteful (Chubb & Moe, 1990). By eliminating the geographic enrollment zones that provide public schools with a captive group of students or by promoting nonpublic alternatives to the traditional public schools, parental choice will change the incentives facing schools and, by analogy to the role of competition in the private sector, induce them to provide higher-quality education at lower cost.

Clearly, if one is to have competition among schools, parents must be free to make choices among schools. In addition, competition requires that schools have significant autonomy in order to have the flexibility to alter their programs to meet parental preferences and to reduce costs. Thus the concepts of parental choice, self-governing schools, and competition are closely linked. Yet while competition requires both parental choice and self-governing schools, the reverse is not true; the case for more parental choice and autonomy for schools need not rely on the concepts of competition or other market processes. As a result, choice in education has much broader political appeal than it would if it were associated only with a right-wing political agenda. This broader appeal provides a powerful explanation of the widespread interest in choice-based reform in education across national boundaries.

Nonmarket Arguments for Choice and Self-Governing Schools

In the U.S. context, a major argument for more parental choice emerges from the cherished value of freedom to choose. Given that people are generally permitted to choose where to live and where to work in the United States, it is reasonable to ask why they are not given more control over where their children go to school. This argument is particularly applicable to urban minority families and economically disadvantaged families, since the traditional education system offers them the least choice and their children end up in the lowest-performing schools. In contrast to these families, more advantaged families can choose schools for their children through choosing where to live or opting for private schools. Howard Fuller, a leading

African American spokesperson for more choice, eloquently gives voice to this view as he makes the case for school choice as a means of empowering urban minorities. As he states: "This is a debate about power. . . . This is about whether parents of low-income African American children should obtain a power that many critics of the choice movement exercise every day on behalf of their own children" (Fuller, 2000, p. 1). Many African Americans apparently agree with him, since polls show strong support among them for voucher programs.

Expanded choice may also promote important educational goals. The traditional view that one size fits all when it comes to education is no longer accepted. Research shows that children differ in their learning styles, and people are increasingly recognizing that alternatives are needed for those who do not function well in the traditional public education system. More choice would allow families to make a better match between the needs of their children and what a school has to offer. That choice could take various forms. One would be to have parents choose from a number of differentiated options provided by the public sector, as, for example, in the controlled choice program in Cambridge, Massachusetts, in which no child has an assigned school and school assignments take into consideration the preferences of families among schools.[1] A second would be for parents to chose between their assigned public school and private schools that were made affordable by the provision of vouchers or other forms of financial assistance.

A somewhat different form of this argument draws on the communitarian literature to highlight the positive role that communities may be able to play in delivering quality public services (Brandl, 1998; Witte, 1996). According to this view, by choosing schools for their children, families will create communities of shared values that will lead to greater cooperation and effort toward the ultimate goal of better education. Supporters of this view point to the shared community values in U.S. Catholic schools to explain their greater effectiveness relative to comparable public schools (Bryk, Lee, & Holland, 1993). This communitarian perspective also provides support for the charter school movement in the United States, in which groups of parents and educators with a shared educational vision are given the opportunity to set up new self-governing schools that receive public funding.

The Role of Community, Parental Control, and Democratic Values

Consistent with these observations, it is interesting to note that in several of the countries described in this volume, the initial steps toward choice and market-based reforms were oriented more toward the notions of parental involvement and community than of market competition and reflected, at least in part, democratic and populist values. As described by Edward Fiske and Helen Ladd in Chapter 2, that was certainly the case in New Zealand, where a Labour government initiated that country's radical reform effort in 1989 by transferring authority from a bureaucratic Department of Education to individual schools run by elected and parent-dominated boards of trustees. Economic pressures in the mid-1980s had brought growing attention to the ways in which the state educational system was failing to meet the needs of significant segments of the population. Hence, the goal was to give all local communities, and particularly the minority communities of Maori and Pacific Islanders, greater control over their schools in the form of a collective-voice participatory process. Thus parental control and self-governance became the centerpiece of the initial reform effort. Not until 2 years later, in 1991, when the more conservative National party returned to power, were enrollment zones abolished and competition among schools aggressively encouraged.

Progressive rather than conservative governments also took the lead in Sweden and Australia. According to Holger Daun in Chapter 4, movement in the direction of more local authority in schooling in that country was initiated by the Social Democrats and justified in terms of values that built on the concepts of "participatory democracy" and "user democracy" that had emerged in the 1960s and 1970s. With respect to Australia, Max Angus describes in Chapter 5 how a Labor government energized private schooling in the early 1970s by proposing additional federal aid based on need for both public and private schools. Though not fully anticipated, the playing out of this funding strategy over time has led to a situation in which one out of three children in Australia is now in a private school.

Nor were competition or other market processes the driving force behind the expansion of parental choice in the urban areas of China, according to Mun Tsang in Chapter 7. Instead, China increased nongovernmental educational options for children primarily in response to parental demands for more control over the schooling of their children. Such demands were in part the product of a political environment that was becoming somewhat more tolerant of differences and of the growth in material well-being that made it possible for some families to afford the higher-quality education they wanted. Such quality was not always available through the public schools because of the low overall level of public education spending and disparities in resources across local governments. The combination of a high cultural value placed on education and large variation in the quality of schools provided strong pressure for making more options available to parents, especially to those parents who were in a position to pay. The provision of such options achieved two goals: It gave wealthy parents some of the control they wanted, and it freed up resources for public schools. In addition, the new nongovernmental schools were sometimes required to pay a portion of their tuition revenue to the government schools.

As emphasized by John Pampallis in Chapter 6, the governance reforms in South Africa largely reflected the need to replace an education system that had treated Blacks and Colored students unfairly during the apartheid era with a more democratic system in which schools would be open to all students irrespective of race. The task was particularly challenging because of limited resources for education and the huge number of underserved Black students relative to White students. The reforms in that country gave significant authority to local schools governed by parent-dominated councils, including the power to set admissions policies (subject to nondiscrimination constraints) and to set fees. Such reforms were designed to retain middle-class White and Black students in the public school system and to generate additional resources for education.

Role of "New-Right" Ideas and Neo-Liberal Market Orientation

Not surprisingly, many of the governance reform efforts also reflected a "new-right" or neoliberal market orientation. The new-right perspective is grounded in the conviction that competition will improve the delivery of most services by reducing provider capture and minimizing transaction costs. Provider capture occurs, according to this perspective, when well-organized public-interest groups such as teachers' unions "capture" agencies and twist public policies in their favor at the expense of the broader public interest. Transaction, or agency, costs arise in ensuring that the incentives of employees who deliver public services are aligned with legislated policy objectives. To avoid provider capture and to minimize transaction costs in the context of education, such thinking calls for minimizing the role of the central government, separating funding from operations, encouraging competition among schools, giving parents and students maximum choice in determining which school to attend, providing information to parents about the performance of schools, weakening the power of unions, and introducing a management system oriented around mission statements, output targets, and performance-based pay.[2]

Such rhetoric played significant roles in general policy making in both Sweden and New Zealand, where serious economic crises in the mid-1980s forced those countries to pay more attention to the themes of deregulation, competition, and efficiency in restructuring their private and public sectors. With respect to education in Sweden, Holger Daun claims that the new-right rhetoric led the Social Democrats to move forward with policies that were not fully consistent with the party's core values. In New Zealand, the election of a conservative National government in 1991 allowed a market-based ideology to prevail over the more democratic and populist perspective of the Labour party, which had inspired the initial decentralization, and to move the education reforms in a decidedly more rightward direction. Similar ideas dominated the policy environment in Australia's state of Victoria under a non-Labor government between 1993 and 1999.

According to Geoffrey Walford in Chapter 3, the discussion in England and Wales throughout the 1980s and 1990s was heavily influenced by new-right and market principles under the long period of Conservative rule, although such ideas did not fully take hold until the late 1980s. In the early 1980s, parental preferences were given some weight in the student assignment process, but at that time those preferences were still balanced against other considerations, such as the efficient use of school facilities and planning for enrollment changes. In the late 1980s the reform proposals took on a stronger market-oriented tenor with the introduction of City Technology Colleges, grant-maintained schools, and supply-side initiatives to promote the establishment of new schools. The City Technology Colleges were officially private high schools established with support from the business community to promote technology and encourage competition. Grant-maintained schools were schools of choice that operated independently of the local education authorities and were designed to promote competition.

Chile is the clearest example of the dominance of new-right thinking. In the late 1970s, the country's military government had disbanded the teachers' union and decentralized administrative responsibility for schools down to the provincial and municipal level. However, as noted by Martin Carnoy and Patrick McEwan in Chapter 1, that administrative decentralization should be understood not as an attempt to generate democratic participation, as was the case in many other countries, but rather as a way to implement central government direction through a military chain of command. During the 1980s, the military government then turned all schools over to local municipalities, thereby making teachers municipal rather than national employees, and set up a new system of education funding designed to separate the funding and operating of schools. Under the new arrangement, a fixed amount of money was provided per pupil, including to those pupils who opted for private schools that did not charge tuition. As a result of this voucher scheme, new unregulated for-profit private schools were established to compete with the traditional public schools.

The power of Chile's right-wing military dictatorship clearly makes that country unique. In other countries, the evidence suggests a more complex story in which neo-liberal ideology played only a limited, or even nonexistent, role in the introduction of more parental choice and other related governance changes. Instead, the prevalence of choice-based governance reform efforts in countries around the world can best be understood as the product of a number of different philosophical strands that converged on similar policy recommendations related to self-governance of schools and parental choice. Moreover, the international experience suggests that in democratically controlled countries, even those reforms driven by new-right principles will inevitably reflect a variety of political compromises.

PUBLIC SCHOOL CHOICE VERSUS
PRIVATE SCHOOL CHOICE

The question of why choice and competition were expanded primarily in the public sector in some countries while in others it was expanded to include private schools is of particular relevance to the choice debate in the United States, where any extension of parental choice to private schools, particularly schools run by religious groups, raises serious red flags for supporters of public education. The evidence in this volume indicates the importance of each country's history and also highlights the importance in the United States of the historical commitment to the separation of church and state. Many other countries have been more willing to blur the distinction between public and private schools either by integrating financially struggling religious schools into the public sector or by subsidizing them.

According to the new-right ideology, there is no reason to distinguish public schools—that is, those that are owned and operated by the government—from schools that are owned and run by nongovernmental agencies. Hence, it is not surprising that Chile's reforms put private schools on a par with municipally run schools. Some reformers in New Zealand would have preferred that the distinction be blurred there as well, but there were good reasons to focus most attention on the public schools. At the time of the reforms only 3.5% of the students were in independent schools, most of which were expensive and catered to wealthy families. This small share reflected the fact that financially strapped Catholic and other religious schools had become part of the public school sector in the mid-1970s. Similarly, the private sector was quite small in England and Wales (with 8% of the students) because the Church of England and Roman Catholic schools had long been incorporated into the state-maintained sector. Thus, in neither of these countries was there a strong group of private schools with relatively low tuition pushing for a publicly funded voucher program. At the same time, declining student enrollments in both countries strengthened the argument for choice within the public sector. In England, the government used the choices of parents to make the politically difficult determination of which schools to shut down. In New Zealand, declining enrollments strengthened the argument that parents should be able to move their child to a preferred school provided the school had excess capacity.

The historical experience in other countries cuts the other way. Unlike England and New Zealand, Australia has not integrated its Catholic and Protestant schools into the public school system and, given its historical commitment to private schools, has faced ongoing political pressure to provide financial support for them. Australia, which has long blurred the distinction between church and state, provided public subsidies to religious schools in the 19th century. After withholding financial assistance to private schools during much of the 20th century, the federal government resumed aid to private schools in the early 1970s in response to concern about the adequacy of education funding in both the public and the private sectors. This new federal assistance energized the private sector, and the interplay of federal and state financing strategies provided unintended incentives for governments to favor private schools. As a result, one in three Australian students is now in a private school.

The main choice-related reforms in China, Hungary, and the Czech Republic all take the form of allowing more nongovernmental schooling options. As described by Randall Filer and Daniel Munich in Chapter 8, the new schools in both those countries are private schools. In China the nongovernment schools are both private and *minban*, or people-run schools, that in some ways resemble charter schools in the United States. In contrast to the United States, however, where new voucher programs and, in most cases, charter schools would make new options more accessible than otherwise to families with low incomes, the motivation for the choice programs in these other countries was to satisfy the preferences of wealthy families who were no longer content with the public school system and were willing to pay to get better schools for their children. This motivation reflects the recent totalitarian histories of countries in which private schools were prohibited. In such an environment, it makes political sense to provide new options first for the wealthy, who are likely to be more vocal about their demands. In many developed countries, including the United States, where wealthy families already have many more options than poor families, nonmarket arguments for expanding choice are more persuasive when applied to poor than to wealthy families.

WHAT CAN BE LEARNED FROM
THE INTERNATIONAL EXPERIENCE?

The experiences of the countries described in this volume shed light on a number of questions about the effects of choice policies. These questions relate to the impacts of competition on schools at the bottom of the performance distribution, on student achievement and costs, on who benefits, on accountability, and on innovation and the diversity of educational offerings.

Will Competition for Students Improve the Schools
at the Bottom of the Distribution?

Of particular interest in the United States is whether the competition for students induced by giving parents more choice over the schools their children attend will provide effective incentives for schools at the bottom of the performance distribution to improve. The international evidence shows that not only is competition unlikely to improve such schools, but it is likely to exacerbate their problems.

The fundamental reason for this conclusion has to do with how parents select schools. As discussed most fully in the New Zealand chapter, but supported by evidence in other countries such as Sweden, England and Chile, parents tend to judge the quality of a school by the socioeconomic and ethnic mix of its students. In Chile, for example, Carnoy and McEwan document that higher-income families are likely to choose schools based on test scores and the average education level of the other parents. Moreover, in their search for quality, families in many of the countries try to move their children out of schools with large proportions of disadvantaged and minority students into schools with more advantaged students. By such moves, they are likely to expose their children to positive spillover effects on motivation, better teachers, and more resources. This behavior makes it difficult for schools that start out with large proportions of disadvantaged and low-performing students to compete successfully for students and thereby makes the playing field of competition uneven.

As a result, schools serving disadvantaged students experience declining enrollments and reduced funding at the same time that they face increasing concentrations of the most difficult-to-educate students and find it more difficult to attract high-quality teachers and administrators. Such problems are compounded in countries such as England and New Zealand by school inspection systems designed to provide the public with full information on the quality of each school. In both countries, the "naming and shaming" of low-performing schools through public reports exacerbates the problems such schools face in attracting students and good teachers. In New Zealand, such schools are referred to as "downwardly spiraling" schools and in England as "sink" schools.

If overall enrollments are declining, such schools can be shut down. However, when overall enrollments are rising, shutting down such schools is politically and practically difficult, given that all children must be served in a compulsory education system. The high costs of setting up new schools as well as the fact that existing schools are reluctant to diminish their reputations by increasing their intakes of disadvantaged and low-performing students means there are few alternatives for the students in the failing schools. The result is that competition among schools relegates many low-performing and disadvantaged students to worse schools than otherwise would be the case. The "market model" fails to achieve desirable results in this context both because the playing field of school choice is not level and because all students must be served.

Even when policy makers try to minimize the adverse effects of competition on the schools losing students, they are often unsuccessful. The experience with England's City Technology College initiative is illustrative. The major goals of that program were to increase technology education with the support of the business community and to provide competition for the traditional public schools to induce them to improve. To keep the new technology schools from skimming off the best students, such schools were required to select students from across the ability spectrum, which in fact they did. However, as a substitute for selection by ability, the schools selected students based on the degree of motivation of parents and children. The result was that the nearby inner-city public schools were made worse off by the loss of their more motivated students and involved parents.

The limitations of choice and competition as a solution to educational problems for the most disadvantaged students emerge clearly from South Africa. In Chapter 6, John Pampallis points out that the vast majority of South African children are Black and poor and live in rural areas or in townships where there is little opportunity to exercise the right to choice. They attend schools with fewer resources, larger classes, and less well educated teachers than is true for schools serving middle-class students. The solution, according to Pampallis, lies not in providing more opportunity for the poor Black children to attend the historically more privileged schools, which are few in number, but rather in improving the quality of the schools in the areas where such children live.

Given that competition does not improve the schools at the bottom, what will? Because the case studies in this volume are focused on choice-based reforms, they provide only limited insight into this issue. Statistical evidence provided by Carnoy and McEwan for Chile (Chapter 1) indicates the value of investments targeted at teacher training and classroom investments. New Zealand provides little direct empirical evidence because it was so slow to acknowledge the fact that competition was having such adverse effects on some schools. However, the indirect evidence from that country suggests that policy makers need to focus attention less on governance reforms and more on teaching and learning in those schools, including attention to the quality of their teachers. Some intriguing insights come from China, where forays into the provision of new options for higher-income families were specifically designed to help improve the low-quality government schools and to mobilize additional resources for the education sector.

Do Choice and Competition Generate Higher Achievement and/or Lower Costs?

The failure of choice and competition to solve the problems of the schools at the bottom of the distribution need not mean that such reforms are undesirable or that they generate no educational benefits. They could still make the overall education system more productive by raising average achievement levels, lowering the costs of providing education, or some combination of both.

Unfortunately, it is often difficult to determine the effects of such reforms on student achievement and on costs. In some cases, such as New Zealand, no national test scores are available and researchers must rely on indirect measures of student learning. In others, such as England, where test scores are available, it is difficult to unravel the effects of choice and competition from those of other simultaneous education reforms, such as the introduction of a national curriculum with regular testing of all students, publication of exam results, and regular inspections. At best one can determine the effects of the whole package of reforms.

One empirical strategy is to ask whether the schools of choice—such as grant-maintained schools in England, or private schools in countries such as Australia, Sweden, or Chile—have higher achievement and/or lower costs than the public schools. The clearest evidence comes from Chile, where detailed data on student test scores and other characteristics of students makes it possible for researchers to separate the effects of school type from the socioeconomic factors that influence student achievement. Emerging from that country's experience is the conclusion that choice and competition do not generate large gains in achievement. Indeed, Carnoy and McEwan (Chapter 1) report lower gains in achievement for the fastest-growing type of private school in Chile, nonreligious for-profit schools, than for the traditional public schools. Although the Catholic schools appear to generate higher achievement than the public schools, the authors attribute this outcome not to their greater productivity but rather to their greater resources. A closely related conclusion is that "all private schools are not created equal" (Chapter 1). Though a simple point, this observation is important to the U.S. debate, where advocates of choice tend to use evidence from one type of private school—namely, Catholic schools—to generalize to an expanded private sector that would inevitably include many different types of private schools.

The other chapters generate no clear conclusions about the impacts of choice and competition on student achievement. In Sweden, for example, student performance is higher on average in the independent schools, but the variation among independent schools is large, and the differences between sectors disappear when researchers control for the socioeconomic status of students or their initial knowledge. In Australia, where the large number of private schools could potentially provide a wealth of information about the productivity of the private sector relative to the public, little or no useful information is available. Neither the federal government nor the state governments have been particularly interested in the impact of choice on

overall academic achievement. Choice among sectors was not introduced in that country out of concern about low academic standards in
the public schools, the public sector does not really want comparisons
between sectors to be made, and the states have opposed national testing. Although Max Angus (Chapter 5) cites some studies that have
shown higher test performance for Catholic schools, perhaps even adjusting for the characteristics of the students, he notes that the adjustments may not be complete. He concludes that the evidence is not
clear.

These comparisons between private and public schools do not tell
the whole story. If competition between sectors successfully forced
the public schools to become more productive, the differences between sectors could disappear over time. Hence, the evidence on how
competition affects the traditional public schools is also relevant.

The most careful empirical investigation of this issue is based on
the Chilean experience. If competition from private schools forces the
public schools to become more productive, one would expect the public schools in Chilean municipalities with large increases in private
enrollment to exhibit greater gains in achievement than those subject
to less competition from the private schools. However, that would be
true only if the analyst were able to fully control for all the factors
that determine the growth of private schools in a municipality that
might be correlated with student achievement. The studies cited by
Carnoy and MacEwan (Chapter 1) use a sophisticated strategy to address this empirical challenge and find at best mixed effects. Although
they find that competition led to modest gains in achievement among
some public schools in Santiago, Chile's capital, they found small negative effects in the rest of the country, which is home to three-quarters of the country's population.

Some limited evidence in support of positive impacts comes from
Filer and Munich's study of the Czech Republic (Chapter 8), in which
they show that school districts facing significant competition from
private schools had greater success in getting their students into university than did other districts. Working in the other direction is evidence from New Zealand showing that the competition among
schools in that country reduced the quality of student learning as perceived by teachers.

Although one might wish for clearer and more consistent evidence of the effects of choice and competition on student achievement
in either a positive or a negative direction, the fact that the effects are
unclear or, at best, mixed is nonetheless important. The international
evidence simply does not support the claims of those who argue in

favor of more parental choice and competition on the instrumental grounds that it will make an education system significantly more productive than it would otherwise be.

Who Benefits from Choice Programs?

In some countries, choice programs have undoubtedly helped some children from poor or minority families enroll in schools that would otherwise not have been available to them. This is certainly the case, for example, in New Zealand, where many Maori and Pacific Island parents have exercised their new opportunities to move their children from one school to another, and in South Africa, where choice opened up to middle-class Black and Colored children many schools that previously served only White children. Overall, however, the international experience suggests that school choice policies tend to favor middle- and upper-income families and those with more White or European backgrounds.

One reason is that poor families are less likely than higher-income families to take full advantage of opportunities to choose their children's schools. They lack equal access to information about schooling options, they often cannot afford the cost of transportation to new schools, they may be reluctant to send their children to "middle-class" schools where they feel unwelcome, and they may face high voluntary fees for schools of choice within the public sector or expensive tuition for private schools. While policy decisions such as paying for transportation, providing good information to all parents, or prohibiting schools accepting vouchers from charging tuition or fees could offset some of these disadvantages, the international experience suggests that governments are not typically willing to undertake all the actions needed to make choice equally available to all parents.

A second reason choice policies favor middle- and upper-income families is the power given to schools to select their students, a power often justified as a logical component of self-governance for schools. Given that parents tend to make judgments about the quality of a school based on the mix of its students, selecting students gives schools an opportunity to enhance their reputations by choosing the more advantaged students. In addition, schools have incentives to enroll the students who are the least costly to educate from among their applicant pools, a policy that also tends to favor students from the middle and upper classes.

The power to select students was granted to all the oversubscribed schools in New Zealand and to the grant-maintained public schools in England. Moreover, England's decision to allow public schools to "specialize," as distinct from "select," in practice led to selection that favored more motivated and advantaged students. South Africa's self-governing public schools were also given the power to select their students, with the proviso that they not discriminate based on the race of the child. In all the countries, private schools retained their power to select students, even in countries such as Australia where private schools received significant public funding. In China, where in some cases the nongovernment schools had to collect fees large enough for a share of the revenue to go to the government schools, schools by necessity had to select students that could pay the fees.

Evidence from the various countries supports the conclusion that choice programs benefit the more advantaged students. In Chile, high-income parents were more likely to choose private voucher schools than were low-income parents, and more educated parents opted for schools with higher test scores and higher proportions of educated parents. In New Zealand, parents of European descent were more aggressive in moving their children out of the schools serving families at the bottom of the socioeconomic and minority distribution than were the parents of Maori and Pacific Island children. In Sweden, among the 7% of the children who have exercised their option of choosing a school other than the one to which they were assigned, children of Nordic origin were more likely than the non-Nordic do so. Moreover, such children typically left schools with large percentages of students of African, Asian, and Arabic descent.

A closely related effect of choice schemes in many countries was increased polarization of the student body. Students within schools became more similar and across schools became more different in terms of income levels, ethnicity, and achievement. That pattern emerges quite clearly in New Zealand and in Sweden, although, according to Walford (Chapter 3), it is a bit less clear in England. In Australia, the evidence indicates that over time higher-income students were increasingly likely to enroll in private schools, leaving the public schools to serve as the residual provider of education to lower-income families. And in South Africa, more affluent families were favored as a result of the fee policy and the encouragement of other forms of private funding.

Reasonable people can disagree about how to evaluate these distributional effects of choice policies. Some might argue that polarization is desirable in that it assures the best education for the middle- and upper-class students who will contribute the most to a country's economy. Others might object that, given today's global economy in which all children require an adequate education to function successfully, leaving some children behind is both economically undesirable and unfair. Still others might use the evidence presented here to oppose new forms of choice unless they are specifically designed to help disadvantaged students. In any case, the evidence from these case studies brings into sharp focus the pressures that must be considered if policy makers attempt to use choice to improve the lot of children from poor families relative to those from more affluent families.

Does Parental Choice Alone Serve as an Adequate Accountability Mechanism?

When parents can choose which school their child will attend, schools have to be more accountable to parents than would otherwise be the case. It is thus reasonable to ask whether this market-based form of accountability will suffice for a publicly funded education system designed to promote student learning. Judging by the decisions made in countries such as England and New Zealand, it will not—unless one counts as part of the market-based system national tests and school inspection systems. According to Walford (Chapter 3), the Conservative government in England "quickly lost its faith in the market as the sole way of raising achievement" and in 1992 established the Office for Standards in Education to ensure quality through its periodic inspections of every school. In New Zealand, the order of events was reversed. As part of its initial reform effort, it set up an inspection system to assure quality within the self-governing schools. The subsequent elimination of the geographic enrollment schemes and introduction of full parental choice in no way replaced the government's view that an inspection system was needed.

Does Choice Lead to More Diversity and Innovation?

As mentioned above, an important educational argument for choice emerges from the understanding that one size does not fit all students. According to this view, student learning would be enhanced if parents had some control over their children's schooling either through a collective choice process at the school level, or choice from among a diverse set of schooling options, or some combination of both.

The international experience suggests that self-governance and choice need not always lead to great diversity in the types of school offerings and educational philosophies among schools. How much diversity in offerings emerges depends on how large a role the state plays in promoting national standards through the introduction of a national curriculum and national tests, how vigilant it is in assuring that public funds are spent wisely, and how willing it is to fund schools operated by different religious groups. The most significant general differences among schools that emerge have more to do with the religious orientation of the schools or with the socioeconomic mix of students that schools serve than with their differing approaches to education. Schools in a competitive environment serving an advantaged group of students tend to be successful and to benefit from the ability to tailor their programs to those students. Schools serving a more disadvantaged mix of students often do not have that luxury, given the pressure they are under to increase their enrollments. The international experience provides only limited examples of schools emerging to serve small niche markets.

The main constraint on diversity is the fact that the public interest in education is so strong. Despite its initial focus on promoting community involvement through self-governing schools that would write their own charters, for example, New Zealand early on reasserted its interest in education by requiring all school charters to incorporate the national education goals, administrative guidelines, and national curriculum framework. In so doing, the charters, which were intended to express each school's unique mission and operating philosophy, became relatively bland and homogeneous. New Zealand's approach to school inspections also tended to make school policies more uniform as schools sought to gain positive reviews.

The pressure for imitation rather than innovation was even greater in England and Wales, where the inspection system was reinforced by national testing. As emphasized by Walford (Chapter 3), the presence of national tests privileges academic outcomes and generates a single-dimensional hierarchy of schools, with examination results serving as a screening mechanism. Despite the fact that parents in fact look at many factors, schools react as if parents have academic factors as their major criterion. The result is greater uniformity and conformity as less successful schools try to imitate the schools that are more successful on the academic dimension.

Although one might have predicted that the new nongovernmental schools in China's urban areas would differ significantly from the public schools, they appear in fact to be quite similar. The reason is that all schools are driven by the same exam system and nongovernmental schools are subject to significant regulation in the areas of school management, finance and accounting, and basic educational standards. Even for the people-run schools, innovation is not a major marketing point. Instead, these schools tend to try to duplicate the instructional model of their parent schools.

The most innovation emerged where it was explicitly promoted by the state or where lack of regulation permitted it. In the mid-1990s, the Conservative government in England addressed the supply side of the market by encouraging the development of entirely new schools, with the proviso that the sponsoring group put up at least 15% of the capital costs. Interestingly, when the Labour party came to power in 1997, it authorized under the program one Seventh Day Adventist secondary school, two Muslim primary schools, and one small community school. All the new schools, however, have to accept the regulations and constraints applicable to other grant-maintained schools, including following the national curriculum.

In both Chile and Australia, the private sectors were not very heavily regulated. A large number of low-quality, for-profit, nonreligious schools emerged in Chile. In Australia, the success of the relatively unregulated private schools in drawing large numbers of students from the public schools has created pressure in some states to diversify the public sector. As noted by Max Angus (Chapter 5), however, diversification may turn out to be a two-edged sword in Australia. On the positive side, setting up new types of public schools would signal the sector's responsiveness to parents. On the negative side, it could weaken overall support for public education by making it less clear what the public sector stands for.

In sum, there is undoubtedly more diversity in education systems that promote self-governing schools and parental choice than in centrally regulated bureaucratic systems. At the same time, the strong public interest in education has tended to limit the diversity of educational offerings and philosophies, and much of the resulting diversity in educational programs ends up reflecting the different socioeconomic mix of the students across schools.

CONCLUSION

The rationale for this book is that policy makers and education theorists have a lot to learn from the experiences of other countries. Such experiences can force one to test presuppositions and can provide new, otherwise unavailable, information on how various policies play out in different situations.

The case studies in this volume do not generate a definitive judgement of choice-based reform programs in education. Given the diversity of choice programs represented and the differing values they reflect, such a judgment would be presumptuous—and also not useful. As is evident from the range of countries represented in this volume, choice-based reforms are likely to be a topic for policy debate for the foreseeable future and to take on different forms in different situations. The real issue in most countries, including the United States, is not whether or not to allow choice, but how to manage it.

The international evidence indicates that the theory of markets has not translated easily into the real world of schools and classrooms anywhere. That conclusion emerges from the experiences reported in this volume and is reinforced by the observation that some of the countries are now backtracking or seeking to offset some of the unintended consequences. Taking this lesson to heart might help to rein in the enthusiasm of policy advocates in the United States, and to focus their attention on questions of policy design. The international experiences can be used to find ways to promote the positive aspects of choice and market mechanisms while minimizing undesirable side effects, especially those on the most vulnerable children.

NOTES

1. For a description of this program and the conditions necessary to make it work, see Fiske (1991).

2. See, for example, New Zealand Treasury Department (1987).

REFERENCES

Brandl, J. (1998). Governance and educational quality. In P. E. Peterson & B. Hassel (Eds.), *Learning from school choice* (pp. 55–81). Washington, DC: Brookings Institution Press.

Bryk, A.S., Lee, V.E., & Holland, P.B. (1993). *Catholic schools and the common good.* Cambridge, MA: Harvard University Press.

Chubb, J., & Moe, T. (1990). *Politics, markets, and America's schools.* Washington, DC: Brookings Institution Press.

Fiske, E. B. (1991). *Smart schools, smart kids: Why do some schools work?* New York: Simon & Schuster.

Fuller, H. (2000). *The continuing struggle of African Americans for the power to make real educational choices.* Paper presented at the Second Annual

Symposium on Educational Options for African Americans. Washington, DC: The Center for Education Reform.

New Zealand Treasury Department. (1987). *Government management: Brief to the incoming government: Vol. 2. Education Issues.* Wellington, NZ: New Zealand Treasury.

Witte, J. (1996). School choice and student performance. In H. F. Ladd (Ed.), *Holding schools accountable: Performance-based reform in education* (pp. 149–176). Washington, DC: Brookings Institution Press.

CHAPTER 1

Does Privatization Improve Education?
The Case of Chile's National Voucher Plan

Martin Carnoy
Patrick J. McEwan

The push to expand public funding for private education—in the form of vouchers or privately managed charter schools—is based on several claims derived from theories of how education markets function.[1] Empirical evidence on opposing claims has been scarce. Yet thanks to recent studies in the United States and in other countries, including Chile, we now know more about educational markets—and hence have more of the information we need to judge whether the claims are valid.[2] This chapter reviews some of the emerging empirical evidence on a national voucher plan in Chile.

Voucher advocates have claimed that because public education is a government monopoly, it inherently denies consumers free choice in their children's education (Friedman, 1955, 1962). This leaves consumers and society worse off than they would be under competitive conditions, for two reasons. First, the preferences of many consumers are less than fully satisfied, since they would choose a different school if they could. Second, public schools are not compelled to produce as many outputs—or as much of any single output, such as achievement—when they are not faced with competition for students. Giving private school vouchers to students may address both of these problems. Vouchers may induce private schools to compete for public school students, perhaps giving consumers educational opportunities not previously available. Second, private schools may produce educational outcomes more effectively and at lower cost, with the added benefit that poorly performing public schools may be forced to improve or lose their students.

Some of these claims, particularly regarding the effectiveness of private schools, have been tested in small-scale programs in the United States.[3] Despite some positive aspects of existing studies, they have limitations (see McEwan, 2000; Carnoy, 2001). They tell us little about the supply response of private education to vouchers, about the potential impact of competition on the performance of students in public schools (see Carnoy, 2001; Greene, 2001; Hoxby, 2001), or about whether private schools would produce outcomes at lower cost than public schools.

Our premise in this chapter is that we can gain insights into these issues by examining school systems where vouchers have been implemented on a large scale and where private school supply has increased substantially. In terms of the size of the voucher program, the length of time it has been in existence, and the degree to which the case conforms to establishing a "market" for educational services, Chile provides an excellent case to study the effects of vouchers.

Influenced by Milton Friedman's proposal, Chile's military government transferred responsibility for public school management from the national Ministry of Education to local municipalities in 1980 and began financing public and most private schools with vouchers. Each school's revenues were henceforth determined on a month-to-month basis by total enrollments and a government-determined voucher. By 1982, most public schools were operated by municipalities and the number of private schools was growing rapidly.

In the following section, we briefly describe the history of Chilean reforms (Gauri, 1998; Jofré, 1988; Parry, 1997a, 1997b). The next section discusses the impact of the reforms on schools and students, and the final section draws several conclusions about the effects of voucher plans—particularly large-scale ones—in Chile and other countries.

EDUCATION REFORM IN CHILE

The Military Regime, 1973–1980

At the time of the military coup d'état in 1973, Chile's education system was one of the most developed in Latin America. It had achieved near-universal enrollment in primary education, a feat that still eludes most Latin America countries (Castañeda, 1992; Schiefelbein, 1991). A *dirigiste* Ministry of Education assumed exclusive responsibility for administering the public schools. Even so, significant numbers of private schools operated, about half of these under the auspices of the Catholic Church (Espinola, 1993). Following a long tradition of public support to private education, many received partial subsidies from the national government that covered about 30% of costs in 1980 (Larrañaga, 1995).

Upon assuming power in 1973, the military government disbanded the teachers' union and fired teachers with leftist views (Parry, 1997a, 1997b). It also initiated a massive administrative reorganization, dividing the country into 13 regions and the regions into provinces and more than 300 municipalities. At each level, the president appointed governors and mayors, drawn mainly from the ranks of the military (Stewart & Ranis, 1994). During the 1970s the Ministry of Education, in addition to other ministries, devolved some powers to Regional Ministry Secretariats (SEREMIs), which were charged with administrative and supervisory duties formerly performed by the central ministry. Despite the apparent move toward decentralization, the system often functioned as a military chain of command, organized to implement central government directives (Parry, 1997a, 1997b; Stewart & Ranis, 1994). Mayors of municipalities would not be elected democratically until 1992.

The Educational Reform, 1980–1990

In 1980 the military government initiated a sweeping reform of the educational system. It first transferred responsibility for public school management from the Ministry of Education to local municipalities.[4] Teachers lost their status as civil servants, reverting to municipal contracts, and schools buildings and land were signed over to municipal control (Gauri, 1998; Parry, 1997a). Initial transfers proceeded rapidly, encouraged by financial incentives; by 1982, around 84% of schools were operated by municipalities.[5] The process was interrupted by economic crisis in 1982, when the central government was unable to cover the costs of transfers, but all schools were transferred by 1987 (Jofré, 1988).

As schools were transferred to municipalities, public teachers were offered severance pay and became municipal rather than national employees (Castañeda, 1992). Instead of conforming to the national Escala Única de Remuneraciones, their wages and working conditions were henceforth governed by the more flexible Código de Trabajo.

(The latter was already applicable to most Chilean workers). Teachers lost guarantees of job security, the right to salary during vacations, standard wage scales, a 30-hour workweek, and the right to bargain collectively (Rojas, 1998). Teachers in private schools also lost some legal protections, including minimum wage guarantees and a system of annual salary adjustments.

In addition to administrative decentralization, the government drastically altered how public and most private schools were financed. Prior to 1980, as in much of Latin America, public school budgets were largely determined by the need to sustain an existing plant of teachers and facilities. If budgets adjusted in response to the level of student enrollments, they only did so at a sluggish pace. Many private schools were already being subsidized by the government before 1980, meeting the rest of their costs with tuition payments and church support. After the reform, the Ministry of Education began disbursing monthly payments to municipalities based on a fixed voucher multiplied by the number of students enrolled in their schools; private schools received equivalent per-student payments if they did not charge tuition. Thus payments to public and private schools began fluctuating in proportion to student enrollments.

The law established a base voucher level, which varied according to the level of education and the location of the school.[6] Though the real value of the voucher was originally intended to keep pace with inflation, it was de-indexed following the economic crisis of the early 1980s. Over the course of the 1980s, as copper prices fell, the real value of the per-pupil voucher declined precipitously, reaching its lowest point in 1988 (see Figure 1.1). It rebounded thereafter as economic growth recovered. It has continued to rise through the 1990s.

The voucher plan precipitated a massive redistribution of enrollment across private and public schools. At the beginning of the 1980s, around 15% of students were enrolled in private voucher schools and almost 80% in public schools. By 1996, around 33% of enrollments were in private voucher schools, although most growth had already occurred by 1990 (see Figure 1.2). Between 5% and 9% of students remained in elite private schools that charged tuition and were not eligible to receive vouchers.

Return to Democracy, 1990

The military ceded power to a democratic government in 1990. The form and function of Chile's voucher system were largely maintained, although new policies were grafted onto the existing system. The gov-

Figure 1.1.   Monthly per-pupil voucher in primary schools, 1981–1996
(1996 pesos).

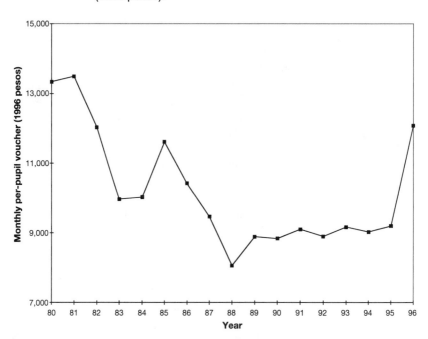

Source: Ministry of Education and authors' calculations.
Note: The base voucher excludes bonuses and deductions, which vary by
municipality and school.

ernment focused on improving the quality of poor primary schools
through direct resource investments. The 900 Schools Program, referred to as P-900, was targeted at high-poverty and low-achieving
schools (Garcia-Huidobro, 1994). Classrooms received a package of basic teaching materials and infrastructure improvements, while teachers received additional in-service training. Funds were also provided
to train and employ local secondary graduates as tutors for the lowest-
achieving students. Eventually, P-900 expanded to include about 2,300
schools. In 1992, the Program to Improve the Quality and Equity of
Pre-Primary and Primary Education (MECE) was initiated with World
Bank financing. More ambitious in scope than P-900, it sought to en-
dow all publicly funded schools with textbooks, libraries, and some
infrastructure improvements (Cox, 1997).

Figure 1.2. Enrollment share in public and private schools, 1981–1996.

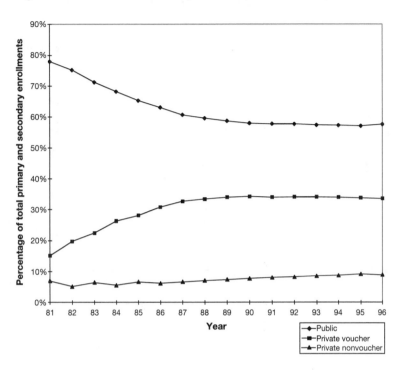

Source: Vargas (1997).

The return to democracy in 1990 brought renewed political pressures from teachers seeking improved wages and working conditions. Negotiation between the government and teachers resulted in the passage of the 1991 Estatuto Docente, a national law that subjected the teacher labor market—particularly for public school teachers—to additional regulation (Rojas, 1998). Wage floors were set for teachers with various levels of experience and training; these minimum wages were legislated to vary in lockstep with the voucher's value. Limits on hiring and firing of public teachers were also introduced. Public school teachers could be hired as either tenured or contracted teachers. Tenured teachers were to be hired through public contests in each municipality, and severe restrictions were placed on their firing or reassignment. Contracted teachers had fewer restrictions placed on their hiring and firing but could account for no more than 20% of a municipality's teacher work force. The contracts of private teachers were still governed by the Código de Trabajo, which permitted significantly more flexibility in hiring and firing.

About 33% of Chilean children now attend a private voucher school in the primary (K–8) grades (McEwan & Carnoy, 2000). Private voucher schools are both religious (mainly Catholic) and nonreligious. The latter, mostly for-profit, account for approximately two-thirds of primary enrollments in private voucher schools. For-profit schools also accounted for most of the substantial growth of the private enrollment share after 1980. Another 8% of students attend nonvoucher private schools that charge tuition and do not receive government financing. Fifty-seven percent of primary pupils still attend schools managed by municipalities, which are also largely financed by vouchers. This figure represents a considerable decline since 1980.

The students who enroll in each type of school are different in many respects (see Table 1.1). Those attending private nonvoucher

Table1.1. Characteristics of primary students and their families, 1994.

	Public DAEM	Public corporation	Catholic voucher	Protestant voucher	Nonreligious voucher	Private non-voucher
Mother's schooling[1]	7.49	8.97	10.70	9.95	9.28	14.20
	(4.80)	(2.77)	(3.45)	(3.17)	(2.98)	(2.26)
Father's schooling[1]	7.68	9.44	11.18	10.53	9.64	15.35
	(5.01)	(2.92)	(3.56)	(2.93)	(3.06)	(2.36)
Monthly household income[2]	1.65	2.29	3.02	2.61	2.88	11.17
	(2.34)	(2.23)	(3.19)	(1.96)	(3.11)	(31.01)
Number of students	16,707	2,740	2,622	227	3,125	1,159

[1]Means of these variables exclude observations for children whose mothers or fathers are absent from the household.

[2]Variable divided by 100,000.

Source: McEwan & Carnoy (2000, Table 1.3).

Note: Standard deviations for continuous variables are in parentheses. Student observations are weighted in order to account for unequal probabilities of selection into the sample. Thus the distribution of student observations across school types does not reflect the population distribution.

schools come from families that have much higher incomes, on average, and are headed by parents with substantially more schooling. The average father of a student in a private nonvoucher school has at least some college, which is not true of any other school type. Differences among students from public and private voucher schools are somewhat less pronounced. Nonetheless, the families of students from private—especially Catholic—voucher schools are still of relatively higher socioeconomic status than public school families.

EVIDENCE ON THE CHILEAN VOUCHER PLAN

This section discusses the impact of the Chilean voucher plan on schools and students, focusing on three issues. First, are private voucher schools more effective and cost-effective than public schools? Second, did the introduction of vouchers and subsequent expansion of private enrollments increase competition, thereby improving public schools? Third, which families are most likely to choose private voucher schools and which characteristics of schools influence their school choices? The following discussion draws on results presented in a series of empirical studies by the authors (McEwan, 2001a; McEwan & Carnoy, 1998, 1999, 2000).

Private School Efficiency

Empirical evidence of improved student outcomes under voucher and charter plans—specifically, student performance in privately run schools—is important to the argument that they make consumers better off. The gain for low-income students is especially crucial given current voucher proposals.

Which category of school—public or private—produces higher academic achievement in Chile? We explored this question using Spanish and mathematics achievement test data collected by the Ministry of Education between 1990 and 1997, as well as background data on students (McEwan, 2001a; McEwan & Carnoy, 2000). Since private schools tend to enroll students of a higher socioeconomic status (SES), a simple comparison of average achievement across school types confuses the distinct effects of schools and families. Thus, we estimated achievement differences across school types, controlling for student SES. Even so, there may be unobserved characteristics of students that lead them to choose private schools more often as well as to achieve at higher levels, resulting in selection bias (Murnane, Newstead, &

Olsen, 1985). To address this, McEwan (2001a) makes further statistical corrections for selection bias.[7] In brief, the analyses in both papers
suggest the following.

Chile's reforms encouraged a rapid growth in private school enrollment in the 1980s that was driven by an expansion of nonreligious
and profit-maximizing voucher schools. Our estimates suggest that
this type of privately run school is marginally less effective than municipal schools in producing Spanish and mathematics achievement
in the fourth and eighth grades, after controlling for SES. However, the
difference in test scores is not large, typically less than 0.1 standard
deviation. Table 1.2 reports the fourth-grade results in the 1990s after
almost 10 years of the voucher plan. Other results, not reported in
Table 1.2, suggest that nonreligious private voucher schools are even
less effective than municipal schools when they are located outside of
the capital of Santiago. McEwan's (2001a) estimates, using eighth-
grade test score data from 1997, corroborated the lower achievement
scores in nonreligious voucher schools. Some evidence suggests that
the gap is explained by different resources in nonreligious voucher

Table 1.2. Fourth-grade achievement differences between public DAEM and
other school types, adjusted for SES.

	1990	1992	1994	1996	Mean effect (1990–1996)
Dependent variable: Spanish test scores					
Public corporation	-0.04	-0.06	-0.08	-0.08	-0.06
Catholic voucher	0.31	0.23	0.25	0.27	0.27
Protestant voucher	-0.17	-0.21	-0.01	-0.16	-0.14
Nonreligious voucher	-0.05	-0.10	-0.07	-0.07	-0.07
Private nonvoucher	0.63	0.61	0.66	0.38	0.57
Dependent variable: mathematics test scores					
Public corporation	-0.04	-0.03	-0.06	-0.09	-0.06
Catholic voucher	0.28	0.19	0.17	0.24	0.22
Protestant voucher	-0.18	-0.27	-0.09	-0.15	-0.17
Nonreligious voucher	-0.04	-0.10	-0.08	-0.08	-0.07
Private nonvoucher	0.67	0.58	0.65	0.40	0.57

Source: McEwan & Carnoy (2000, Table 4).

Note: See text for definitions of school types. Unless indicated by "n.s.," all
results are statistically significant at 5%. For full details on the data and
methods, see McEwan & Carnoy (2000).

schools, such as a greater percentage of teachers with short-term contracts (McEwan & Carnoy, 2000).

At the same time, we found that students in Catholic private voucher schools score higher than students in public (municipal) schools even when SES differences among students in the two types of schools are held constant. Correcting for selection bias using the 1997 eighth-grade survey reduces this difference, but students in Catholic voucher schools still appear to score higher (McEwan, 2001a).

Although they produce somewhat lower test scores, nonreligious private schools cost about 13% less than public schools after controlling for test scores, student SES, and school location (see Table 1.3), suggesting they are more cost-effective. Further controlling for school resources, such as class size, explains only a small portion of this difference (see the final column in Table 1.3; for more details, see McEwan & Carnoy, 2000). The differences in costs are probably attributable to regulations imposed on municipal schools but not on private voucher schools. These include higher public-sector wages for teachers and other personnel and less public-sector flexibility in managing infrastructure investments.

Catholic voucher schools produce somewhat higher test scores, but they are equally cost-effective once we control for test scores, student SES, and school location (see Table 1.3). McEwan and Carnoy (2000) offer the explanation that Catholic schools spend more in absolute terms than public schools, thereby producing greater achieve-

Table 1.3. Cost differences between public DAEM and other school types, 1996.

	Cost difference adjusted for:		
	SES, location	SES, location, municipal dummies	SES, location, municipal dummies, school characteristics
Public corporation	n.s.	n.s.	n.s.
Catholic voucher	n.s.	n.s.	5.0%
Protestant voucher	-9.3%	n.s.	n.s.
Nonreligious voucher	-14.9%	-13.2%	-11.2%
Private nonvoucher	13.8%	14.0%	12.2%

Source: McEwan & Carnoy (2000, Table 4).

Note: See text for definitions of school types. Unless indicated by "n.s.," all results are statistically significant at 5%. For full details on the data and methods, see McEwan & Carnoy (2000).

ment, even though their *cost-effectiveness* is similar to that of public schools.

The fact that our analysis of relative student performance in public and private schools begins in 1990, a decade after the initial implementation of the voucher plan, could mean that we are just measuring the positive result of competition between private and public schools. Thanks to vouchers and a public school response to increased competition, the average scores of pupils in public schools may have increased by 1990 to the point where public school effectiveness achieved parity with private schools. We explored this issue in a separate analysis and briefly discuss it below.

Competition

Milton Friedman suggested that vouchers would "permit competition to develop," thus leading to the "development and improvement of all schools" (1962, p. 93). Despite its importance, the assertion is just beginning to be explored by empirical researchers. The few studies that exist generally have been conducted in educational systems that do not use vouchers, such as that of the United States (e.g., Dee, 1998; Hoxby, 1994; McEwan, 2000; Sander, 1999). More recently, two studies, one in Florida (Greene, 2001) and the other in Michigan, Milwaukee, and Arizona (Hoxby, 2001), purport to show that vouchers and charter school competition have a positive effect on public school performance (Carnoy, 2001).

The empirical challenge facing researchers is to relate a proxy of market competitiveness, such as the local share of private school enrollments, to outcome measures, such as academic achievement. Greater competition, proxied by the enrollment share, is hypothesized to increase achievement, all else being equal. Unfortunately, partial correlations between private enrollments and achievement, even controlling for a wide range of background variables, are likely to provide biased estimates of the effects of competition.

There are at least two reasons for this. First, private enrollments may be correlated with unmeasured determinants of achievement. In Chile, for example, private enrollments tend to be higher in more privileged municipalities. If we do not perfectly control for municipal wealth or socioeconomic status—both likely determinants of achievement—then we confound the effects of competition and unmeasured municipal characteristics. Second, private enrollments and achievement may be simultaneously determined; that is, increasing private enrollments may lead to higher achievement in public schools, but low levels of achievement in public schools may encourage more parents to choose private schools.

To address these biases, we constructed a data set that includes repeated observations of public school achievement and local private enrollment shares between 1982 and 1996 (McEwan & Carnoy, 1999). By differencing the panel data, we were able to control for unobserved determinants of outcomes that might bias estimates of competition effects.[8]

We found that the effect of competition is positive in the metropolitan region, though modestly so, accounting for a roughly 0.2 standard deviation increase in test scores over 15 years. Outside the metropolitan region, where three-quarters of Chile's primary students live, competition has small negative effects. Other evidence suggests that the P-900 program had positive effects of 0.1–0.2 standard deviation on Spanish and mathematics achievement.

There are at least two potential explanations for the lack of competitive effects. First, some public schools may lack the proper incentives to compete, in spite of declining enrollments and revenues. As one example, Gauri (1998) documents how some Chilean municipalities faced "soft" budget constraints during the 1980s. When voucher revenues declined, these municipalities lobbied the national government for extra budget allotments, instead of improving quality. Second, some public schools may not possess the means to improve quality, even given proper incentives. These schools generally employ the least-qualified teachers and enroll impoverished students who are ill prepared to succeed in the classroom. When these schools are faced with declining enrollments, they may simply lack the financial, administrative, or pedagogical resources that are necessary to raise achievement.

Our results neither refute nor provide strong support for the notion that competition will lead to improvements in the quality of public schools. Instead, they suggest that the effects of competition may exist in some contexts, but not in others. In this respect, they resemble the mixed findings from U.S. research, which are based on data from a variety of states, time periods, and institutional contexts (McEwan, 2000).

The Chilean experience demonstrates that many stakeholders will seek to alter the form and function of voucher policies, often with great success (for additional examples, see Gauri, 1998). This modifies the incentives and constraints faced by public school managers and, ultimately, the effects that vouchers will have on student outcomes. A cogent lesson from Chile is that an economic understanding of vouchers and competition cannot divorce itself from the larger political economy of school choice (Gauri, 1998).

It is worth noting that between 1980 and 1990 the Chilean voucher plan was implemented under a military dictatorship. In many respects, its provisions during that first decade met many of the conditions favored by many voucher advocates, including the weakening of collective bargaining (in Chile, teachers' unions were abolished in the 1980s, but restored in the 1990s) and the expansion of relatively unregulated for-profit private schooling.[9] If the effect of competition on public education was diminished in a strongly authoritarian context, it is plausible that it would also be at least as diminished in politically democratic societies, where political opposition to vouchers could not be easily squelched.

Competition encourages a large-scale sorting of students across public and private schools. This certainly occurred in Chile, and some empirical evidence suggests that it assumed the form of "cream-skimming," in which able or privileged students were the first to exit public schools (Gauri, 1998; Parry, 1996). If peer effects are important (McEwan, 2001b), then it is probable that the exit of these students negatively affected the outcomes of students remaining in public schools. Nevertheless, we do not have good empirical evidence on the full magnitude of sorting effects. It is clear, however, that a full evaluation of the Chilean reform—or any voucher plan, for that matter—should weigh the beneficial effects of competition against the potentially harmful effects of sorting.

A curious feature of the voucher literature is that advocates and critics have a tendency to emphasize one of these effects and to ignore or downplay the others. For example, advocates have emphasized the positive effects of competition (e.g., Greene, 2001; Hoxby, 1998, 2001), while skeptics have focused on the negative effects of sorting and cream-skimming (e.g., Fuller, Elmore, & Orfield, 1996). To adequately evaluate the impact of vouchers, we need to consider both.

Parent Choice

Several researchers have shown that Chilean parents with more schooling and higher incomes are more likely to enroll their children in both private voucher and nonvoucher schools, relative to public schools (Aedo & Larrañaga, 1994; Gauri, 1998; Winkler & Rounds, 1996). Though informative, such findings do not explain why parents have increasingly tended to choose private schools. One method of assessing this is to compare the characteristics of the school actually chosen by parents—public or private—to other schools in their choice set. In this fashion, we can examine the revealed preferences of parents for certain school characteristics, such as test scores or the socioeconomic background of other parents in the school.

To make this comparison, we estimated conditional logit models of the determinants of parental choice among public, private voucher, and elite private schools where tuition is paid (McEwan & Carnoy, 1998). We find that parents in private voucher schools have higher levels of schooling and income relative to public school parents. Moreover, parental school choice is sensitive to school attributes such as test scores and the educational background of other parents in the school. Nevertheless, we find that families have a relatively stronger preference for schools that enroll students with more highly educated parents. We also find that preferences for school attributes vary strongly in relation to parental education. Less-educated parents, for example, opt for schools with lower test scores and with less-educated parents. The opposite is true of more-educated parents.

These findings are at odds with the hypothesis that less-educated parents respond to the offer of higher-performing, higher-social-class schools to a similar degree as do more-educated parents, even when these schools are available in equal numbers and even when their cost is approximately the same.[10] Our results should not be interpreted as meaning that less-educated parents are "irrational." For example, Wells and Crain (1992) have argued that school choice is governed not only by resource availability but also by access to information and internalized viewpoints associated with social status.

Lower-income parents may not have full information concerning school quality because such information is costly to obtain or interpret, a sentiment echoed by Levin (1991). Existing evidence on Chile suggests that information about test scores may not be fully disseminated or available to all parents (Gauri, 1998). Even with full information on school quality, however, members of lower-social-class groups could be "either intimidated by, distrustful of, or resistant to members of the dominant group and therefore [would] remove themselves from competition for seats in the 'best' schools" (Wells & Crain, 1992, pp. 77–78). Lower-income parents might not be as likely to choose higher-performing schools with higher-social-status student bodies even when their children might qualify for these schools or they could afford to pay the somewhat higher costs associated with them.

Certainly these explanations must be considered in the Chilean context, where the income distribution is highly unequal and class divisions are strong. Schools with educated parents may reinforce these perceptions by dissuading less-educated parents from placing their children there. This would be rational behavior on the part of schools if they believed that lower-status children could affect the school's desirability to other parents, especially those with more education.

CONCLUSIONS

Chile's national voucher plan led to a rapid growth in private enrollments, driven by the expansion of nonreligious, for-profit schools. The empirical evidence discussed in this chapter suggests that such schools are slightly less effective than public schools in producing academic achievement but that they are more cost-effective. In contrast, established Catholic schools are more effective than public schools, although they are similarly cost-effective. Increasing competition from private schools may have led to small improvements in achievement for a subset of public students in Santiago, but not nationwide. For students in areas outside Santiago, competition may have produced slight declines in achievement. Lastly, evidence suggests that parents make choices about where to enroll their children based on school characteristics such as test scores and the socioeconomic background of other children in the school. The latter characteristic is particularly important. Moreover, highly educated parents are more likely than less-educated parents to base their decisions on these characteristics.

Taken together, these findings suggest several lessons for the debate on vouchers, in Chile and other countries. First, it is clear that all private schools are not created equal. This may be obvious, but it is difficult to extract this conclusion from most research in the United States, which usually focuses on a single category of private schooling (often Catholic). There exist excellent, thoughtful studies explaining why Catholic (secondary) education in the United States may produce higher achievement and attainment than public high schools for lower-SES students (e.g., Bryk, Lee, & Holland, 1993). However, much research that argues for markets in education overgeneralizes the positive aspects of private schooling and the negative aspects of public schools (see, e.g., Chubb & Moe, 1990). The Chilean experience suggests that any generalization conceals a great deal of heterogeneity and is unlikely to provide useful guidance on the potential effectiveness and costs of private schools that may arise under vouchers. It is especially important to understand the differences between private schools operated by religious and nonreligious (especially for-profit) organizations. Research in Chile suggests that their outcomes and costs are quite different. Undoubtedly, their objectives, resources, and constraints are also distinct, although existing theory and evidence provide little basis for predicting or interpreting these differences.

Second, there is no consistent evidence that vouchers lead to important gains in academic achievement, even for low-income students, the target of most voucher experiments in the United States. The largest category of private schooling—nonreligious voucher schools—appears to produce somewhat less academic achievement than public schools among similar kinds of students, on average. In contrast, other categories of schools, such as Catholic or nonvoucher private schools, may produce greater achievement. Even so, the evidence suggests that this achievement is obtained by using more resources than do public schools.

Third, there is not much evidence that the small differences in effectiveness between public and nonreligious voucher schools are the result of market competition. Competition may have led to modest improvements in the achievement of some public schools in the capital. However, gains of a similar magnitude appear to have been achieved via the P-900 program, a straightforward investment in textbooks and in-service training. Outside the capital, where the majority of Chileans live, competition appears to have had small negative effects on achievement. These findings are not consistent with the notion that vouchers will produce across-the-board gains in student outcomes. Regional variation in the effects of competition may stem from several features of the institutional and educational context. For example, many public schools may have lacked the proper incentives or means to respond by improving quality, despite losing enrollments.

Fourth, there is consistent evidence that nonreligious voucher schools produced student achievement at lower cost than public schools even when controlling for test scores and student SES. In this respect, for-profit private schools in Chile are more cost-effective than public schools. A great deal of cost savings may be due to lower teacher salaries in private schools and other constraints placed on public school resource allocation. While this can be viewed as an argument for private schooling, it can also be given a broader interpretation. If public schools operated in the same regulatory environment— regardless of whether schools are financed by vouchers—there seems little reason why they could not become as efficient as private schools (at the very least, this is an empirical question). In other words, the apparent benefits of vouchers are principally a result of a more favorable regulatory environment for private school entrepreneurs.

Finally, the evidence from Chile provides a cautionary tale regarding equity. It suggests that voucher plans that are comprehensive in their coverage are less likely to benefit the poor. Research on the revealed preferences of families suggests that less-educated parents are less likely to make choices based on school quality. Furthermore, the best-quality voucher schools, operated by the Catholic Church, enroll students of higher SES than nonreligious voucher schools and charge higher tuition co-payments. Most poor students attend public or nonreligious voucher schools. Furthermore, the majority of private schools are still located in urban areas with higher-income and better-educated families. Despite 20 years of voucher reform, public schools are still the only option for a large fraction of primary students, particularly in rural areas. Finally, competition appears not to have improved the achievement of the poor public school students outside of Santiago.

NOTES

This chapter is based on research conducted under a grant from the Ford Foundation in 1998–1999. We would like to thank the foundation for its support. The views expressed here are, however, the authors' and should not be attributed to the foundation. This chapter is partially based on another work by the authors, "Privatization Through Vouchers in Developing Countries: The Cases of Chile and Colombia."

1. For recent examples of such claims, see Chubb and Moe (1990); Greene, Peterson, and Du (1998); and Hoxby (1998). McEwan (2000) also describes a simple economic framework that underlies voucher proposals.

2. For reviews of the U.S. evidence, see Goldhaber (1999), Levin (1998), McEwan (2000), and Carnoy (2001).

3. For example, see the quasi-experimental evaluations of the small-scale voucher program in Milwaukee (Greene et al., 1998; Rouse, 1998; Witte, 1998). Also see the recent experimental evaluations of small-scale private scholarship programs in New York, Dayton, and Washington, D.C. (Howell & Peterson, 2000; Howell, Wolf, Peterson, & Campbell, 2000; Peterson, Myers, & Howell, 1998; Wolf, Howell, & Peterson, 2000).

4. Once transferred to municipalities, schools were placed under the control of one of two kinds of institutions. Most opted to manage their schools with a Departmento de Administración de la Educación Municipal (DAEM). DAEMs exist under the larger umbrella of the municipal bureaucracy and, as such, are governed by municipal rules. Corporations are nonprofit organizations that are not subject to direct mayoral control, though the mayor does preside over a governing board. Their operations are generally subject to fewer regulations. In contrast to DAEMs, the corporation head is not

required to be a teacher and corporation employees are not subjected to municipal rules regarding the hiring and remuneration of municipal employees.

5. Municipalities received an overhead grant of 3% to 5% of total municipal wages and salaries as an inducement to begin administering schools (Parry, 1997a; Winkler & Rounds, 1996).

6. Chilean law specifies a factor by which the base voucher is adjusted for students at every grade level. Furthermore, selected municipalities receive ad hoc "zone assignments" to compensate for high poverty or isolation. Since 1987, rural schools within municipalities have received upward adjustments. For details, see Parry (1997a).

7. Such corrections for selection bias depend vitally on the choice of exclusion restrictions, that is, on the variables that are posited to affect the probability of attending a private school, but not achievement. McEwan (2001a) uses the local availability of private schools, which is strongly related to the probability that students attend a private school. It is not correlated with achievement after conditioning on student SES.

8. We initially first-differenced the data (akin to including "fixed effects", or dummy variables for each school). First-differencing controls for unobserved determinants of outcomes that are constant across time for individual schools. We then differenced the data a second time, a "difference-in-difference" approach that controls for unobservables that have a constant time trend.

9. Advocates such as Friedman (1962) and Chubb and Moe (1990) have argued strongly for school deregulation and the elimination of the "control" of teachers' unions over education.

10. Most voucher programs in the United States are aimed at low-income parents, who are seen as most likely to respond to vouchers because the public schools their children attend are of such low quality (see Hoxby, 2001).

REFERENCES

Aedo, C., & Larrañaga, O. (1994). Sistemas de entrega de los servicios sociales: La experiencia chilena. In C. Aedo & O. Larrañaga (Eds.), *Sistema de entrega de los servicios sociales: Una agenda para la reforma* (pp. 33–74). Washington, DC: Banco Interamericano de Desarrollo.

Bryk, A., Lee, V. E., & Holland, P. B. (1993). *Catholic schools and the common good.* Cambridge, MA: Harvard University Press.

Carnoy, M. (2001). *Do school vouchers improve student performance?* Washington, DC: Economic Policy Institute.

Castañeda, T. (1992). *Combating poverty: Innovative social reforms in Chile during the 1980s.* San Francisco: ICS Press.

Chubb, J. E., & Moe, T. M. (1990). *Politics, markets, and America's schools.* Washington, DC: Brookings Institution Press.

Cox, C. (1997). La reforma de la educación chilena: Contexto, contenidos, implementación. Programa de Promoción de la Reforma Educativa en América Latina (PREAL). Washington, DC: Inter-American Dialogue.

Dee, T. S. (1998). Competition and the quality of public schools. *Economics of Education Review, 17*(4), 419–427.

Espinola, V. (1993). *The educational reform of the military regime in Chile: The system's response to competition, choice, and market relations.* Unpublished doctoral dissertation, University of Wales, United Kingdom.

Friedman, M. (1955). The role of government in education. In R. A. Solo (Ed.), *Economics and the public interest* (pp. 123–144). New Brunswick, NJ: Rutgers University Press.

Friedman, M. (1962). *Capitalism and freedom.* Chicago: University of Chicago Press.

Fuller, B., Elmore, R. F., & Orfield, G. (Eds.). (1996). *Who chooses, who loses? Culture, institutions, and the unequal effects of school choice.* New York: Teachers College Press.

Garcia-Huidobro, J. E. (1994). Positive discrimination in education: Its justification and a Chilean example. *International Review of Education, 40*(3–5), 209–221.

Gauri, V. (1998). *School choice in Chile: Two decades of educational reform.* Pittsburgh, PA: University of Pittsburgh Press.

Goldhaber, D. D. (1999). School choice: An examination of the empirical evidence on achievement, parental decision making, and equity. *Educational Researcher, 28*(9), 16–25.

Greene, J. P. (2001). *An evaluation of the Florida A-Plus Accountability and School Choice Program.* New York: Manhattan Institute for Policy Research, Center for Civic Innovation. http://www.manhattan-institute.org/html/cr_aplus.htm.

Greene, J. P., Peterson, P. E., & Du, J. (1998). School choice in Milwaukee: A randomized experiment. In P. E. Peterson & B. C. Hassel (Eds.), *Learning from school choice* (pp. 335–356). Washington, DC: Brookings Institution Press.

Howell, W. G., & Peterson, P. E. (2000). *School choice in Dayton, Ohio: An evaluation after one year.* Program on Education Policy and Governance, Harvard University, Cambridge, MA.

Howell, W. G., Wolf, P. J., Peterson, P. E., & Campbell, D. E. (2000, September). *Test-score effects of school vouchers in Dayton, Ohio, New York City, and Washington, DC: Evidence from randomized field trials.* Paper prepared for the American Political Science Association meeting, Washington, DC.

Hoxby, C. M. (1994). Do private schools provide competition for public schools? National Bureau of Economic Research Working Paper No. 4978, Cambridge, MA.

Hoxby, C. M. (1998). What do America's "traditional" forms of school choice teach us about school choice reforms? *Federal Reserve Bank of New York Economic Policy Review, 4*(1), 47–59.

Hoxby, C. M. (2001). *School choice and school productivity (or, could school choice be a tide that lifts all boats?)*. Unpublished manuscript, Harvard University and National Bureau of Economic Research.

Jofré, G. (1988). El sistema de subvenciones en educación: La experiencia chilena. Estudios Públicos, (32), 197–237.

Larrañaga, O. (1995). Descentralización de la educación en Chile: Una evaluación económica. *Estudios Públicos, 60*, 243–286.

Levin, H. M. (1991). The economics of educational choice. *Economics of Education Review, 10*(2), 137–158.

Levin, H. M. (1998). Educational vouchers: Effectiveness, choice, and costs. *Journal of Policy Analysis and Management, 17*(3), 373–391.

McEwan, P. J. (2000). The potential impact of large-scale voucher programs. *Review of Educational Research, 70*(2), 103–149.

McEwan, P. J. (2001a). The effectiveness of public, Catholic, and non-religious private schooling in Chile's voucher system. *Education Economics, 9*(2), 103–128.

McEwan, P. J. (2001b). *Peer effects on student achievement: Evidence from Chile*. Unpublished manuscript, University of Illinois at Urbana–Champaign.

McEwan, P. J., & Carnoy, M. (1998). *Choice between private and public schools in a voucher system: Evidence from Chile*. Unpublished manuscript, Stanford University.

McEwan, P. J., & Carnoy, M. (1999). *The impact of competition on public school quality: Longitudinal evidence from Chile's voucher system*. Unpublished manuscript, Stanford University.

McEwan, P. J., & Carnoy, M. (2000). The effectiveness and efficiency of private schools in Chile's voucher system. *Educational Evaluation and Policy Analysis, 22*(3), 213–239.

Murnane, R. J., Newstead, S., & Olsen, R. J. (1985). Comparing public and private schools: The puzzling role of selection bias. *Journal of Business and Economic Statistics, 3*(1), 23–35.

Parry, T. R. (1996). Will pursuit of higher quality sacrifice equal opportunity in education? An analysis of the education voucher system in Santiago. *Social Science Quarterly, 77*(4), 821–841.

Parry, T. R. (1997a). Achieving balance in decentralization: A case study of education decentralization in Chile. *World Development, 25*(2), 211–225.

Parry, T. R. (1997b). Decentralization and privatization: Education policy in Chile. *Journal of Public Policy, 17*(1), 107–133.

Peterson, P. E., Myers, D., & Howell, W. G. (1998). *An evaluation of the New York City school choice scholarships program: The first year*. Mathematica Policy Research and Program on Education Policy and Governance, Harvard University, Cambridge, MA.

Rojas, P. (1998). Remuneraciones de los profesores en Chile. *Estudios Públicos, 71*, 121–175.

Rouse, C. E. (1998). Private school vouchers and student achievement: An evaluation of the Milwaukee parental choice program. *Quarterly Journal of Economics, 113*(2), 553–602.

Sander, W. (1999). Private schools and public school achievement. *Journal of Human Resources, 34*(4), 697–709.

Schiefelbein, E. (1991). Restructuring education through economic competition: The case of Chile. *Journal of Educational Administration, 29*(4), 17–29.

Stewart, F., & Ranis, G. (1994). *Decentralization in Chile.* Human Development Report Occasional Papers No. 14, United Nations, New York.

Valdes, J. G. (1995). *Pinochet's economists: The Chicago School in Chile.* Cambridge, UK: Cambridge University Press.

Vargas, J. (1997). Mercado,competencia y equidad en la educación subvencionada. *Persona y Sociedad, 11*(2), 59–69.

Wells, A. S., & Crain, R. L. (1992). Do parents choose school quality or school status? A sociological theory of free market education. In P. W. Cookson (Ed.), *The choice controversy* (pp. 65–81). Newbury Park, CA: Corwin.

Winkler, D. R., & Rounds, T. (1996). Municipal and private sector response to decentralization and school choice. *Economics of Education Review, 15*(4), 365–376.

Witte, J. F. (1998). The Milwaukee voucher experiment. *Educational Evaluation and Policy Analysis, 20*(4), 229–251.

Wolf, P. J., Howell, W. G., & Peterson, P. E. (2000). *School choice in Washington, DC: An evaluation after one year.* Program on Education Policy and Governance, Harvard University, Cambridge, MA.

CHAPTER 2

School Choice in New Zealand: A Cautionary Tale

Edward B. Fiske
Helen F. Ladd

In 1989 New Zealand embarked on a two-stage restructuring of its state education system that was more complete and far bolder than is typically the case for major educational reforms. The first step came when a Labour government abolished the country's long-standing, and bureaucratically stifling, centralized system of school governance and turned operational control of each of the country's 2,700 primary and secondary schools over to locally elected school-specific boards of trustees dominated by parents. Two years later, in 1991, a newly elected National government pursuing an aggressive new-right agenda ratcheted the reform stakes up a notch by abolishing enrollment zones and giving parents the right to seek to enroll their child in any public school. These reforms are known as the Tomorrow's Schools reforms.

The importance of the Tomorrow's Schools reforms in New Zealand comes from the fact that the ideas they embraced—decentralization of authority to individual schools, parental choice, and market competition—are part of the global marketplace of ideas about education reform that are the object of experimentation, debate, and controversy in many other countries. The boldness of New Zealand's reforms makes it relatively easy for outsiders to observe the effects, positive and negative, of these central ideas. In addition, the reforms were sustained for 10 years, which means that they were in place long enough for observers to see how they evolved over time, how they played out in practice, and what new and unexpected policy challenges they inspired.

Our analysis covers the years 1989 to 1998, the period during which the reforms were initiated by a Labour government, expanded by a National government, and subsequently adjusted in various ways in response to political and practical realities.[1] We did most of the research for this chapter during 1998, while the National government was still in power and was still strongly supportive of the reforms. The following year, control of the government reverted to the Labour party, which has since begun to reverse or modify some of them.

It is a fair question to ask how the experience of this island nation of only 3.8 million people (and 48 million sheep) is relevant to other countries around the world, especially those with large, diverse urban populations. In fact, most New Zealanders live in urban areas, and the research summarized below focuses on how the reforms played out in the country's three main urban areas of Auckland, Wellington, and Christchurch. As is the case in other countries, minority groups are disproportionately represented in these areas. In the New Zealand context, minority groups include the Maori, who account for about 14% of the total population, and Pacific Islanders, who account for about 6%. Members of these ethnic groups tend to have lower income and to exhibit lower levels of educational attainment and achievement than their more affluent counterparts of European background. Thus they impose greater educational challenges for the education system.

New Zealand also has a long-standing international reputation for social innovation. In the field of literacy, New Zealand was the birthplace of Reading Recovery, an approach to reading instruction that has been widely emulated in the United States and other countries. On international tests, New Zealand students rate near the top in reading and recently scored well on the twelfth-grade international tests of science and math.

It should be noted at the outset that, because New Zealand does not carry out systematic national testing, we cannot determine whether the combination of self-governing schools in a competitive environment has increased average student achievement. The best we can do is to draw inferences from piecemeal evidence on school-leaving exams and from perceptions of impacts on the quality of student learning from surveys of principals and teachers administered throughout the reform period.

CHARACTERIZING THE REFORM PACKAGE

With respect to its self-governance component, the New Zealand reform package resembles the U.S. charter school phenomenon, which gives significant flexibility to boards of individual schools that are publicly funded. Since 1989, every school in New Zealand has been self-governing and therefore, in principle, free to innovate and to respond to the needs and wishes of its local community. The Department of Education, which formerly operated the schools, was abolished and replaced with a smaller Ministry of Education charged with establishing policy rather than managing schools. Each school receives public funding for operating expenses that varies with the number of students in the school. The government maintained ownership of the school buildings and is responsible for major renovations, modernization, and new facilities. Each school also drafts a charter document that specifies its mission and objectives.

With respect to parental choice, the closest U.S. analogy to the New Zealand reform is the concept of public school choice. Since 1991, New Zealand parents have, in principle, been free to choose among all public schools. The public schools include not only "Crown-owned schools" but Roman Catholic and other religious schools that have a "special character" and are run by boards that are accountable both to the Ministry of Education and to the sponsoring agency. Such schools were "integrated" into the public school system during the 1970s, when the country's Catholic school system was going through a financial crisis and church leaders were threatening to force the state system to absorb tens of thousands of additional students. Although they own their own physical plants, integrated schools are fully funded by the state for operating and new capital expenses. As of the mid-1990s, only 3.5% of the country's children were in independent private schools and therefore outside the system of public school choice.

New Zealand might also be described as having a "quasi-voucher" system in that parents choose among schools, a school's revenue is closely tied to the number of students it can attract, and the available choices include the integrated religious schools that were formerly outside the public school system. However, one must be careful in characterizing the New Zealand system as a voucher system, because it has few, if any, mechanisms or incentives for new schools to be established. Thus, in contrast to a true voucher system, in which vouchers would provide a financial incentive for new private schools to be created to compete with the traditional public schools, New

Zealand's reforms encouraged competition primarily among the existing schools, both Crown-owned and integrated.

THE GENESIS OF THE TOMORROW'S SCHOOLS REFORMS

Like any change of such magnitude, the Tomorrow's Schools reforms came about for multiple reasons. First of all, reform of the education sector was part of a general restructuring of New Zealand's private and public sectors that was necessitated by a major economic crisis in the mid-1980s. In both the private and public spheres, the themes of the day were downsizing, deregulation, competition, and efficiency. Initial reforms were designed to reduce the power of unions and to make public-sector enterprises operate more like private-sector firms (Boston, Martin, Pallot, & Walsh, 1996). The attention of the reformers then turned toward the social policy areas of health and education.

Significantly, the Tomorrow's Schools reforms emerged less from a sense that the old educational system had failed than from the conviction that governance reform could make it work better. Over the years a series of official commissions had warned that the system had become top-heavy, ponderous, and unresponsive; that school administrators were unnecessarily restricted in doing their jobs; and that the Department of Education's outdated structures were undermining the quality of teaching and learning that the country required if it was to remain competitive in the emerging global economy.

The reforms were shaped by the three distinct ideological currents that we characterize respectively as democratic/populist, managerial/business, and new right/market (Fiske & Ladd, 2000). Each of these currents brought its own analysis of the fundamental problem to be addressed and, by implication, of the appropriate remedy.

Proponents of the democratic/populist approach believed that the state education system was failing to prepare a broad base of New Zealand's young people to take their place in the emerging global economy, and they attributed this problem to the fact that the system had lost touch with the students and communities it served. Such thinking was particularly strong among Maori, Pacific Islanders, and others concerned about issues of equity. To them, education should be a partnership among parents, communities, and school professionals, and the way to achieve this was to build greater parental and community "voice" into the running of schools. This objective could be achieved by transferring operating control to individual schools and by letting elected boards of trustees define the mission of each school through a school charter.

Adherents of the managerial/business current supported the idea of a strong state education system. The problem, as they saw it, was that the current system was too large, cumbersome, and unresponsive to student needs to carry out this function effectively. To them the solution lay in importing managerial principles that had proved effective in corporations and other large institutions into the state education system. They were open to democratic/populist ideas of community involvement in school management because they believed a decentralized system would increase efficiency.

Those who advocated the new-right/market approach agreed with the managerial/business analysis that the state education system was inefficient and needed to be overhauled. To them, however, the way to do this was not through the actions of managers but by the establishment of a competitive environment. They also argued that even if the existing system were running efficiently, it infringed on the rights of parents and students to shape their own educational experience. This problem, too, would be solved by the creation of a market environment in which parents exercised choice and local schools competed for students.

Although the three currents were present from the outset, their relative influence varied significantly over time. The vision of education that was embodied by the initial enabling legislation of Tomorrow's Schools was for all practical purposes a combination of the first and second currents—mixing community involvement with management reforms. Over time, democratic/populist ideas were gradually pushed out, and the ideological balance of power in New Zealand's state education system shifted to a combination of managerial/business and new-right/market concepts. Local school charters, supposedly the centerpiece of community voice, did not live up to their early billing, and the new institutions intended to promote community involvement in education were stillborn.

SELF-GOVERNING SCHOOLS

The Tomorrow's Schools reforms can be thought of as establishing a "tight–loose–tight" governance structure for education. Under this arrangement, the goals and missions of the schools would be clear (that is, tight), schools would have significant responsibility for how they operate (the loose part), and schools would be held tightly accountable to the center for outcomes. For a number of reasons, New Zealand has not fully achieved a governance structure of this type, but its efforts to move in that direction provide insight into the challenges of implementing such a structure.

Governance

The principle of self-governing schools is the bedrock on which the Tomorrow's Schools reform package was constructed in 1989. The reforms created a system whereby each school was run by a board of trustees elected at the school level. These boards were controlled by parents and had the authority to hire and fire the principal and the teachers and to allocate funds. In the spirit of self-governance, schools that were at capacity were given the authority to set their own enrollment policies regarding which students they would accept.

The initial design for self-governance provided for each school to have a local charter that would provide it with "clear and explicit objectives" reflecting "both national requirements and local needs." These charters would constitute a "contract between the community and the institution, and the institution and the state."[2] Under this three-way contract the various parties would have different responsibilities but would relate as equals. The state would fund schools and provide national guidelines, while boards of trustees would make local policies and run the schools in line with community interests.

This design proved to be unworkable for a variety of reasons, including concern about the ministry's capacity to negotiate and approve 2,700 new charters in a short period of time and concern on the part of the central government about its legal obligations to provide adequate funding for schools. Thus the charter framework quickly evolved from a three-way contract among equals to a one-way statement of the obligations of local schools to promote national objectives.

Funding

While governance was to be decentralized, funding remained a function of the central government and came in two forms. First, the government provided each school with an operations grant, much of which was distributed on a per-pupil basis, to cover expenses such as teaching materials, maintenance, and utilities. Second, each school received an entitlement of a specific number of teachers, and the government paid the salaries of these teachers directly. The teacher entitlement reflected the government's policy decisions about appropriate teacher–pupil ratios by grade level, and it varied by school in accordance with the number of students in each grade. Schools hired their own teachers and allocated them among classes as they chose.

This two-part funding system was not what had been originally envisioned. In keeping with the spirit of self-governance, the Tomorrow's Schools enabling legislation called for a "bulk funding" system under which the government would give each school a single grant with two components—one for operating expenses and one for teacher salaries. However, the Labour government chose not to implement this part of the reform immediately. Its reasons were that the details had not yet been fully worked out, that the new boards of trustees already had their hands full dealing with all the other changes, and that one important source of the Labour party's political support, the teachers' unions, was adamantly opposed. Consequently, bulk funding of teacher salaries was put on hold and teacher slots were funded separately.

When the National party regained power in 1991, the new minister of education, Lockwood Smith, put the bulk-funding issue back on the agenda. Despite Smith's strong support for bulk funding, however, he, too, had to back off in the face of a revolt within his own caucus. Members of Parliament of his own party were being pressured by schools and trustees opposed to the plan, and the prime minister reportedly had reservations based on the strong opposition of the teachers' unions and concern that the National's majority in Parliament might be jeopardized. Smith worked out a compromise that permitted a voluntary trial of bulk funding. Schools that opted for this method would receive funding for the number of teachers to which they were entitled, based essentially on average teacher salaries by school type. With this arrangement, schools with large numbers of inexperienced, and hence low-salaried, teachers had greater incentives to volunteer than schools with a large number of higher-salaried teachers.

Much was at stake in the debate over bulk funding of teacher salaries (Fiske & Ladd, 2000). At one level the issue was simply how much flexibility the schools should have to move funds from one category to another. On a number of other levels, however, the debate raised some fundamental political, economic, and educational issues and took on great symbolic significance to many of the groups involved. Critics charged that bulk funding was merely a cover for agendas that included breaking the teachers' unions, moving toward privatization, or setting up a system whereby the government needed to pull only a single lever in order to reduce funding for education.

One notable feature of New Zealand's education reforms was a recognition that disadvantaged students were more costly to educate than other students. In the early 1990s, the Ministry of Education developed a system of assigning decile rankings to schools based on the socioeconomic and ethnic characteristics of the students they attracted. These deciles were developed so that supplementary funding could be distributed to the schools with the most challenging-to-educate students. Low-decile schools, which serve large proportions of minority children and students from disadvantaged backgrounds, are eligible for more funding per pupil. Students in high-decile schools tend to come from predominantly affluent and well-educated European families.

Accountability

The move to self-governance of local schools meant that New Zealand had to rethink the way in which schools were held accountable to the central government, which bore the ultimate responsibility for maintaining the system of compulsory education. Given its roots in the British education system, with its long tradition of school inspectors, it is no surprise that New Zealand opted for an inspectorate model for holding its newly self-governing schools accountable. For this purpose, the initial reform legislation established a new agency, the Education Review Office (ERO), that would be independent of the Ministry of Education and charged with monitoring the schools.

The main function of the new agency was to provide an independent and arms-length evaluation at least every 2 years of how well each school was performing. To that end, the ERO sent a review team made up of former teachers to each school. The teams, which had from two to five members, visited classes, pored over school documents and records, discussed draft reports with the schools, and issued final public reports laying out both the school's strengths and any deficiencies that needed to be addressed. Significantly, the ERO had no enforcement authority. Although the ERO got off to a halting start, the agency gained respect and credibility after the 1991 appointment of a strong and effective new chief review officer, Judith Aitken.

The inspectorate system in general worked reasonably well in New Zealand. It was effective in part because of its independence from the Ministry of Education. In addition, it had credibility because of the high quality of the professionals on its staff and its strong leadership. However, a number of issues and concerns arose over the years.

The intent of the reformers was for the ERO to monitor how well each school was meeting the "clear and specific aims and objectives, expressed as outcomes" specified in each school's charter.[3] However, as already described, the charter failed to emerge as the definitive document envisioned, and the ERO was put in the position of having to determine for itself what it should monitor.

Aitken's solution was to introduce two distinct types of audit: assurance and effectiveness. The assurance audits, which began in 1992, were designed to verify that the boards of trustees were meeting their legal obligations to the Crown as specified in the school's charter, including adherence to the National Education Guidelines, and that they were fulfilling other agreements between the state and the schools, such as the schools' property agreement. In retrospect, it was clear that such audits were necessary, especially during the start-up period. During 1992–1993, only 12% of the boards of trustees were operating in a fully lawful way. By 1998, the proportion had reached 90%.

In 1993 the ERO added the second type of audit—the effectiveness audit—to its arsenal as a means of shifting attention to student achievement. Because New Zealand has no compulsory national tests, the ERO has no good way to compare student achievement in one school either with that of other schools or with national standards. Instead, effectiveness audits are process-oriented and pose two specific questions to local boards of trustees: What do you expect the children in the school to learn? And how will you know that learning has occurred?

Despite this effort to focus more on educational outcomes, the ERO has been criticized for its focus on administrative and educational processes rather than on student outcomes. To be sure, some of the processes are related to outcomes, such as whether the curriculum is being delivered and whether boards of trustees have any way of knowing what the students are learning. Nonetheless, the reviews often became mechanistic. They were heavily focused on management procedures and did not necessarily foster better educational outcomes. Moreover, the ERO provided no evidence in support of its general view that "the quality of school governance and management is a reliable indicator of the quality of educational service provided."[4] That said, the reviews were undoubtedly useful to many schools. A 1999 survey of primary schools, for example, indicated that 56% of the principals found them "helpful" and another 21% "very helpful." In addition, most (72%) of the schools made minor changes as a result of the review, and 13% made major changes, mainly in the areas of assessment, curriculum, and performance management (Wylie, 1999).

Overall Satisfaction with the New System

In general, the new system of self-governing schools in New Zealand worked quite well, although, not surprisingly, it worked better for some types of schools than for others. Schools in New Zealand were generally happy with their new self-governing status, and virtually no one wanted to return to the highly controlled system of the past, when schools could not even make unilateral decisions about the color of classroom walls.

As a general rule, schools serving predominantly middle- and upper-income constituencies had no trouble mustering board members with the skills needed to carry out the responsibilities of self-governance. Most trustees in such schools were sophisticated enough to organize the search for a principal, read a budget, and engage in strategic planning, and they understood subtleties such as the distinction between governance and management. When board members in such schools lacked specific skills, such as legal or financial expertise, they usually had little difficulty co-opting other parents with the necessary skills onto the board.

Problems for Low-Decile Schools

The situation was quite different in low-decile schools—those serving large proportions of disadvantaged and minority students—where the sort of cultural capital that middle-income schools take for granted was largely missing. In 1998 the Education Review Office analyzed reports that its review officers had filed for 236 decile-1 and 231 decile-10 schools. It found that 24% of the low-decile schools were judged inadequate in terms of their compliance with the legal requirements of Tomorrow's Schools versus only 5% of the high-decile schools.[5] Not only did board members in schools serving low-income areas frequently lack technical skills, but they often lacked the sophistication that would allow them to challenge decisions by the principal. In recent years the Ministry of Education has taken steps to consolidate the boards of several low-decile schools in order to draw on human resources from a wider area.

Impacts on Innovation

The new system did not generate much diversity and innovation. Of course there were exceptions, such as a high school in Christchurch that set up a sports academy, a primary school in Auckland that organized its curriculum around theories of multiple intelligences, and new programs and schools serving Maori students. The programs for Maori students, however, were the result of broader national policies toward the Maori and should not be viewed as an outcome of the Tomorrow's Schools reform.

Various factors account for the limited amount of diversity and innovation. The main one is that the incentive system of New Zealand's competitive model did not encourage schools to look for niche markets. The strategic objective for most schools was to maximize the number of their students—at least up the school's capacity—and thereby to maximize funding and, as we discuss below, gain control over their student intake. Consequently, schools were more interested in offering broad traditional programs aimed at attracting a large number of students than in designing programs targeted to particular types of students. A second explanation is the state's early reassertion of its interest in educational missions and its requirement that all school charters include the National Education Guidelines. In this way the state made it clear that local goals would be secondary to those imposed from the center. A third and related reason was the existence of national school-leaving exams. Results on these exams provided a common benchmark for parents to use in comparing secondary schools and constituted a strong incentive for schools to work toward common goals. Most of the differences that did emerge among schools had more to do with the socioeconomic and ethnic mix of students that schools were serving than with explicit attempts by schools to innovate.

PARENTAL CHOICE

Once geographic zones for schools were abolished in 1991, parental choice became an integral part of compulsory education in New Zealand. Parents, including many Maori and Pacific Island families, did not hesitate to make use of their expanded right to choose among schools, and the choices they made had large and systematic effects on enrollment patterns. In particular, parental choice led to a distinct movement of students away from low-decile schools (serving high proportions of disadvantaged and minority students) and toward high-decile schools (serving a more advantaged clientele).

In the relatively slow-growing Wellington area, for example, enrollment in the three lowest deciles of secondary schools decreased by about 25% between 1991 and 1996.[6] Enrollment declined by a smaller percentage on average in the middle-decile schools and increased somewhat in the high-decile schools. In fast-growing Auckland, the patterns for secondary school students were clearest at the two ends of the distribution, with decile-1 schools losing about 20% of their students and decile-10 schools growing by more than 15%. In Christchurch (which had no decile-1 secondary schools) there was a clear shift of students between decile-2 and -3 schools and decile-4 and -5 schools. Comparisons between these enrollment changes and changes predicted based on the numbers of school-age children in each area from the New Zealand census of population indicate that the patterns cannot be explained by changes in the pattern of residential locations of families with children.

Parental Preference for Higher-Decile Schools

The pattern of these enrollment shifts suggests that parents tended to use the mix of students in a school as a proxy for the quality of the school. In particular, parents tended to view schools with more White and more advantaged students as superior to those with more minority and disadvantaged students. At the secondary school level, parental judgements of this type were fully consistent with publicly reported league tables showing that students in high-decile schools typically perform better on school-leaving exams than do those in lower-decile schools. But even if parents were astute enough to recognize that the average level of test scores says more about the socioeconomic composition of a school's students than about the contribution of a school to a child's learning, their tendency to use the mix of students as a proxy for quality could be quite rational.

From the perspective of parents, higher-decile schools may well have been preferred because they were likely to attract higher-quality teachers[7] and their mix of students could well generate positive spillover effects on the motivation of other students.[8] In contrast to low-decile schools, with their heavy concentrations of students who are challenging to educate, higher-decile schools were able to devote less time to pastoral care and more time to teaching and learning. In addition, such schools had access to a larger stock of parental resources to complement the budgetary resources available to the school. We note, however, that what is rational for individual families may not be rational for the system as a whole.

Role of Policy

Also affecting the enrollment patterns were three policy decisions related to the implementation of parental choice. The first was the country's decision not to finance transportation costs in urban areas. This policy meant that it was easier for middle- and upper-income families to choose schools outside their local neighborhood than it was for low income families. The second was the decision to encourage schools to supplement their public funding with revenue from local sources, including activity fees from parents. While schools were prohibited from making such fees compulsory, the fees undoubtedly played a role in some parents' decisions about where to enroll their children.

Third, and probably most important, was New Zealand's decision, fully consistent with the spirit of self-governing schools, to let a school that had more applications than spaces draft an "enrollment scheme" spelling out the criteria it would use for selecting students. Although parental choice had been introduced initially at a time when many schools had excess capacity, it did not take long for the more popular schools, typically the higher-decile schools, to reach their capacities and thus to earn the right to establish enrollment schemes. By establishing such a scheme, schools gained effective control of which students they would accept and which they would turn down. In such situations, parental choice, in effect, gave way to school choice. By 1997, more than 50% of urban secondary school students were in schools that had enrollment schemes, and the percentage was above 60% in the fast-growing Auckland area. In the Christchurch area, by 1997 every school with a decile ranking above 6 was at capacity and had an enrollment scheme.[9] Even at the primary level, more than 50% of students in Auckland and Christchurch (but only 30% in Wellington) had such a plan.

Thus the particular model of choice adopted by Tomorrow's Schools fell short of the ostensible goal of offering choice on an equal basis to all students. Some families, especially those with low incomes, were not in a position to exercise choice, in part because they could not afford the transportation, fees, and other costs of enrolling in a preferred school and in part because they were denied access to their preferred school because of the enrollment schemes. In addition, because no student had a guaranteed school of attendance, some families found it difficult to enroll their child in any school within a reasonable commuting distance. This last consideration has been a major rationale for the recent retrenchment in parental choice under the new Labour government.

Polarization of Student Enrollment

The expansion of choice was beneficial for many families and their children, including many Maori and Pacific Islanders who seized the opportunity to choose new schools. Although both White and minority families participated in the movement from low- to high-decile schools, the former were more aggressive in taking advantage of the choice options than Maori or Pacific Islanders. As a result, the system of parental choice had the undesirable effect of increasing the ethnic and socioeconomic polarization of the education system, particularly at the bottom end of the distribution of schools.

Between 1991 and 1996, for example, the share of minorities in decile-1 primary and intermediate schools in the capital city of Wellington rose from 76% to 82%—a shift that cannot be explained by changes in ethnic residential patterns as measured by census data.[10] At the secondary level even greater changes occurred, although the patterns were a bit more complex, as some minorities moved from decile-1 to decile-2 schools while Europeans fled from both. The net effect was a large increase in the proportion of minorities in the low-decile schools. Piecemeal evidence from a ministry-financed study indicates that school enrollments also became more segregated in terms of socioeconomic status.[11]

One can reasonably ask whether the increased ethnic and socioeconomic polarization is a problem. We believe it is. The Hippocratic oath taken by new physicians begins with the declaration, "First do no harm." While state school systems cannot be expected to solve all social problems, they should at a minimum not exacerbate existing inequities. Ideally, they should serve to offset them. Although other countries might design a competitive system somewhat differently from New Zealand, the forces unleashed by parental choice, including the use of student mix as a proxy for academic quality, are likely to push systems toward greater ethnic and socioeconomic polarization whatever the circumstances.

COMPETITION

The greater inequality across schools might be acceptable if the reforms raised the quality of education throughout the system. Indeed, one of the standard arguments for expanding parental choice and giving more operating flexibility to schools is to force schools to compete for students and thereby to induce them to provide higher-quality education at lower cost. The absence of good data on student achievement makes it difficult to determine how the introduction of competition in New Zealand affected student learning. However, evidence from surveys of primary school teachers and principals, interviews with principals of urban secondary schools, and observations of how the competitive system played out in practice shed some light on this issue.

Survey Responses of Primary School Principals and Teachers

One important source of information emerges from surveys administered in 1996 to a random sample of principals and teachers in about 10% of New Zealand's primary schools.[12] One series of questions solicited the views of principals and teachers on the impact of the Tomorrow's Schools reforms on the quality of children's leaning and various other outcomes. More than half the principals believed that the reforms had had a positive impact on the quality of children's learning, the content of teaching, and teaching styles. A similar picture emerges from the responses of teachers. Almost half of the teachers believed that the reforms had a positive impact on the quality of children's learning; 67%, on teaching content; and 59%, on teaching styles. Significantly, the teachers separated their views about the impacts on teaching from their views about job satisfaction; 57% said the reforms had a negative impact on their own professional satisfaction.

The generally positive assessments of the impacts of the reforms on student learning, teaching content, and teaching style provide little, if any, information by themselves about the impact of competition per se on educational outcomes. This conclusion follows because not all principals and teachers viewed their own schools as being in competition with other schools and because competition was only one component of the overall reform package. Other relevant components include the accountability system, which by the mid-1990s had focused external attention on teaching and learning within the school, and the new national curriculum guidelines of 1993 that were accompanied by additional professional development opportunities for teachers.

To separate the effects of competition from other elements of the reforms, we made use of the fact that not all primary schools were in a competitive situation. The survey responses indicated that only about one-third of the schools were directly competing with other primary schools for students. A multivariate statistical analysis that controlled for the decile rankings of the schools, as well as for the rates of enrollment change in some of the specifications, generated the following conclusions (Ladd & Fiske, 2001b). According to the teachers' responses, the effects of the reforms on the quality of student learning, teaching content, and teaching style were more negative for schools facing competition than for schools not facing competition. Similar patterns emerged for school principals, but for them the results were not statistically significant. Thus we conclude that instead of improving the quality of student learning, competition among schools at the primary level appears to diminish it.[13]

In addition, the teachers' equations indicated that competition had negative effects on their relations with parents, with teachers in other local schools, and on their job satisfaction. These findings suggest that competition in education could well reduce the attractiveness of teaching as a profession.

Views of Secondary School Principals

Our interviews with urban principals of secondary schools suggested that the introduction of competition for students kept principals on their toes and made them more alert to the needs of their students. However, competition also generated some undesirable side effects, including a decline in professional collegiality. Principals and even teachers became less willing to share pedagogical and other ideas with their counterparts at schools with which their school was competing for students. In addition, some urban principals reported being under such pressure from their boards to increase student enrollments that they engaged in recruiting practices that made them ethically uncomfortable, such as using secretive methods to get school lists from schools that traditionally fed other schools.

We observed situations in New Zealand where two or more secondary schools operating on a level playing field were engaged in vigorous competition for students that probably redounded to the benefit of all of them. In one comfortable suburb of Wellington, for example, Heretaunga College increased its enrollment between 1992 and 1998 at the expense of nearby Upper Hutt High School. Both were viable high schools, though, and the competition appears to have energized them both. In that case, competition was healthy because both schools were competing for the same group of middle-class students.

The Uneven Playing Field of School Choice

The problem is that the playing field was not always level. The fact that parents tended to use the composition of a school's student body as a proxy for school quality meant that schools serving disadvantaged students found it hard to compete successfully for students. Even if they were well managed and had a high "value added," they would still lose students to schools that served a more advantaged student body. After controlling statistically for other determinants of enrollment change, our multivariate statistical analysis of enrollment changes indicated that the greater the share of minority students in a school in 1991, the greater the decline in that school's enrollment (or the smaller the growth) in the following 5-year period.[14]

This unevenness of the playing field meant that minority and economically disadvantaged students ended up being overrepresented in schools that were unable to compete successfully in the new educational marketplace. In the Auckland area, for example, as of 1997, about 30% of the students were minority in the secondary schools that were not successful in attracting students, in contrast to about 10% in the schools that were successful.[15] The differences were comparable in the Wellington and Christchurch areas. Similarly great were the differences in the decile rankings: Schools that were successful in attracting students had much higher decile rankings than schools that were not successful.

A consequence of this widening of the differences among schools is that between 1992 and 1997 (the longest period for which comparable test score data were available) test scores on school-leaving exams went up in the successful schools and down in the schools that were losing students.[16] Thus, as measured by levels of test scores, some schools were getting better and others worse. Whether the value added of the schools in either category had changed, however, is impossible to determine. The rise in test scores in the successful schools could well simply reflect the new mix of students in those schools, while the fall in test scores in the unsuccessful schools could reflect the fact that they were serving a greater concentration of hard-to-educate students.

Schools at the Bottom

It took the New Zealand Ministry of Education a long time to acknowledge that a competitive marketplace in education would not solve the problems of the schools at the bottom of the distribution. In the private sector, firms that are unable to compete go out of business, and, if there are profits to be made, other firms will enter and take over the customers of the failed firm. In the education sector, however, closing down schools is more complicated, largely because elementary and secondary education is compulsory and all children must be served. Given the greater challenges of educating disadvantaged students and the fact that successful schools have little desire to take in students that may lower the quality, as perceived by parents, of the education they offer, it turned out to be difficult to close down schools serving the most disadvantaged students.

The result was an even greater concentration of difficult-to-teach students—those from poverty-stricken homes, those whose English was weak, and those with learning difficulties—in schools at the bottom. Statistics on students who were suspended for disciplinary reasons show that such students were far more likely to end up in a lower-decile school than to move up the decile ladder.[17] The loser schools have commonly been described as "spiraling" downward. Once they began to fall behind in the educational marketplace, downward-spiraling schools found their problems compounding and feeding on one another. Lower student enrollments meant fewer teachers, which meant a less attractive academic program, which meant even fewer students. Schools became losers; so did the students and families served by them.

Not until the late 1990s did the ministry recognize the need to intervene in such schools, and by 1998 it was still struggling with how to do so. Its initial interventions were heavily oriented toward improving the schools' management, the only type of intervention that could be rationalized within the theory of an educational marketplace. Only later did it appreciate the systemic nature of the problem, including the fact that such schools had difficulty attracting high-quality teachers and that more vigorous intervention by the central government was required.

CONCLUSIONS

A major lesson from New Zealand's experience with self-governing schools, parental choice, and competition is that it served to polarize enrollments along ethnic and socioeconomic grounds. Only with careful attention to the design of such a system can this polarization be avoided. Another clear conclusion is that governance changes of this type will not solve the problems of the schools at the bottom, and they may well exacerbate them.

The New Zealand experience also offers insights about the need to balance the legitimate but competing interests of the system's multitude of stakeholders, from students and parents to employers and the body politic. The original Tomorrow's Schools reform plan called for a number of mechanisms to balance interests, including the creation of community forums to deal with local conflicts and the use of lotteries to decide which students would be admitted to oversubscribed schools. Largely for political reasons, however, these mechanisms fell by the wayside.

Instead, primacy was given to the rights of current parents in a particular school. Thus when the boards of several primary schools decided to add two more grades so their parents would not have to send their children to the local intermediate school—a decision with significant consequences for other schools and parents in their areas— they were free to pursue their own self-interest. The new system also showed its faith in the capacity of an educational marketplace to balance competing interests by giving oversubscribed schools the right to accept and reject students with little reference to how their decisions would affect other schools or the system as a whole.

Over the years, as the consequences of a laissez-faire approach to the balancing of interests became clear, the Ministry of Education was forced to inject some balancing of the interests of various stakeholders into the process. Primary schools no longer have carte blanche to add grades, and new regulations related to enrollment schemes now guarantee access to a "a reasonably convenient school."

Are the results that emerged in New Zealand the inevitable outcomes of an education system with self-governing schools operating in a competitive environment? Not fully. In retrospect it is clear that different policy decisions could have been made. For example, other countries need not follow New Zealand's lead in giving schools control over enrollment policies. Nevertheless, given the importance that families ascribe to the mix of students, it is likely that there will be intense pressure for ethnic polarization in any system of parental choice.

Any market-based system is also likely to create losers unless the government takes explicit action to improve teaching and learning in those schools. It is noteworthy that low-decile schools in New Zealand had operational autonomy, strong incentives to improve the quality of their offerings, some good managers, and, under a progressive funding system, more funding per pupil than high-decile ones. Still, they were unable to compete successfully.

The demonstrable conclusion is that school autonomy and strong incentives to attract students are not sufficient to overcome the serious challenges faced by schools with disproportionate shares of low-performing students. New Zealand provides little evidence about what might constitute effective intervention because the ministry was slow to act, and when it finally did so it focused mainly on managerial improvement. Still, the implication is clear: Policies are needed that address more directly the challenges of teaching and learning in such schools.

Institutions or procedures can also be introduced to balance competing interests. For example, parents could be invited to express their preferences for particular schools, but assignment could be made centrally with an eye toward balancing the racial makeup of schools and other factors. The point is that explicit attention to the balancing of interests of various stakeholders is needed. The invisible hand will not do the job.

Finally, New Zealand's experience with self-governing schools in a competitive environment teaches that there are no panaceas in school reform. Instead, trade-offs must be made between various worthy policy objectives: improved quality, enhanced parental involvement, managerial efficiency, and equity. The architects of Tomorrow's Schools put their faith in simple governance solutions to complex questions of educational quality, and they found them wanting. Grasping for simplistic solutions can cause considerable harm to both individuals and schools unless policy makers are willing to anticipate the limitations of such solutions from the outset and to build in appropriate safeguards.

Any country that seeks to follow New Zealand's lead by introducing market-based reforms into its school system would do well to understand the problems built into this approach to school reform and to make efforts to address them from the outset.

NOTES

The chapter draws heavily on Edward B. Fiske and Helen F. Ladd (2000), *When Schools Compete: A Cautionary Tale*. The authors are grateful to the Fulbright Association and the Smith Richardson Foundation, which funded the research on which the book was based.

1. Much of our research was completed during the 5 months we spent in New Zealand in early 1998 with the support of a Fulbright grant. During that period, we visited nearly 50 schools, primarily in the three urban areas of Auckland, Wellington, and Christchurch. We gathered and analyzed data on enrollment patterns, funding, and teachers from the Ministry of Education and other sources, and we interviewed a substantial number of policy makers in the Ministry of Education, Treasury, and elsewhere. See Fiske and Ladd (2000) for a more complete discussion of our analysis and sources.

2. These phrases come from the report of the Task Force to Review Education Administration, often referred to as the Picot Report. See Task Force (1998 p. xi).

3. Task Force (1988, p. 60).

4. Education Review Office (1994, p. 6).

5. Education Review Office (1998, appendix 2). Also reported in Fiske and Ladd (2000, Table 4–4).

6. These and the following figures can be found in Fiske and Ladd (2000, Chapter 7). The enrollment changes are based on calculations by the authors based on data provided by the Ministry of Education. Projected enrollment changes are based on census data by small geographic area from *Statistics New Zealand*.

7. Evidence to support this claim about the distribution of teachers can be found in Fiske and Ladd (2000, Table 7–7).

8. How large such spillovers are in practice, and indeed whether they are necessarily positive, has been the subject of extensive, but not fully decisive, research (Jencks & Mayer, 1990). What matters for parental decisions, however, is not that the peer effects be large and positive in fact but that the parents believe that they are.

9. Based on calculations by the authors based on data from the Ministry of Education. See Fiske and Ladd (2000, Chapter 8).

10. Calculations made by the authors, reported in Fiske and Ladd (2000, Figure 7–5).

11. Lauder and Hughes (1999). This book is the outgrowth of the Smithfield Project, a multiphased study of how competition played out in a few urban areas during the early 1990s supported by the Ministry of Education. See Smithfield Project (1994, 1995).

12. From 1989–1999, the New Zealand Council for Educational Research periodically surveyed principals, teachers, and trustees of 239 randomly selected primary and intermediate schools about their views on the Tomorrow's Schools reforms and their effects. The 239 schools represented about 10.5% of all such schools in 1989 and were proportionately representative of the 1989 distribution by type of school, location of school, enrollment size, proportion of Maori enrollment, and whether the school was state owned or was a religious school that had been integrated into the public school system. The figures in this paragraph come from Wylie (1997) and refer to the

1996 schoolyear. They are also reported in Fiske and Ladd (2000, Tables 8–8 and 8–9).

13. Some people might be tempted to dismiss the teachers' results on the grounds that teachers simply do not like market-based reforms in education and, according to this view, will try to subvert them by asserting that such reforms reduce the quality of student learning. Significantly, however, the conclusions about competition are based not on teachers' responses in general but rather on the differences between the responses of teachers who happened to find themselves in a competitive environment after the reforms and those who did not. For a more detailed discussion of the methodology, see Ladd and Fiske (2001b).

14. This conclusion is based on multivariate regressions reported in Ladd and Fiske (2001a).

15. For these and the other figures in this paragraph, see Fiske and Ladd (2000, Table 8–1).

16. Fiske and Ladd (2000, Table 8–2).

17. See Fiske and Ladd (2000, Tables 8–5 and 8–6).

REFERENCES

Boston, J., Martin, J., Pallot, J., & Walsh, P. (1996). *Public management: The New Zealand model.* Oxford University Press.

Education Review Office. (1994). *Annual report, July 1993 to 30 June 1994.* Wellington, NZ: Education Review Office.

Education Review Office. (1998). *Good schools, poor schools.* Wellington, NZ: Education Review Office.

Fiske, E. B., & Ladd, H. F. (2000). *When schools compete: A cautionary tale.* Washington, DC: Brookings Institution Press.

Jencks, C., & Mayer, S. (1990). The social consequences of growing up in a poor neighborhood. In L. E. Lynn Jr. & M. G. H. McGreary (Eds.), *Inner-city poverty in the United States* (pp. 111–86). Washington, DC: National Academy Press.

Ladd, H. F., & Fiske, E. B. (2001a). The uneven playing field of school choice: Evidence from New Zealand. *Journal of Policy Analysis and Management, 20*(1), 43–64.

Ladd, H. F., & Fiske, E. B. (2001b). *Does competition generate better schools? Evidence from New Zealand.* Sanford Institute Working Paper, Sanford Institute of Public Policy, Duke University, Durham, NC.

Lauder, H., & Hughes, D. (1999). *Trading in futures: Why markets in education don't work.* Buckingham, NZ: Open University Press.

Smithfield Project. (1994). *The creation of market competition for education in New Zealand.* Phase 1, first report. Wellington, NZ: Ministry of Education.

Smithfield Project. (1995). *Trading in futures: The nature of choice in educa-*

tional markets in New Zealand. Phase 1, third report. Wellington, NZ: Ministry of Education.

Task Force to Review Education Administration. (1988). *Administering for excellence: Effective administration in education.* Wellington, NZ:

Wylie, C. (1997). *Self-managing schools seven years on: What have we learnt?* Wellington, NZ: New Zealand Council for Educational Research.

Wylie, C. (1999). *Ten years on: How schools view educational reform.* Wellington, NZ: New Zealand Council for Educational Research.

CHAPTER 3

School Choice and Educational Change in England and Wales

Geoffrey Walford

Many countries of the industrialized world in the 1980s and 1990s saw the dramatic reorganization of state-maintained educational systems giving greater choice of school to families with the explicit aim of encouraging competition between schools. These moves towards a quasi-market have often been accompanied by greater financial and ideological support for the private sector and a greater blurring of the distinction between private and state-maintained schooling. The result is that, in many countries, state-maintained schools are now in a situation more resembling the competitive market that was once the province of the private, fee-paying sector alone. The official aims of such changes have usually been couched in terms of increasing the efficiency and effectiveness of schooling by introducing competition between schools. The extent to which this has occurred is difficult to evaluate, in particular because many other changes have usually accompanied the move to the quasi-market. In contrast to these positive claims, it has been consistently argued by many researchers that increased choice and competition have led to greater inequalities between schools and increasing differences in the educational experiences of children from different genders, social classes, and ethnicities.

The extension of market ideas into education has been a highly controversial issue, and there has been considerable debate about the effects and desirability of such moves. Many critics believe that education should be viewed as a public good and that it is a grave error to treat the provision of schooling as a marketable commodity (e.g., Wringe, 1994). In practice, all market-oriented schemes so far introduced have accepted this argument to some degree. The nature of the market introduced into education is not identical to that found in manufacturing or even in major service industries. It is generally recognized that the schooling of a society's young holds benefits for the individual, the family, and the society itself, and all Western societies have legislated to ensure that children receive some education whether or not the family or child wishes it. While some commentators argue that the benefits of competition will only accrue where there is a totally free, open market for schooling (e.g., Tooley, 2000), in practice only quasi-markets have been introduced.

The term *quasi-market* (Glennerster, 1991; Le Grand, 1991; Le Grand & Bartlett, 1993) indicates that the market forces introduced into schooling differ in some fundamental aspects from classical free markets in respect to both the demand and supply sides. One essential difference is that money need not change hands between the "purchaser" and the "supplier." A second is that society forces all families to make some sort of "purchase" from what is already on offer or to provide a similar "product" itself. On the supply side, the institutions providing schooling are not necessarily privately owned, nor do they have profit maximization as their main objective. Further, entry of new suppliers is regulated and subject to strict controls. Consumers do not have the freedom to choose any product, but only products that have been deemed to meet relatively strongly defined and inspected criteria. On the demand side, the purchaser is not necessarily the "consumer" of what schools offer. There are a variety of beneficiaries, and this particular quasi-market may be conceptualized in terms of a diversity of purchasers and consumers. Moreover, the market forces introduced into schooling differ from those of the classical market in that the act of choosing can directly transform the product. Market forces in schooling lead to some schools becoming full while others remain empty—a choice for a small school is made invalid if it expands to meet the demand (Carroll & Walford, 1996).

A BRIEF HISTORY OF CHOICE IN ENGLAND AND WALES

Prior to the 1980s, real choice of a particular school in England and Wales was mainly available only to those families able and willing to pay high fees for private schools. The private sector is smaller than in most industrial countries, as most of the Church of England and

Roman Catholic schools were incorporated into the state-maintained sector following the 1870 and 1944 Education Acts. In consequence, although there is considerable diversity within the sector, the private schools are generally more prestigious, more academically and more socially selective than in other countries. The whole private sector now serves about 8% of the school-age population (Walford, 1991; Whitty, Edwards, & Fitz, 1989). Within the state-maintained sector, alongside schools provided and organized by the Local Education Authorities, are so-called voluntary schools run by the Church of England and the Roman Catholic Church, as well as a small number run by Jews and Methodists. Before the 1980s, families could choose which type of school they wished to use and where available, whether they wished to use a single-sex or coeducational school, but there was very little choice of individual school. Each school—whether denominational or nondenominational, single-sex or coeducational—drew its students from a defined zone or catchment area. If families wished to choose a particular school, they had to move into the appropriate catchment area of the desired school. This led to what has been called "selection by mortgage," whereby the location of a home within the zone of a popular school added greatly to its value.

Superimposed upon this map of catchment areas was a further set of zones for selective grammar schools. The 1944 Education Act not only introduced secondary education for all students but, indirectly, produced a bipartite system of grammar and secondary modern schools in most Local Education Authorities. A proportion of children were selected, mainly through examination at age 10, to be given the right to attend their local grammar school. Parents of such children were able to decline this place, but parents of children who were not selected had no right to insist on a grammar school place. During the 1960s and 1970s there was growing concern about the inequity of selection at age 10, and the selective system of secondary schooling was gradually replaced by comprehensive schools (Simon, 1997). In many cases the move to comprehensive education was accompanied by a decrease in single-sex schools. These comprehensive schools were still provided by the Local Education Authorities as well as by the religious bodies. By 1979, about 90% of secondary-age children in the state-maintained sector were in comprehensive schools. About 28% of primary-age pupils and 17% of secondary-age pupils were in voluntary schools. Across all ages, 22% of pupils were in voluntary schools, made up of 11% Church of England, 9% Roman Catholic, and less than 1% each of Jewish and Methodist (O'Keeffe, 1986). These schools have all their current expenditure funded by the state and have to provide only 15% of any new capital expenditure.

The idea that parents should be given some right to state a preference for a school was first included in the 1944 Education Act for England and Wales, but the relevant sections were designed only to ensure that parents could indicate their wishes with regard to the religious denomination of schools, not to give choice between individual schools (see Walford, 1994). While some parents gradually began to question and appeal the placement of their child in a particular school, most were prepared to accept their catchment area school when there was an obvious shortage of accommodation following World War II. However, in England, the number of 10-year-olds reached its peak in 1975, and there was a decline of some 30% in the years until 1987. It is often forgotten that it is this dramatic demographic change that does most to explain the increased interest in choice of school in Britain in the late 1970s and into the 1980s. From the mid-1980s, this demographic feature was combined with the Conservative government's growing belief in "the market" as having greater efficiency and effectiveness than central or local democratic planning.

Over the last two decades the state-maintained educational system of England and Wales has been subjected to a plethora of changes, many of which have been justified in terms of introducing "market discipline" into education by giving families a greater choice of school. While these changes affect entry to both primary schools at age 5 and secondary schools at age 11, the bulk of the research and concern has focused on entry to secondary schooling. Only recently have the effects at the primary level been researched. It is important to recognize that increased choice was introduced at a time when belief in comprehensive schooling up to age 16 was strong. By 1980, about 90% of children in English state-maintained secondary schools were in comprehensive schools that served all academic abilities. Belief in the value of such schools, both academically and socially, was firmly held by the majority of people of all social classes (Pring & Walford, 1997). While there was a clear wish among some of the Conservative new right to abolish comprehensive schools, any open attempt by the central government to reintroduce selective education would certainly have failed (Walford & Jones, 1986). If a Conservative central government wished to make secondary schooling less comprehensive, it had to do so indirectly.

In the following description it will be shown that during the long years of Conservative rule, there was a series of changes that had the effect of weakening the comprehensive principle. These include the introduction of the Assisted Places Scheme in 1980; the granting of greater opportunity for parents to "express a preference" for particular state-maintained schools following the Education Act of 1980; the development of City Technology Colleges beginning in 1986; the 1988 restructuring of the education system through grant-maintained schools, local management of schools, and open enrollment; and the 1993 Education Act's even greater emphasis on choice and diversity and the development of "specialisms" within comprehensive schools. While the Labour government elected in 1997 began to phase out the Assisted Places Scheme and, from September 1999, brought grant-maintained schools into a Local Educational Authority (LEA) framework as Foundation or Voluntary schools, the fundamental changes that the Conservative government made to parents' rights on choice of school remain unchanged.

Mrs. Thatcher's newly elected Conservative government of 1979 rapidly moved to implement a slightly greater degree of choice through the 1980 Education Act. From 1982, parents were given the right to "express a preference" for a school, and the LEA was obliged to take this preference into account. However, the act still gave LEAs considerable powers so that they could manage falling school rolls and plan the overall provision of school places in their areas. It allowed the benefits of the community as a whole to override the benefits to individual parents by giving LEAs the right to refuse parents' preferences if this would lead to some less-popular schools having unviable numbers.

Stillman and Maychell (1986; Stillman, 1986) have shown that the effect of this legislation throughout England was extremely variable. Some LEAs tried to encourage choice, while others endeavoured to restrict it. Those offering minimal choice justified their behavior in terms of catchment area schools fostering better links with the local community. They also argued that catchment areas ensured that the LEA could engage in long-term planning and hence benefit from the most efficient and effective use of resources. There were many examples of both Conservative and Labour LEAs offering only very restricted choice.

The next development that gave some families greater choice of school was the City Technology College (CTC) initiative, announced in 1986. City Technology Colleges are schools that cater to 11- to 18-year-olds in selected inner-city areas. These are officially private schools, run by educational trusts with close links to industry and commerce. The governing bodies of these schools include representatives from industry and commerce but exclude both parent and teacher governors. The CTCs charge no fees, but sponsors are expected to cover the extra costs involved in providing a highly technological curriculum and were originally expected to make substantial contributions to both capital and current expenditure. In practice the bulk of both capital and current expenditure has been provided by the state. These CTCs select children with a broad range of academic abilities who apply to the school from a large catchment area. Significantly, these new schools were also supposed to act as "beacons of excellence" for nearby LEA schools and thus raise educational standards overall.

The desire to increase technological education was a major feature of the plan, but many political speeches at the time of the original announcement showed that CTCs were also designed to encourage competition, weaken the comprehensive system, and reduce the powers of the Local Educational Authorities. As the title of the promotional booklet, *City Technology Colleges: A New Choice of School* (Department of Education and Science [DES], 1986), made clear, the development was to be justified and legitimized through the ideology of increased choice and the idea that greater choice within an educational quasi-market would improve educational standards for all.

All of the CTCs are required to provide education for children of different abilities who are wholly or mainly drawn from the area in which the school is situated. An early study by Walford and Miller (1991) of the first CTC showed some of the potential problems. This CTC selects children from a tightly defined catchment area that includes eight LEA secondary schools and is thus in direct competition with these other schools for pupils. Parents are required to apply for admission to the CTC on behalf of their child. The child takes a simple nonverbal reasoning test, which is used to ensure that children with a range of abilities broadly representative of those who apply are selected. They are also interviewed with a parent. The parents and the child also have to state that they intend the child to continue in full-time education until age 18. The research showed that the college took great care to ensure that it was taking children with a wide ability range, but the whole entry procedure means that selection was based instead on the degree of motivation of parents and children. Children and families with a low level of interest in education simply did not apply.

In interviews, heads and teachers in the nearby LEA schools claimed that the CTC was selecting those very parents who had the most interest in their children's education and those children who

were most keen and enthusiastic. They argued that the CTC was selecting children who, while they might not be particularly academically able, had special skills and interests in sports, art, drama, or
other activities. These children were seen as invigorating the atmo-
sphere of any school, providing models for other children, and being
rewarding for teachers to teach. Heads and teachers in nearby schools
thus saw their schools as having been impoverished by the CTC's
selection of these well-motivated pupils. They saw the CTC as having
only a negative effect on their schools.

In practice, the CTC idea was not a success. Business and industry were not prepared to invest in the colleges, and the whole pro-
gramme stalled at just 15 colleges. Moreover, as the colleges follow
the national curriculum, there have not been any great innovations in
curriculum or pedagogy (Edwards & Whitty, 1997; Whitty, Edwards, &
Gewirtz, 1993). However, the symbolic significance of the CTCs is
disproportionate to the number of pupils involved. Fundamentally,
the CTC idea made it clear that the Conservative government wished
to develop a more market-based educational system and that it was
prepared to accept, if not encourage, inequality of provision and the
selection of children for those schools with the best facilities, funding,
and support. The CTCs may have been a faltering start to this change,
but the idea rapidly led to more radical developments.

CHOICE IN THE 1988 EDUCATION REFORM
ACT AND BEYOND

The 1988 Education Reform Act for England and Wales introduced
a wide range of changes designed to hasten market processes within
education (Walford, 1994). Through the introduction of grant-maintained schools and in the interlinked ideas of local management of
schools and open enrollment, the major thrust of the act was designed
to increase competition between schools and to encourage parents to
make choices between schools. Funding to individual schools is now
largely related directly to pupil numbers, and schools have their own
delegated budgets that they can use as they wish, including decisions
on how many staff to employ. Popular schools gain extra funding as
they attract more pupils, while less popular schools lose funding as
their numbers decline. Local Education Authorities have lost much of
their power to give extra support in areas of special need or to tempo-
rarily adjust funding to particular schools to ensure that future needs
are met. At a time of falling school rolls, this means that the choice

of which schools will close is left largely to the summation of the decisions of existing parents. The needs of future parents, or the society as a whole, are forgotten.

Both grant-maintained schools and open enrollment were designed to increase competition between schools and to encourage families to make choices between schools. However, once schools become oversubscribed, it is the schools that are able to select children and families rather than families being able to choose a school. Very little money was provided to enable popular schools to expand. One early study (Fitz, Halpin, & Power, 1993) agreed that grant-maintained schools were increasingly popular and that a large proportion of grant-maintained schools were selective, but argued that (at the time of the research) there was little evidence for a widespread return of a selective system. In contrast, a second study (Bush, Coleman, & Glover, 1993) showed that 30% of the supposedly comprehensive schools in its grant-maintained sample were using covert selection and one had introduced a selection examination. These authors argued that the grant-maintained policy was leading to the development of a two-tier system. What is interesting is that, in spite of heavy capital investment and continued additional current expenditure, there was little evidence that grant-maintained schools offered much that was distinctively different from that provided in LEA schools (Fitz, Halpin, & Power, 1997; Power, Halpin, & Whitty, 1997). Often parents and pupils saw no difference between grant-maintained schools and the LEA schools—apart from better facilities and greater attention to the symbols of academic elitism, such as logos and school uniforms. Where they were perceived as different, it was that they offered a "better"-quality education of the same sort as before (Bush et al, 1993; Fitz et al, 1993). Recent research (Levačić & Hardman, 1999) has shown that while in crude terms the grant-maintained schools produced a greater proportion of children with high examination results, this was only because they had a reduced proportion of children from deprived backgrounds. Once social background was taken into account, they did not do better; their relative success was simply due to increased selection.

Before 1993 it was not legal for schools to introduce selection without a full public enquiry. However, in mid-1993, new Department for Education (DFE) guidelines on admissions announced that all schools were to be allowed to "specialize" and to select up to 10% of their intake on the basis of abilities in such areas as music, art, sports, and technology without any need for official approval. The government of the day argued that such specialization need not lead to selection, but it is difficult to see how this can be correct. Once there are more applications than places, selection must inevitably increase. The current Labour government has continued with this semantic obfuscation.

Further quasi-market mechanisms were introduced through the 1993 Education Act. First, grant-maintained schools and voluntary aided schools were encouraged to appoint sponsor governors from business and become City Technology Colleges specializing in science, technology, and mathematics. This involved finding at least £100,000 from sponsors, and in return the schools received more than matching extra resources from the DFE. Obviously, some schools are far better able to attract initial sponsorship than others. Such extra resources going to a limited number of schools can lead to substantial differences between the learning environments of neighboring schools. While overt selection was not necessarily introduced, self-selection can operate in a similar way to the original CTCs. The scheme was later extended to include specialist language schools and was opened to a broader range of secondary schools. This was later further expanded to allow schools to specialize in sports and arts; by mid-2000, there were about 500 such specialist schools.

Second, the 1993 Education Act began to encourage the supply side of the quasi-market. While the 1988 act introduced grant-maintained schools, it did nothing to encourage the development of entirely new schools. In contrast, the 1993 Education Act made it possible for the governors of existing private schools or groups of independent sponsors to apply to the Secretary of State to establish sponsored grant-maintained schools. These schools may be based on particular religious or philosophical beliefs—such as Islam, Hinduism, or evangelical Christianity—or may be designed to follow particular teaching methods or subject specialties. However, to have a chance of acceptance sponsors have to be able to find at least 15% of the funding for buildings and land, and be prepared to accept the regulations and constraints applicable to all other grant-maintained schools—including following the national curriculum (Walford, 1997b, 1998).

The legislation came into operation in April 1994. In the period up to the general election of May 1997, seven schools in England were granted sponsored grant-maintained status. All of the seven schools had religious foundations—six Roman Catholic and one Jewish—and all provided substantially more than 15% of the capital costs. Seven more schools in England have been given grant-maintained status under the Labour administration. While there are some interesting contrasts between the schools receiving sponsored grant-maintained status under the Conservative government and those receiving such status under the Labour government, one would not expect a complete discontinuity. Because the new government wished to restructure the whole schooling system, no further applications were accepted after May 1997, so the Labour government was making decisions on applications that had been put forward under the Conservatives. However, it is clear that some of the most recent applications were made in the expectation that a Labour government would be retained in office, since they would have had little chance of success under the Conservatives. We do not know what decisions another Conservative government would have made, but we do know that the Labour decisions marked some dramatic changes in policy. While all of the successful schools under the Conservative government were either Roman Catholic or Jewish, and thus showed no decisive break with the past, the Labour government has granted four out of seven applications that may be of considerable political and social significance. It has supported the applications of one Seventh Day Adventist secondary school, two Muslim primary schools, and one small community school, each of which serves a particular minority population (see Walford, 2000a, 2000b). However, in all cases but one, these seven schools made substantial contributions to capital costs. For example, the trust that runs one of the existing private Muslim schools in Birmingham paid 50% of the capital costs of providing a new building for a larger number of students.

Since the 1988 Education Standards and Framework Act, a formerly private Sikh secondary school has entered the state-maintained sector. While these changes have obviously led to greater diversity within the state-maintained sector, they have not increased the diversity of overall provision. On becoming state-maintained schools, they have had to implement the full national curriculum, associated testing, and all other regulations imposed by the central government. In practice, they have become more like other state-maintained school than before.

THE EFFECTS OF CHOICE

Following the 1980 Education Act and, in particular, the 1988 Education Reform Act, there has been a growing number of research projects into the effects of increased school choice in the state-maintained as well as the private sector. Many of these studies have been summarized by Walford (1997a). The studies by Stephen Ball and his colleagues have been particularly influential (Ball, 1993; Ball, Bowe, &

Gewirtz, 1995, 1996; Ball & Gewirtz, 1997; Ball & Vincent, 1998; Gewirtz, Ball, & Bowe, 1995; Reay & Ball, 1997). They interviewed a broad spectrum of parents who had recently decided which secondary school to send their child to, and examined in detail the ways in which various families responded to the market situation in which they found themselves. Ball argues that families are privileged or disadvantaged by the values that inform their conceptions of choice making. Indeed, "choice" is a socially and culturally constructed concept that has different meanings for different families. Government policy, he claims, is predicated on a consumerist vision that is most likely to be embraced by the middle class. Ball (1993) argues that:

> the implementation of market reforms in education is essentially a class strategy which has as one of its major effects the reproduction of relative social class (and ethnic) advantages and disadvantages. (p. 4)

Gewirtz and colleagues' (1995) study of the workings of choice and the market since 1988 has examined in detail the way in which various families responded to the market situation they found themselves in. They identify three broad groups of parents, defined in terms of their position in relation to the market—the privileged/skilled choosers, the semiskilled choosers, and the disconnected—and show the ways in which working-class or newly immigrant families were disadvantaged in the market. They present a picture of a complex situation where patterns of choice are generated both by choice preferences and opportunities, and where reputation and desirability are played off against other factors. But they also show that the way in which parents played the market was strongly related to social class, and that working-class parents were much more likely than middle-class parents to see the child's views as decisive. This last finding is supported by other research (e.g., Carroll & Walford, 1997b).

Gewirtz and colleagues (1995) also indicate that, where curriculum specialisms were being introduced by schools, they were sometimes acting as selection mechanisms for high academic ability and middle-class children. In particular, the development of specialties such as dance or music indirectly discriminated against working-class children and allowed schools a greater chance to select what they deemed to be "appropriate" children. They show that, in practice, rather than schools becoming more diverse, the pressures of competition between schools has led to schools becoming more similar in what they offer, but within a hierarchy of perceived ability to offer advantage. They conclude that local hierarchies of schools were developing where resources flowed from those children with greatest need to those with the least need.

A recent series of articles from Gorard and Fitz (1998a, 1999b, 2000; Gorard, 1999a, 1999b, 2000) has partly challenged this general picture developed from qualitative research. In these articles, they draw year-by-year comparisons using statistical data available from government sources of the social composition of schools. Using indicators such as the percentage of children in each school who have the right to free school meals (which is a commonly used indicator of poverty), they argue that in most cases social segregation is actually decreasing rather than increasing, as the qualitative studies have found. Their methodology is relatively simple. In most of their work they take the Local Education Authority as the unit of analysis and compute the "expected" percentage of students eligible for free school meals in each school. They then compare the "expected" percentage with the "actual" percentage in each school in each year of the analysis and show that the differences have declined since families have been given greater choice of school. They find reduced segregation in 84 out of 122 English LEAs. In their recent studies they have also used alternative indicators of deprivation, such as the percentage of children with special educational needs or for whom English is a second language. In all these cases, their calculations lead them to conclude that, overall, increased marketization has not led to increased segregation. While they do find some cases where segregation appears to have increased, the balance of their evidence points in the opposite direction. One of their interesting arguments is that, while market forces may theoretically have a polarizing effect, because they were introduced into a system that was already deeply polarized through "selection by mortgage," the result has been that preexisting polarization has decreased. Their work is important, but it has been the subject of some criticism. Gibson and Asthana (1999, 2000), for example, have argued that the unit of analysis taken by Gorard and Fitz is inappropriate. They claim that while LEA-level statistics may well show decreased polarization, within competitive local markets there may still be increasing differences. More importantly, they argue that schools may be becoming increasingly stratified in terms of academic performance. Levačić and Woods (1999) also argue for the importance of studies of groups of local schools. Their study of more than 300 schools, which they have tracked in detail over the period 1991–1998, broadly supports the work of Gorard and Fitz, and they estimate that between 30% and 40% of localities have experienced increased social polarization. However, they find that social polarization is more likely to have occurred where there are high levels of competition between schools and greater diversity of school type. It may simply be that polarization has not occurred in local areas where competition has not been great. They also argue, in support of Gibson and Asthana, that segregation indexes can fail to identify widening local school hierarchies. For certain schools at the bottom of the hierarchy, the effects of the market have been so great that they have led to school closure. Such closures reduce the overall polarization effect, but only following a period of greater polarization.

However, there are three further comments on this work worth making. First, the indicators used are all indicators of deprivation. Only about 20% of children are eligible for free school meals, and the percentage of children with special education needs or for whom English is a second language are smaller. These are measures of social disadvantage, not social advantage, and are used as bipolar either–or indicators. Further, taking "English as a second language" as a single category, for example, conceals the known differences in academic performance of children from different backgrounds and ethnic groups. These single bipolar indicators do not give information on the whole distribution of social polarization, but only on how particular extreme (but still sometimes heterogeneous) groups have coped with marketization compared with the rest. It is certainly not unimportant that these groups may not have fared as badly as expected, but such data give no information at all about how the most advantaged or even the average students have fared. We need research that uses the full range of social-class, income, and wealth variables to enable a true test of the polarization hypothesis. The qualitative and quantitative research are not necessarily in disagreement.

Second, as Gorard and Fitz (2000) acknowledge, we do not know what has actually caused the decrease in segregation that they have found. In particular, their findings could be caused by local and national demographic changes.

Third, while the usual social indicators of social class, income, wealth, ethnicity, and gender are important, the detrimental effects of marketization do not depend on disadvantage being linked to these variables. Several of the detailed small-scale studies already discussed have shown that families are differentially placed before the market. Choosing a school has now become a complicated process in which local knowledge, interest in education, and degree of motivation of parents and children have become vital indicators of successful acceptance of a child in a leading school. Children and families with a low level of interest in education simply do not give this process sufficient attention. Put crudely, if there is a hierarchy of schools, someone has to attend those at the bottom of the hierarchy if others are selected for the schools at the top. With a quasi-market, the children at the bottom are likely to be those with the greatest need for high-quality schooling—whether or not this need can be identified by standard social indicators of class, gender, and ethnicity.

REASONS FOR CHOICE AND ACADEMIC PERFORMANCE

One further focus of research has been on the reasons for choosing a particular school, and one way of conceptualizing these aspects is through "process" and "product" criteria (Elliott, 1982). "Process" criteria involve factors indicative of the capacity for human relationships, such as the happiness of the child, while "product" criteria refer to such outcomes as examination results. Early studies showed that parents were more concerned with "process" than "product" criteria. For example, early studies carried out by Alston (1985), Boulton and Coldron (1989), Webster, Owen, and Crome (1993), and Woods (1992) have all shown that "parents are just as, if not more concerned with 'process' issues than measured outcomes when choosing schools" (Webster et al., 1993, p. 18). Other studies reporting similar findings include those by Hunter (1991) and West (1992a, 1992b).

However, work by David, West, and Ribbens (1994) and Carroll and Walford (1997a) has suggested an increase in the emphasis given to examination results by parents, but the ways in which examination results of particular schools are taken into consideration by families may be complex. While it is rarely the only criterion, or even the major criterion, examination results seem to act as a screening mechanism—deselecting particular schools from consideration. For many parents, schools have to show that their examination results are above an acceptable minimum before they become potentially acceptable.

The latest large-scale study of choice conducted by Woods, Bagley, and Glatter (1998) takes this one stage further. Their study takes a case study approach and focuses on three contrasting groups of secondary schools selected such that they can be seen as representing three separate local competitive markets. Within each of these areas, two main aspects were investigated. First, based on interviews with school personnel and a variety of local qualitative data, the reactions of each of the 11 research schools to increased choice were explored.

Second, through mailed questionnaires, parents' views on the school choice process were examined. A total of about 6000 questionnaires were completed by parents.

Their findings about the relative importance of "academic-centered factors" and "child-centered factors" in choice are complex. They find differences between the three groups of schools studied. Overall, they do not find that academic concerns are generally of greater importance to parents, but that they are roughly equal. However, even though this is true, they find that the schools themselves have reacted *as if* parents have academic factors as their major criterion. They find that "there is a sharpening of the focus on the academic in most schools and that, further than this, there is a privileging of the academic" (Woods et al, 1998, p. 162). They find that, when school managers talk about the attractiveness of their school, they talk of academic progress and examination performance. These are "the major and widely accepted currency of 'good schooling' in the climate of enhanced emphasis on choice" (p. 163).

Now, of course, there is nothing wrong with schools attempting to improve the academic performance of young people! What is at issue here is that this seems to be becoming almost the one and only way in which schools judge themselves and expect others to judge them. Not only does this suggest a corresponding decrease in the emphasis given to social, cultural, and aesthetic activities, it also implies that schools can be ranked within a single hierarchy. Thus, rather than leading to greater diversity of schooling, within the English and Welsh context, greater choice appears to be leading to greater uniformity and conformity. Schools have attempted to become more like each other, in the sense that they are either "better" or "worse" than competitor schools on this single criterion. Once schools are seen as being placed within a single hierarchy, they become less or more popular. The popular schools are able to attract and select those young people who will enhance their examination successes, and the differences between schools will widen.

This leads directly to a consideration of whether the introduction of greater school choice has led to improvements in academic performance, as was predicted by the advocates and the Conservative government. While several of these advocates have asserted that this is true, the situation is actually too complex to unravel. It is certainly true that academic performance, as measured by examination successes at age 16 and 18, has improved greatly since the introduction of greater choice, but such success does not necessarily indicate a causal relationship. In England and Wales greater school choice was accompanied by the introduction of a national curriculum with regular testing of all pupils, and this was fairly swiftly followed by two separate yet linked developments—the publication of the examination results of all schools and the introduction of regular inspection of schools with, again, the results being made public.

The national curriculum was designed to standardize what should be taught in schools, and the associated assessment of children within each school was designed to provide information to existing and prospective parents on the quality of each provider. This, then, suggested that schooling was much like any other consumer product. There were a variety of possible suppliers of this service and parents could choose between providers on the basis of information they supplied.

Following the 1988 act, successive legislation tried to ensure that more information was available about schools so that families could make a more reasoned choice. The 1992 Education (Schools) Act, for example, gave new powers to the Secretary of State to require all schools (including private schools) to provide more information. The aim was to assist parents in choosing schools for their children and, as is made explicit within the act itself, to "increase public awareness of the quality of the education provided by the schools concerned and of the educational standards achieved in those schools" (Her Majesty's Stationery Office [HMSO], 1992, p. 11). The government was acting to improve the information available on the range of possible providers in a similar way to listing the ingredients on food packaging. The implication was that, once parents had sufficient information, they would act together to drive the poor producers out of the market.

This last aspect—driving poor-quality providers out of the market—is central to any understanding of how markets might raise educational performance, yet it is only feasible in very restricted circumstances. One feature of the 1988 act that is rarely discussed is that it coincided with a period of dramatic decline in the school-age population. Between 1982 and 1989, the number of children in all schools in the United Kingdom fell from 9.93 million to 9.01 million—a decrease of more than 9%. This led to some schools being closed, but not nearly in line with the decline in pupil numbers. The student–teacher ratio improved from 17.8 to 16.9 in the same period, mainly because the decline in the number of schools and teachers did not keep pace with the decline in student numbers. Although many welcomed this improvement in student–teacher ratios, it was not necessarily the result of a deliberate policy. The truth is that schools are very difficult for local authorities to close. In almost every case, parents tend to object to the proposed closure of their local school. The closure process becomes politically sensitive and can extend over very many years. Additionally, the LEA had responsibility to think about the future needs of the area, when there might well be an expansion in student numbers that could not be accommodated if some existing schools were closed.

What I am saying here is that the 1988 Education Reform Act, with its emphasis on increased choice, was, in part, designed to deal with this specific problem of falling school rolls and the perceived need to "rationalize provision"—that is, to close schools. At a time of oversupply of school places, it was seen as desirable to encourage parents to make choices about the schools they wished to use and to use the summation of these choices to lead to the closure of particular less popular schools. Parents' choices helped to make decisions about which school should be closed—the assumption being that these would be the "bad" schools and that other schools would increase their quality to ensure their survival within this market.

However, once sufficient schools had been closed, such that the number of places available roughly matched the number of students, this direct pressure of competition (even if all the assumptions were correct) would be insufficient to ensure that quality was continually improved. Once the number of places roughly meets the number of students, there is no direct threat of closure. If quality is to be maintained and enhanced through market competition, there needs to be an oversupply of places and the ability of new suppliers to enter the market.

In fact, of course, the Conservative government itself quickly lost its faith in the market as the sole way raising achievement. While the ideology of the market was still evident in government rhetoric, the same 1992 legislation that gave greater powers to the Secretary of State to demand further information from schools also established the Office for Standards in Education and ushered in a new era of school inspection. Teams of registered inspectors conducting regular inspections of all schools every 4 years were now seen as the way to ensure quality. To report on "the quality of the education provided by the school" is the first of the four general reporting duties of any registered inspector (HMSO, 1992, p. 6). This is followed by the duty to report on standards, on finance and on the spiritual, moral, social and cultural development of pupils.

The 1992 Education Act's confusing, if not contradictory, messages about the means to raise achievement are also to be found in the 1993 act. In the 1993 Education Act the market was potentially strengthened through the publication of even more information on schools but, most importantly, through the inclusion of the legislation that encouraged new providers to enter the state-maintained school market. But while the number of providers and the nature of provision were expanded at the same time, the 1993 Education Act showed that the government had increasing doubts about the ability of the market alone, through parents' choices, to ensure the quality of schooling. While the 1992 Education act had made provision for action plans to follow Office for Standards Education inspection reports and for the monitoring of the implementation of those action plans for failing schools, it was left to the 1993 act to give specific powers to LEAs to introduce special measures to deal with failing schools. This act also gave powers to the Secretary of State to establish education associations where it was felt that the LEA was unable or unwilling to deal satisfactorily with a failing school. Subsequent legislation by both Conservative and Labour governments has given even greater powers to the Secretary of State to intervene if a school is perceived, as a result of inspection, to be failing. Since the 1997 election, schools can find themselves designated as being "under special measures" or "failing" and be put in a position where bids can be made by private companies and others to run the school. Because of this "naming and shaming," it has become almost impossible for a "named" school to improve, since it immediately becomes very unpopular with parents.

The fact that Office for Standards Education inspection was established so quickly after the introduction of market mechanisms into state-maintained schooling means that it is almost impossible to make judgments about the independent effects of these conflicting strategies for maintaining and improving academic achievement. Advocates of choice often point to increasing examination success since the 1988 Education Reform Act, but the cause of such an increase may be more closely linked to the introduction of the national curriculum, the inspection of schools, and changes within the work force and wider society than to school choice. We simply do not know, and it is simply not possible to investigate the independent effects of choice in England and Wales.

CONCLUSION

Since 1997, under Labour, the Department for Education and Employment has become even more directive than it was under the previous Conservative government and has supported particular pedagogic practices as well as directing what curriculum content should be "delivered." At the primary level, the Literacy Hour was introduced in 1998 and the Numeracy Strategy followed in 1999. In both, primary teachers are "encouraged" to follow particular ways of teaching literacy and numeracy, even extending to how many minutes should be spent on group work and how much teaching should be "from the front of the classroom." While not at present legally compulsory, these pedagogic interventions have been taken to be so by most teachers, even though very many oppose them. The threat of inspection and pressures from parents make it very difficult for schools to *not* follow the government's plans. Centralization of the curriculum has now been extended to a growing centralization of pedagogy, and schools are increasingly being judged within a single hierarchy of academic success. The Labour government has established a new framework for schools, such that there are now foundation, voluntary aided, voluntary controlled, and community schools. In theory, foundation and voluntary aided schools can be established by any sponsoring group, but most have a religious foundation. The traditional Christian denominational schools have been supplemented by some schools supported by Muslims, Seventh Day Adventists, and Sikhs. All of these types can be selective or nonselective, single-sex or coeducational. Superimposed on this matrix are further chances for schools to be designated as specialist schools or beacon schools. Just outside the maintained system, the City Technology Colleges remain as private schools mainly supported by government, and in 2000 the Labour government announced a very similar category of schools—the City Academies. It is not worthwhile describing the differences between these various schools in detail for, while there appears to be a greater variety of schools than before in terms of type, there is actually greater uniformity in what is taught and the way it is taught.

Moreover, in England inequality of provision has been directly and indirectly encouraged. City Technology Colleges were explicitly established with the intention that they would be funded at a higher level than other schools. Specialist schools have to find an initial contribution from business and industry and are rewarded with even greater additional funds from government. Schools are encouraged to "bid" for particular programs in competition with each other. Thus the schools with the most active and innovative staff, parents, and governors get extra funding. The schools that already have support from business and industry get further extra funding. Those schools at the bottom drift farther down the hierarchy. Ironically, it is the schools that least need extra funding that have often received higher funding.

There is some hope that this trend of unequal funding will be reduced under Labour. The Educational Action Zones policy was introduced in 1998 to try to bring extra resources to needy urban schools. They are an explicit attempt to give additional funding to schools in poorer areas, yet they still rely on the initiative of teachers and local bodies to make bids for funding. Moreover, improvement in examination success is the prime objective of these Education Action Zones—not, in itself, a bad thing, of course, but it reinforces the idea that schools should be judged on the single criterion of academic success. It has reinforced the moves toward conformity.

The title of the 1992 White Paper that preceded the 1993 Education Act was *Choice and Diversity* (DFE, 1992). It was expected that the introduction of a quasi-market would bring with it greater diversity of provision. Yet the situation is now such that increased centralized control of the curriculum and pedagogy has led to greater uniformity within a framework of pseudo-diversity. Within such a system, some parents and children will be more highly motivated, more concerned, and better informed about schooling than others. Some parents are better able to pay for the transport of their children to school and may be better able to ensure that their choices become a reality. Some schools will be able to draw on national, local, and parental financial support for new buildings and equipment or to pay for additional teachers and helpers. Other schools will not be so lucky. As choices are made and pupils selected, it must be expected that schools will become more differentiated—but only in their ability to achieve examination successes with particular selected intakes. We are moving toward a school hierarchy in which the examination success of schools is the main criterion for choice and the diversity of other talents that children have are being devalued. There is no evidence that increased choice, in itself, has acted to increase examination success; but, coupled with the initiatives of a more centralist government, choice has led to a narrowing of the focus of schooling onto examinations. This is not necessarily a desirable outcome.

NOTES

The work reported in this chapter was in part made possible by a grant from the Spencer Foundation. The data presented, the statements made, and the views expressed are solely the responsibility of the author.

REFERENCES

Alston, C. (1985). *Secondary Transfer Project. Bulletin 3: The views of parents before transfer*. London: Inner London Education Authority.

Ball, S. (1993). Education markets, choice and social class: The market as a class strategy in the UK and the USA. *British Journal of Sociology of Education, 14*(1), 3–19.

Ball, S., Bowe, R., & Gewirtz, S. (1995). Circuits of schooling: A sociological exploration of parental choice of school in social class contexts. *Sociological Review, 43*(1), 52–78.

Ball, S., Bowe, R., & Gewirtz, S. (1996). School choice, social class and distinction: The realisation of social advantage in education. *Journal of Education Policy, 11*(1), 89–112.

Ball, S., & Gewirtz, S. (1997). Girls and the education market. *Gender and Education, 9*(2), 207–222.

Ball, S., & Vincent, C. (1998). "I heard it on the grapevine": "Hot" knowledge and school choice. *British Journal of Sociology of Education, 19*(3), 377–400.

Boulton, P., & Coldron, J. (1989). *The pattern and process of Parental Choice Project Report*. Sheffield, UK: Sheffield City Polytechnic.

Bush, T., Coleman, M., & Glover, D. (1993). *Managing autonomous schools. The grant-maintained experience*. London: Chapman.

Carroll, S., & Walford, G. (1996). A panic about school choice. *Educational Studies, 22*(3), 393–407.

Carroll, S., & Walford, G. (1997a). Parents' responses to the school quasi-market. *Research Papers in Education, 12*(1), 3–26.

Carroll, S., & Walford, G. (1997b). The child's voice in school choice. *Educational Management and Administration, 25*(2), 169–180.

David, M., West, A., & Ribbens, J. (1994). *Mother's intuition? Choosing secondary schools*. London and Washington, DC: Falmer.

Department for Education (DFE). (1992). Choice and diversity. London: Her Majesty's Stationery Office.

Department of Education and Science (DES). (1986). *City Technology Colleges: A new choice of school*. London: Author.

Edwards, T, & Whitty, G. (1997). Marketing quality: Traditional and modern versions of educational excellence. In R. Glatter, P. Woods, & C. Bagley (Eds.), *Choice and diversity in schooling: Perspectives and prospects* (pp. 24–80). London and New York: Routledge.

Elliott, J. (1982). How do parents choose and judge secondary schools? In R. McCormick (Ed.), *Calling education to account* (pp. 71–92). Milton Keynes, UK: Open University Press.

Fitz, J., Halpin, D., & Power, S. (1993). *Grant maintained schools*. London: Kogan Page.

Fitz, J., Halpin, D., & Power, S. (1997). "Between a rock and a hard place":

Diversity, institutional identity and grant-maintained schools. *Oxford Review of Education, 23*(1), 17–30.

Gewirtz, S., Ball, S. J., & Bowe, R. (1995). *Markets, choice and equity in education.* Buckingham, UK: Open University Press.

Gibson, A., & Asthana, S. (1999, April). *Schools, markets and equity: Access to secondary education in England and Wales.* Paper presented at the annual meeting of the American Educational Research Association, Montreal.

Gibson, A., & Asthana, S. (2000). What's in a number? Commentary on Gorard and Fitz's "Investigating the determinants of segregation between schools." *Research Papers in Education, 15*(2), 133–153.

Glennerster, H. (1991). Quasi-markets and education. *Economic Journal, 101,* 1268–1271.

Gorard, S. (1999a). "Well, that about wraps it up for school choice research": State of the art review. *School Leadership and Management, 19*(1), 25–47.

Gorard, S. (1999b). Keeping a sense of proportion: The "politician's error" in analysing school outcomes. *British Journal of Educational Studies, 47*(3), 235–246.

Gorard, S. (2000). Here we go again: A reply to "What's in a number?" by Gibson and Asthana. *Research Papers in Education, 15*(2), 155–162.

Gorard, S., & Fitz, J. (1998a). Under starters orders: The established market, the Cardiff study and the Smithfield project. *International Studies in Sociology of Education, 8*(3), 299–314.

Gorard, S., & Fitz, J. (1998b). The more things change . . . the missing impact of marketisation. *British Journal of Sociology of Education, 19*(3), 365–376.

Gorard, S., & Fitz, J. (2000). Investigating the determinants of segregation between schools. *Research Papers in Education. 15*(2), 115–132.

Her Majesty's Stationery Office (HMSO) (1992). Education (Schools) Act 1992.

Hunter, J.B. (1991). Which school? A study of parents' choice of secondary school. *Educational Research, 33*(1), 31–41.

Le Grand, J. (1991). Quasi-markets and social policy. *Economic Journal, 101,* 1256–1267.

Le Grand, J., & Bartlett, W. (1993). *Quasi-markets and social policy.* London: Macmillan.

Levačić, R., & Hardman, J. (1999). The performance of grant maintained schools in England: An experiment in autonomy. *Journal of Education Policy, 14*(2), 185–212.

Levačić, R., & Woods, P. A. (1999, September). *Polarisation and inequality between secondary schools in England: Effects on school practice and performance.* Paper presented at the annual conference of the British Educational Research Association, University of Sussex, Sussex, England.

Lpo (1994). *Läroplan för grundskolan,* 1994 [Curriculum for the Comprehensive School, 1994]. Stockholm: Swedish National Board of Education.

O'Keeffe, B. (1986). *Faith, culture and the dual system*. London & Washington, DC: Falmer.

Power, S., Halpin, D., & Whitty, G. (1997). Managing the state and the market: "New" educational management in five countries. *British Journal of Educational Studies, 45*(4), 342–362.

Pring, R., & Walford, G. (1997). (Eds.) *Affirming the comprehensive ideal*. London and Washington, DC: Falmer.

Reay, D., & Ball, S. (1997). "Spoilt for choice": The working classes and educational markets. *Oxford Review of Education, 23*(1), 89–101.

Simon, B. (1997). A seismic change: Process and interpretation. In R. Pring & G. Walford (Eds.), *Affirming the comprehensive ideal* (pp. 13–31). London and Washington, DC: Falmer.

Stillman, A. (Ed.). (1986). *The balancing act of 1980. Parents, politics and education*. Windsor, UK: National Foundation for Educational Research/ Nelson.

Stillman, A., & Maychell, K. (1986). *Choosing schools: Parents, LEAs and the 1980 Education Act*. Windsor, UK: National Foundation for Educational Research/Nelson.

Tooley, J. (2000). *Reclaiming education*. London and New York: Cassell.

Walford, G. (Ed.). (1991). *Private schools: Tradition, change and diversity*. London: Chapman.

Walford, G. (1994). *Choice and equity in education*. London and New York: Cassell.

Walford, G. (1997a). Diversity, choice and selection in England and Wales. *Educational Administration Quarterly, 33*(2), 158–169.

Walford, G. (1997b). Sponsored grant-maintained schools: Extending the franchise? *Oxford Review of Education, 23*(1), 31–44.

Walford, G. (1998). Reading and writing the small print: The fate of sponsored grant-maintained schools. *Educational Studies, 24*(2), 241–257.

Walford, G. (2000a). A policy adventure: Sponsored grant-maintained schools. *Educational Studies, 26*(2), 247–262.

Walford, G. (2000b). From City Technology Colleges to sponsored grant-maintained schools. *Oxford Review of Education, 26*(2), 145–158.

Walford, G., & Jones, S. (1986). The Solihull adventure: An attempt to reintroduce selective education. *Journal of Education Policy, 1*(3), 239–253.

Walford, G., & Miller, H. (1991). *City Technology College*. Buckingham, UK: Open University Press.

Webster, A., Owen, G., & Crome, D. (1993). *School marketing: Making it easy for parents to select your school*. Bristol, UK: Avec Designs.

West, A. (1992a). Factors affecting choice of school for middle class parents: Implications for marketing. *Educational Management and Administration, 29*(4), 213–221.

West, A. (1992b). *Choosing schools: Why do parents opt for private schools or schools in other LEAs?* (Clare Market Papers No.1). London: Centre for Educational Research, London School of Economics.

Whitty, G., Edwards, T., & Fitz, J. (1989). England and Wales: The role of the private sector. In G. Walford (Ed.), *Private schools in ten countries: Policy and practice* (pp. 8–31). London and New York: Routledge.

Whitty, G., Edwards, T., & Gewirtz, S. (1993). *Specialisation and choice in urban education. The City Technology College experiment.* London and New York: Routledge.

Woods, P. (1992). Empowerment through choice? Towards an understanding of parental choice and school responsiveness. *Educational Management and Administration, 20*(4), 204–211.

Woods, P.A., Bagley, C., & Glatter, R. (1998). *School choice and the public interest: Markets in the public interest?* London and New York: Routledge.

Wringe, C. (1994). Markets, values and education. In D. Bridges & T. H. McLaughlin (Eds.), *Education and the market place.* London and Washington, DC: Falmer.

CHAPTER 4

Market Forces and Decentralization in Sweden: Impetus for School Development or Threat to Comprehensiveness and Equity?

Holger Daun

The market forces and decentralization introduced into the Swedish education system at the beginning of the 1990s have been both a stimulus for school development and a threat to the conception of "equivalent education" for all students (Lpo, 1994). These new policies are best understood against the background of the relative decline of the Swedish economy in world markets during the 1960s and 1970s, rapidly expanding public expenditures, and pressure from neo-liberal and political-participatory discourse that emerged in the 1980s.

This chapter gives a brief account of the implementation of the educational policies governing comprehensive school since 1962, including the restructuring measures introduced at the end of the 1990s. The reasons for these reforms are summarized and some of the general outcomes of the reforms are discussed. The most important and disturbing of these outcomes so far is that a homogenization of individual comprehensive and secondary schools and a heterogenization of the collective education system have begun. This decreasing diversity of students within individual schools and increasing diversity between schools threatens to undermine the fundamental tenet of equality of educational opportunity in Sweden.

BACKGROUND

Sweden has long been known for educational policies in which equality of education for all students has been given priority, regardless of their socioeconomic, geographic, and ethnic backgrounds. Following World War II, gross national product (GNP) levels in Sweden were among the highest in the world, and the construction of an extensive social welfare state ensued. Over time a consensus developed that linked the major stakeholders—the Social Democratic party, the other branches of the labor movement, and the employers' federation—with the state in a corporatist arrangement (Johnson, 1987). This consensus resulted in the development and institutionalization of a welfare system that covered individuals from the cradle to the grave.

At the beginning of the 1960s, all the parties except for the Conservatives argued for a radical reform of the education system. Supporters proposed moving from a selective to a comprehensive school system requiring 9 years of education for all students (Isling, 1980). A compromise arrangement was implemented that included the 9 years of compulsory education in comprehensive schools but also included some differentiation in the later grades. Schools that had followed a national curriculum prior to the reform were now subjected to inspection by provincial officers under the authority of the National Board of Education. As part of the reform, national standardized tests were distributed periodically to the schools and new, centralized criteria for teacher training and competence testing were established.

With the massive expansion of female participation in the labor market in the 1970s and 1980s, the need for preschool and out-of-school arrangements increased rapidly. Due to the high costs of public preschools and pressure for the expansion of institution-based learning, the Social Democrats (SDs) suggested that voluntary school be implemented for 6-year-old children in 1991. These children were given the right to a place in a primary school if the parents so wished (SMES, 1997). The number of schools enrolling children of this age has increased rapidly. In 1998, preschool institutions were administratively integrated into the formal education system.

After briefly losing power during the previous election cycle, the SDs returned to power in 1982 and adopted the neo-liberal discourse on the state, welfare, and education. Two principal measures were embraced: (1) the decentralization of administrative bodies and the devolution of decision making to lower levels in the state apparatus; (2) the privatization or exposure to market forces of public companies and service units as well as the reduction of public expenditures (Montin, 1992). The decisions implemented by the SDs at this time were remarkable because they were in conflict with the core principles of social democracy (Dow, 1993) and so were not compatible with traditional SD values held by the "core groups" of the party, the electorate, and other branches of the labor movement. Nevertheless, further reorientation within the SDs took place around 1985, when a subgroup suggested the introduction of choice within the public education sector and a more liberal attitude toward private schools (Englund, 1996; Schüllerquist, 1996). Similar changes took place within the Liberal party. During the late 1980s, full choice across the sectors and larger subsidies to private schools had been suggested by three of the biggest opposition parties. As a result, at the end of the 1980s schools were "municipalized" and teachers, who used to be state employees, became municipal employees.

During this period of change, education was increasingly cited as a measure of competence and human capital. A 1990 document concerning long-term development stated that "the aim of education is to make it possible for the pupils to successively find their comparative advantages and their own direction of interest" (SOU, 1990, p. 22). The SDs now claimed that decentralization was justified as a means of improving democracy and efficiency (Lindblad & Wallin, 1993; SOU, 1988).

In 1994 upper secondary education was reformed, as was the curriculum in comprehensive education. The structure was changed and a new curriculum was introduced, including 16 nationally determined programs of study. Students who are unable to choose among these programs have two other options: a special program or an individual program. All programs last 3 years and include eight core subjects. Apart from the core subjects, the curriculum allows for a great deal of local adaptation. For example, many schools have started cooperating with companies that provide either workplace-based training or workshops for practical training.

EDUCATION IN SWEDEN TODAY

The basic principle dominating the Swedish education system today is that "all students should have access to an equivalent education, regardless of their sex, ethnic or social background, or place of residence" (SMES, 1997, p. 7). At the central state level, the National Agency for Education monitors the achievement of this and other national goals. Each municipality is expected to have a plan for its schools indicating how the national goals are to be achieved. In turn, every school theoretically has a plan compatible with the municipal plan, specifying how the national and municipal goals are to be attained at the school level. Finally, each teacher is supposed to develop his or her own work plan that must then be approved by the school director.

The financing of primary and secondary education is shared between the state and the municipalities. In 1996, subsidies from the state provided approximately 50% of total educational revenues. The remaining portion is provided by the municipality. Payments from the central government to municipalities are block grants that fund all activities administered by the municipalities, however, including social welfare, health, and education. This means that the municipalities themselves decide how much of the state subsidies should be spent on education, although municipalities are responsible for guaranteeing that a certain level of educational quality is maintained and that the principle of equal education is respected (SMES, 1997). Municipalities vary in size and type of population and therefore generate varying levels of tax revenue. The lump-sum amounts provided by the state are determined in such a fashion as to help compensate poorer municipalities for some of this variance, but the fact remains that municipalities differ in the levels of funding available for education.

In spite of extensive immigration during the 1960s and 1970s, the Swedish culture continues to be a relatively homogeneous one. By the 1990s, approximately 10% of the population were either immigrants or children of immigrants. Immigration has presented challenges to education policy. In areas where high percentages of immigrants live, unemployment rates tend to be high and fewer taxes are collected. At the same time, educational expenses for native-language instruction and courses in Swedish as a second language are very high.

Immigration and urbanization have made it increasingly difficult to maintain the 4,000 small municipalities that existed in the beginning of the 1950s. Municipalities have been consolidated, and by the mid-1990s their number had decreased to 288, although small school units have been maintained in remote and rural areas. This rural policy helps account for lower school enrollment and student–teacher ratios as well as a higher per-pupil cost of education in rural areas (Organisation for Economic Cooperation and Development [OECD], 1996).

Reforms of the curriculum, grading system, and student advancement policies for compulsory and upper secondary education were implemented in 1991 (Carlgren, 1995). In the previous curricula, comprehensive schools had to strictly follow a detailed, centrally approved curriculum. The new national curriculum spells out the broad areas to be covered and the minimum and maximum time to be spent on each area. The focus of the curriculum is on goal attainment, but it allows room for local adaptation and individual tailoring for students (Lpo, 94).

Policies concerning student advancement and grading have also changed. Before 1994, students were, in practice, automatically advanced to the next year regardless of their school performance. There was a 5-point grading scale but no "pass" or "fail." Students from compulsory levels having only 1s (the lowest achievement) could still apply for admission to upper secondary education. Since 1994, students must pass all of their subjects, and they can move to the next grade only with the approval of the teacher and the school director. National standardized tests continue to be administered in grades 5 and 9 for both public schools and independent schools. Apart from the national tests, broader national evaluations, including ones evaluating school processes and their quality, have been introduced. The first of the evaluations was made in 1992.

MAJOR SHIFTS IN EDUCATIONAL POLICY

Three important changes in educational policy occurred between the mid-1980s and mid-1990s: decentralization, the introduction of choice, and the stimulation of private schools. While changes in other policies—such as curriculum, grading, national evaluation, and guaranteed placement for 6-year-old children in school—represented significant departures from the past, it is these three that have had the largest effect on education in Sweden so far.

Decentralization and School-Based Management

During the latter half of the 1960s, demands concerning lifestyles, moral values, and participatory democracy emerged that had never been raised before. The established parties and organizations were not able to handle these demands. The quest for direct and participatory democracy became stronger, manifesting itself in the creation of thousands of *byalag*, principally in urban areas. These "teams for common works" had previously existed in Sweden until the beginning of the 20th century, when the industrialization of the country and the implementation of a national welfare system made them obsolete. The new *byalag* often acted on their own behalf and before the elected municipality parliaments and boards had made their decisions, sometimes undermining the power of the boards (Åkerman, 1972). Also, demands for *user democracy* emerged within the SD party during the 1970s, which meant that the user, not the owners, should make decisions concerning the management of residences and so on (Eliasson, 1972). Both of these phenomena contributed to the decentralization that later was implemented by the national government, including the delegation of decision-making authority from the state to the municipalities and, in turn, from the municipalities to school principals.

Choice

Before 1991, it was practically impossible for a student to choose his or her own school. Each public school had its catchment area and was obligated to accept all pupils living within this area. Independent schools generally received very low subsidies. Fewer than 1% of primary school students attended independent schools at the end of the 1980s.

Since 1991, however, public schools are allowed to take in other students as long as there are available space and adequate teaching facilities. Schools are expected to market themselves in order to attract the maximum number of students. Consequently, many schools have sought to develop a particular profile. When the 1995–1996 schoolyear started, two-thirds of all the municipalities in Sweden offered some sort of choice option within the public education sector (Skolverket, 1996a).

How Choice Affects Families

Although a majority of municipalities now offer choice, choice is not yet available to the majority of students and their families. Especially in rural areas, prohibitive commuting distances and the lack of independent schools effectively limit which schools students can attend. Therefore school choice, in reality, is most commonly determined by the commuting distance to the school rather than by pedagogical preferences or other considerations (Skolverket, 1996g).

On the other hand, school choice can be interpreted as a way for parents to exert pressure on the schools and on the teachers to improve the school. In the mid-1990s a study showed that eight of ten parents wanted to have the option to choose a different school for their children, even if they would never use it (Skolverket, 1996a). Choice and competition in 10 municipal schools serving more than 13,000 students were evaluated in 1996. From July 1994 to July 1996, 7% of students in the evaluation group had chosen a school (public or private) other than the one to which they "belonged" from an administrative point of view (Skolverket, 1996a). Among those choosing another school, 40% had opted for a public school within the same residential area, 40% had chosen a public school outside the area, and the remaining 20% had chosen an independent school. For the most part, parents reported that they chose schools that had "good teachers and clear guidelines/requirements." However, parents also considered commuting distance when making their selection; the closest schools were chosen if they were perceived by parents to give the children a satisfactory education (Skolverket, 1996a).

Ethnicity and parental education levels have played a major role in which students exercise choice options. Students of Nordic origin changed schools more often than could be predicted from their socioeconomic background. It was found that 6% of the Swedish parents and 12% of immigrants from Nordic countries have exercised their school choice right (Skolverket, 1996a). For many of these parents, the opportunity to hear and speak the Swedish language properly, as well as home-language instruction, seem to be the important factors affecting their choices. Also, students whose parents have a postsecondary education were more likely to take advantage of their right to school choice.

How Choice Affects Schools

In urban areas, school choice affects class composition and the way classes are organized. Due to the flow of students between schools, schools are becoming more and more distinct from one another in their way of organizing the classes (Skolverket, 1996a, 1996f, 1996g). Some of the findings reveal a tendency toward increased segregation as a result of student migration from schools situated in areas that are socioculturally heterogeneous (Skolverket, 1996a). Thus, individual schools have become more segregated even though the actual residence areas around the school remain unchanged (Skolverket, 1996a). One case study conducted in a large municipality with a high percentage of immigrants looked at what happened when an independent school was established close to a public school. Nordic pupils left the public school for the independent school and for other public schools with a lower percentage of non-Nordic immigrants. At the public school, the total number of students declined by 30% and the percentage of pupils with African, Arab, and Latin American backgrounds increased from 34% to 52% during the first 3 years the independent school was operating (Daun, 1998).

School choice clearly benefits some schools. For schools that are frequently selected, school competition creates stimulating challenges and fosters motivation for school improvement. This has been observed by inspectors from the national agency and reported by the school principals when interviewed by the national evaluation teams (Skolverket, 1996a, 1999c). Schools with a large *inflow* of students can be classified into two categories: (1) new public or independent schools and (2) public schools that traditionally have existed in economically well-off areas. The latter type of schools tend to have a good reputation and are generally more stable in terms of educational performance and discipline. Although neither type of school actively markets itself, they nevertheless attract new students (Skolverket, 1996a).

Other schools are affected by choice as well. Schools losing students tend to have large proportions of immigrant and/or lower-class students. The outflow of students consists to a large extent of those students who typically possess more cultural capital. Schools with large outflows react in different ways. Some strengthen their efforts to innovate and market new pedagogical profiles. Others do not take any such measures. Among those unable or unwilling to market themselves, some are still able to break the downward trend and create a larger inflow than outflow of students. Schools with a declining number of students are forced to make budget cuts and to dismiss teachers. In some cases, this downward trend is caused not only by the introduction of choice but also by declining cohorts of school-age children. To date, however, there have not been any reports of school closures because of large outflows of students (Skolverket, 1996a, 1999b, 1999d).

A study conducted in another large municipality illustrates several of the issues mentioned above. There are no independent schools in this municipality, but there is considerable student flow between the public schools (grades 7–9). Choice is exercised according to the traditional reputation of the schools. It has been found that choice has cumulative effects on schools. Schools that gain more pupils than they lose have accumulated surplus revenues during the 7 to 8 years that school choice has been available. These schools have been able to buy new equipment and spend more on in-service training of the teachers. A couple of schools losing students initially continued to spend on such items, but they accumulated large deficits (Söderqvist, 1999). In 2000, it was decided that these schools had to pay back their debts, and so they have had to revise their budgets accordingly.

According to some studies, small schools and those in rural areas do not significantly differ from larger schools in urban areas in quality or in student achievement. However, small and rural schools have a limited range of options available for their students, and school choice continues to be based on commuting distance rather than pedagogical preference (Skolverket, 1996g).

Independent Schools

The percentage of compulsory school-age students at independent schools has increased from less than 1% in 1991 to 3% in 1998 (see Table 4.1), with large variations between the municipalities. One-fourth of all independent schools are located in the Greater Stockholm area (Skolverket, 1999e), with only six independent schools situated in remote areas (Skolverket, 1996g, 1998c). Fewer than half of all municipalities have an independent school (118 out of 288 municipalities). The number of independent schools at the compulsory level

Table 4.1. Percentage of pupils and number of schools in independent compulsory and upper secondary schools, 1992–1993 through 1998–1999.

	1991–1992	1992–1993	1993–1994	1994–1995	1995–1996	1996–1997	1997–1998	1998–1999
Compulsory education (grades 1–9)								
Nationally	0.9	1.1	1.5	1.8	2.1	2.5	2.7	3.0
Max.	—	—	—	—	9.6	10.0	11.5	—
Min.	—	—	—	—	0.0	0.0	0.0	—
Number of schools	90	112	172	218	244	72	302	337
Upper secondary (grades 10–12)								
Nationally	—	1.7	1.8	1.9	2.3	.7	3.1	3.5
Max.	—	—	—	—	20.2	2.5	23.2	—
Min.	—	—	—	—	0.0	0.0	0.0	—
Number of schools	—	—	57	59	61	0	77	82

Sources: Skolverket (1997b, 1998a, 1999a, 1999b).

Table 4.2. Percentage of pupils and number of schools in independent compulsory and upper secondary schools, 1992–1993 through 1998–1999.

	1992–1993	1993–1994	1994–1995	1995–1996	1996–1997	1997–1998	1998–1999
Compulsory education (grades 1–9)							
Nationally	1.1		1.8	2.1	2.5	2.7	3.0
Number of schools	112		218	244	272	302	337
Upper secondary (grades 10–12)							
Nationally	1.7	1.8	1.9	2.3	2.7	3.1	3.5
Number of schools	—	57	59	61	70	77	82

Sources: Skolverket (1997b, 1998a, 1999a, 1999b). In 1991–1992, there were 90 independent compulsory schools (see Skolverket, 1998e).

tripled from 112 in 1992–1993 to 337 in 1998–1999. At the secondary level, the number of independent schools has increased from 57 (less than 2% of the students) to 82 (more than 3% of the students) nationally (see Table 4.2). The independent secondary schools are distributed in a geographically similar way to the independent comprehensive schools, although they are situated mainly in urban areas. Subsidies are provided according to a national average, a fact that makes the economic situation difficult for low-income municipalities when independent upper secondary schools are established.

In 1991–1992,[1] 39% of the independent schools were run by voluntary organizations or associations, and 11% were run by companies. Seven years later, the percentage of independent schools run by companies had increased to 30% (Skolverket, 1999e). Increased subsidies have made it possible to establish a number of small independent schools. Many small public schools were forced to close in the early 1990s, but several of them were immediately reopened by parents and/ or teachers as independent schools (Skolverket, 1998b, 1999g). Independent schools are, on the average, considerably smaller than public-sector schools; the smallest private school had fewer than 20 pupils in 1999 (Skolverket, 1999b). Many independent schools do not actively market themselves. Instead, they rely on the positive reputation they have been able to establish. When an independent school is created, parents are generally directly or indirectly involved through formal and informal information channels (Daun, 1998; Skolverket, 1996a).

Case studies show that a great deal of voluntary and nonpaid work is performed by parents and relatives of the students, at least in small independent schools (Brattlund, in press; Daun, 1998).

The most significant increase in student enrollment in independent schools occurred in the big cities, although the number grew least in the industrial urban areas that traditionally have had a leftist political majority reluctant to support private initiatives in the public sector. In some urban municipalities such as Stockholm, the percentage of students attending independent schools has been increasing steadily since 1991 and has now surpassed 10%.

Student Performance

On average, student performance has always been higher at independent schools. During the 1995–1996 schoolyear, for instance, ninth-graders in the Swedish public schools obtained an average score of 3.22 on a 5-point scale, while those at the independent schools averaged 3.54. There are significant differences between the various types of schools in the private sector, however. Students at independent schools with a general profile had an average score of 3.67, while those at religious/ethnic-oriented independent schools had an average score of 3.12.

In a study investigating student performance on the reading comprehension tests, pupils in grades 7–9 were tested in a sample of public and independent schools. Those attending independent schools rated significantly higher on reading comprehension than those attending public schools. In 1996, with the new assessment system, 13% of ninth-graders in the public schools earned the highest grade in the basic English course, as compared to 34% in the independent schools. However, the variation among independent schools is larger than the variation between the sectors (Skolverket, 1997b). Most of the studies investigating differences in student performance between public and independent schools generally support the claim that differences disappear when student socioeconomic background and/or initial level of knowledge is controlled for.

With the change of the grading system in 1994, it is not possible to make any straightforward assessment of the development of performance as measured by grades. However, 20% of the students in the public schools and 25% in the independent schools did not achieve passing scores in all core subjects (Skolverket, 1999a). Private-sector schools are required to employ teachers with pedagogical training, but it is difficult for the National Agency to enforce compliance with this requirement prior to the application evaluation. Moreover, since the mid-1990s, there has been a shortage of trained teachers. For example, in 1998 only 57% of teachers at independent schools fulfilled the national training requirements, compared to 85% at public schools (Skolverket, 1999e).

School Costs

There are large variations in costs not only between the sectors but also among individual schools within each sector. A study of the differences in per-pupil costs in 10 municipalities reveals that five variables explain 50% of the variation between municipalities: residential distance (average distance between the inhabitants in the municipality), percentage of immigrants, political majority, number of pupils per school, and tax power. The first variable alone explains 27% of the variation (Skolverket, 1996e). At the high school or upper secondary school level, the difference in costs between public and independent schools has been large, independent schools being more expensive than the public schools (Skolverket, 1996c, 1997d, 1999b). At this level, there is a great deal of diversity among schools in both the public and the private sectors.

Homogenization

Many of the denominational and ethnic or linguistic schools are owned and operated by religious groups (e.g., various Christian and Muslim associations). In 1997, the National Agency for Education evaluated these schools. It found that denominational schools were most commonly chosen by parents with low formal education as a means of maintaining the culture and religion of their home country. One of the conclusions drawn by the evaluator was that self-segregation of this nature contributed to the overall segregation in society (Skolverket, 1997d).

With the implementation of comprehensive education in 1962, efforts were made to increase student diversity in terms of socioeconomic and cultural background in order to enhance and diversify student experiences and to train students to exercise democracy and tolerance. Some national reports argue that choice, including increased support for independent schools, has not resulted in increased segregation (e.g., Skolverket, 1999c). However, other studies conducted at the municipal or district level indicate that there has been a considerable flow of students between schools in certain urban areas. For example, students of Swedish/Nordic origin have left schools that have a large percentage of students of African, Asian, and Arabic descent. This phenomenon has resulted in increased segregation and inequality (Daun, 1998; OECD, 1994; Skolverket, 1996a, 1996f, 1997d). The reasons parents give for choosing a specific independent school are the same reasons they give for choosing among public schools (Skolverket, 1996a). In urban areas, students of Nordic origin are more likely than other students to choose independent schools regardless of their parents' level of education. Among non-Nordic pupils, on the other hand, parent educational level is the single most important factor in determining whether or not they attend an independent school.

DISCUSSION AND CONCLUSIONS

The educational policy shift that took place in Sweden marked a dramatic break with Swedish tradition. Educational policies in Sweden were, until the mid-1980s, predominantly conditioned by internal forces such as interest groups and popular movements, on one hand, and the ambitions of the state to achieve equality and the development of national human capital, on the other (Dahllöf, 1984). The strong relationship that existed among the Social Democratic party, the labor movement, and the employers' federation was firmly entrenched in the political and social culture. The system of education, as measured by international assessments, had a history of strong performance. There was little dissatisfaction with either the system or its performance.

It is remarkable that any shift in education policy could overcome such inertial forces. Equally remarkable was the alacrity with which the reforms were proposed and implemented. In Sweden, changes in public policy are normally evaluated and discussed by political parties, state authorities, and interest groups for a long time before they are brought to the national parliament. In fact, there is a special expression for this in the Swedish language—*förankra*, or anchoring a decision. However, the shift in education policy was not preceded by consultation with or "anchoring" in the societal interests affected by the proposed changes; it was a surprise not only for educational researchers but also for those working in the schools.

Nevertheless, other factors sufficiently outweighed these traditions to prompt the change in policies. One important factor was the national economy. Economic growth in Sweden from the 1950s until the 1990s was among the lowest of the OECD countries; the world-wide recession of the 1980s added to this sluggishness. Nevertheless, until the early 1970s total government expenditure as a percentage of GNP was one of the lowest among the OECD nations. However, from the mid-1970s through the 1990s state expenditures continued to increase even as revenues were declining (OECD, 1990; World Bank 1979, 1986, 1991). The economy became increasingly export-oriented and dependent on conditions in the world economy (Petersson, 1990). As production in Swedish-owned units abroad increased more rapidly than the exports from the country (Petersson, 1990), the state could no longer guarantee that Swedish companies would invest and create employment within the country. It was evident that something had to be done to jump-start the economy.

Another factor leading to the shift in education policy was the cost of education. During this time, total expenditures on education as a percentage of GNP and per-pupil cost as a percentage of gross domestic product (GDP) were among the highest in the OECD countries (World Bank, 1979, 1986, 1991, 1995), although this was because the number of students per teacher in Sweden was the lowest or one of the lowest among the OECD countries (OECD, 1996). A third factor prompting the changes in education policy was the emergent demand for user democracy and the devolution of authority over governmental services, including education, from the central to the local level.

Overall, the most important results of the educational restructuring are that (1) a great variety of activities have started and more decision making is taking place at the school level; (2) a new type of dynamic among public schools in densely populated areas has emerged since students have been allowed to choose among schools; and (3) the student populations within schools are becoming more and more homogeneous even as the education system is becoming more heterogeneous.

In theory, much decision-making authority has been delegated from the national parliament to the municipalities, and in turn from the municipalities to school principals. In practice, different municipalities interpret the new rules and regulations in different ways. Consequently, the extent to which de facto decision making has been moved to the school level differs greatly from one municipality to the next. The municipalities are supposed to establish school plans, but as late as 1997 a large proportion of them did not yet have such plans (Skolverket, 1999c). Municipalities are also supposed to report on efforts they have made to improve the quality of education, but many do not produce such reports (Dagens Nyheter, 2000).

The results of the decentralization process can be summarized as follows:

- Most school principals are supportive of the current changes concerning decentralization, but opinions among teachers are more divided (Falkner, 1997; Francia, 2000; Möller, 1995; Skolverket, 1996a, 1996c, 1996d, 1996e, 1996f).
- Many municipalities and schools lack concrete strategies and specific plans for attaining the national goals. The concept of equal education seems to be rather vague for many municipal politicians and educational administrators, partly because it is a difficult concept to define and partly because municipal politicians and administrators take a local rather than a national perspective. Moreover, the work plans produced by the schools in each municipality often fail to reflect the municipal school plan (Skolverket, 1997c, 1999c).
- The division of responsibility among different actors in the municipality is not very clear (politicians versus administrators; politicians/administrators versus school principals; school principals versus teachers; schools versus parents, and so on). Furthermore, it seems as if school principals have not adopted one of their most important roles, that of being *pedagogical* leaders. Principals were found to spend too much of their time on detailed and ineffective administrative tasks. This is because a lot of the decision making continues to take place at the same levels and in the same manner as it did prior to the introduction of decentralization. Another reason may be that the school principals are overloaded with administrative work and with trying to solve problems in meeting the needs of their students, especially those with special needs. In only a few schools was systematic support being organized for students who were not achieving the national goals (Skolverket, 1997c, 1999c).
- School principals and teachers have not sufficiently dedicated themselves to a systematic and thorough search for improving the quality of education they provide, nor have schools followed up on actions that are taken. Rather, they have relied on the national test scores to monitor performance (Skolverket, 1997c).
- In rural areas, the lump-sum subsidies make it possible for the municipalities to spend more in areas other than education.

As far as decentralization is concerned, it is evident that there is a great deal of confusion as to who should make what decisions. In some municipalities, the local politicians and administrators as well as the school principals have been given new roles, while in others, the decisions more or less follow the same paths as before. Also, parental access to and involvement in school life differ considerably by parents' socioeconomic background and educational level. Generally, it is not evident that parents have a stronger say than before in the life of the schools. Instead, they exert their influence by choosing or by the fact that choice is a potential option.

Apart from decentralization, the response to the reforms from the grassroots level has been weak. After the 7 or 8 years that have passed since choice was introduced and public support for private schools was increased, the number of children attending private schools remains small, though the percentage has tripled. Meaningful choice opportunities do not exist in sparsely populated areas. In the largest cities, on the other hand, there is full competition between schools. It is not clear to what extent school factors, which principals and teachers can manipulate, make schools losers or winners. When parents are choosing, schools are judged to a large extent on the basis of the socioeconomic and ethnic character of the geographic area in which they are situated. The result is that schools situated in well-off areas do not have to make any particular efforts to gain more students, while schools in other areas lose students no matter what they do. In the latter instance, few of them are able to maintain a stable number of students or to recover students who leave. According to "pure" market principles, schools losing students should eventually close down. As far as it has been possible to confirm, one of the independent schools in a remote area has been closed for economic reasons, while two have been closed by the National Agency.[2] Otherwise, there is little evidence that competition has led to the closing of schools.

In urban areas, choice creates competition with polarizing effects. Choice allows flow between the schools, and this flow makes each school more homogeneous socioeconomically, ethnically, and in regard to academic motivation and achievement among the students. It means, on the other hand, that schools become more and more different in their profiles and quality. Processes of both homogenization and heterogenization are thus taking place that seem to challenge the ability of the Swedish education system to offer an equivalent education. Moreover, the meaning of equivalency seems to have changed from being associated with equality to being associated with individualism and freedom of choice (Francia, 2000).

Despite the systemic shift, overall educational policies remain unchanged: Education should serve equality and the common good, among other things. Educational researchers in Sweden debate intensely whether it will be possible to attain such goals because the means and arrangements that have resulted from the policy shifts in the 1990s seem incompatible with these fundamental goals (Carlgren, 1995; Lindblad & Wallin, 1993; Kallos & Nilsson, 1995).

NOTES

1. In January 2000, there was a debate within the leading group of the Social Democratic party about whether or not to forbid privatization and *bolagisering* (companyization) of public activities such as health care and education (Dagens Nyheter, January 20, 2000).
2. The school in the remote area was a public school that closed in 1993 due to the low number of pupils. It was reopened as an independent school by the parents. The two schools closed by the National Agency were Islamic schools that were closed in mid-1990s due to economic and administrative mismanagement, among other things. However, one of them was reopened in the ownership of another Islamic association (Brattlund, in press).

REFERENCES

Åkerman, N. (1972). *Demokratibegreppet* [The concept of democracy]. *Det nya samhället, 7.* Stockholm: Tidens förlag.
Brattlund, Å. (in press). *The state and Islamic primary schools in Europe. Case studies in Sweden and England.* Stockholm: Institute of International Education.
Carlgren, I. (1995). National curriculum as social compromise or discursive politics? Some reflections on a curriculum-making process. *Journal of Curriculum Studies, 27*(4), 411–430.
Dagens Nyheter. (January 20, 2000). [Un-titled newspaper article.] *Dagens Nyheter.*
Dahllöf, U. (1984). Contextual problems of educational reforms: A Swedish perspective. In T. Husén, and M. Kogan, (Eds.), *Educational research and policy. How do they relate?* Oxford: Pergamon.
Daun, H. (1998). Comprehensive schooling in the intersection of market, state and civil forces: Two Swedish case studies. In A. Tjeldvoll (Ed.), *Education and the Scandinavian welfare state in the year 2000. Equality, policy and reform.* New York: Garland.
Dow, G. (1993). What do we know about social democracy? *Economic and Industrial Democracy, 14,* 11–48.
Eliasson, T. (1972). Rörelsen och demokratin eller Mera makt åt folket. [The movement and democracy or more power to the people]. In N. Åkerman

(Ed.), *Demokratibegreppet* [The concept of democracy]. *Det nya samhället 7.* Stockholm: Prisma.

Englund, T. (1996). Varför en ny läroplan? (Why a new curriculum?) In T. Englund (Ed.), *Utbildningspolitiskt systemskifte?* (Systemic Shift in Educational Policy). Stockholm: Stockholm School of Education.

Falkner, K. (1997). *Lärare och skolans omstrukturering: Ett möte mellan utbildningspolitiska intentioner och grundskollärares perspektiv på förändring i den svenska skolan [Teachers and school restructuring: An encounter between education policy intentions and teachers' perspective on change in the Swedish School].* Uppsala, Sweden: Uppsala University.

Francia, G. (2000). *Policy som text och som praktik. En analys av likvärdighetsbegreppet i 1990-talets utbildningsreform för det obligatoriska skolväsendet [Policy as text and as practice. An analysis of the equivalency concept in the 1990s' reform of comprehensive education].* Stockholm: Pedagogiska institutionen, Stockholms universitet.

Isling, Å. (1980). Kampen för och emot en demokratisk skola [The struggle for and against a democratic school]. Stockholm: Sober förlag.

Johnson, N. (1987). *The welfare state in transition.* Brighton: Wheatsheaf Books.

Kallos, D., & Nilsson, I. (1995). Defining and Re-Defining the Teacher in the Swedish Comprehensive School. *Educational Review, 47*(2), 173–188.

Lindblad, S., & Wallin, E. (1993). On transitions of power, democracy and education in Sweden. *Journal of Curriculum Studies, 25*(1), 77–88.

Möller, M. (1995). *Educational management and conditions for competence.* Unpublished master's thesis. Stockholm: Stockholm University, Institute of International Education.

Montin, S. (1992). Privatiseringsprocesser i kommunerna—teoretiska utgångspunkter och empiriska exempel [Processes of privatization in the municipalities—theoretical points of departure and empirical examples]. *Statsvetenskaplig tidskrift, 1*(1), 31–56.

Organisation for Economic Cooperation and Development (OECD). (1996). *Education at a glance. OECD indicators.* Paris: Author.

OECD (1990). *Education in OECD countries 1987–1988.* Paris: OECD.

OECD (1994). *School: A matter of choice.* Paris: OECD.

Petersson, L. (1990). Den svenska ekonomins internationalisering (The internationalization of the Swedish economy). In G. Hansson & L.-G. Stenelo (Eds.), *Makt och internationalisering* [Power and internationalization]. Stockholm: Carlsons.

Schüllerquist, U. (1996). Förskjutning av svensk skolpolitisk debatt under det senaste decenniet [Shift in the Swedish school debate during the last decade]. In T. Englund (Ed.), *Utbildningspolitiskt systemskifte?* [Systemic shift in educational policy]. Stockholm: Stockholm School of Education.

Skolverket. (1996a). *Att välja skola—effekter av valmöjligheter i grundskolan. [Choosing school—effects of choice in comprehensive education].* Stockholm: National Agency for Education.

Skolverket (1996c). *Skolan i siffror, 1996. Del 1: Betyg och utbildningsresultat [The school in figures. Part 1: Marks and educational results]*. Stockholm: National Agency for Education.

Skolverket (1996d). *Skolan i siffror, 1996. Del 2: Elever och lärare [The School in figures. Part 2: Pupils and teachers]*. Stockholm: National Agency for Education.

Skolverket (1996e). *Skolan i siffror, 1996. Del 3: Kostnader [The School in figures. Part 3: Costs]*. Stockholm: National Agency for Education.

Skolverket (1996f). *Varför kostar elever olika? En analys av skillnaderna i kommunernas kostnader for grundskolan [Why do the pupils costs vary? An analysis of the differences in the municipality costs for the comprehensive school]*. Stockholm: National Agency for Education

Skolverket (1996g). *Finns skolklassen? En studie i elevsammansättningen i grundskolan [Does the school class exist? A study of pupil composition in the comprehensive school]*. Stockholm: National Agency for Education.

Skolverket (1997b). *Resultat från en kunskapsmätning 1995*. Rapport nr 139 [*Results from a test of knowledge 1995*. Report No. 139]. Stockholm: National Agency for Education.

Skolverket (1997c). *Ansvaret för skolan—en kommunal utmaning [The responsibility for the school—a challenge for the municipalities]*. Stockholm: National Agency for Education.

Skolverket (1997d). *Barn mellan arv och framtid. Konfessionella, etniska och språkligt inriktade skolor i ett segregationsperspektiv [Children between inheritance and future. Confessionally, ethnically, and linguistically oriented schools in a segregation perspective]*. Dnr 97:810. Stockholm: National Agency for Education.

Skolverket (1997e). *Beskrivande data om skolverksamheten 97 [Descriptive data on the school activities 97]*. Stockholm: National Agency for Education.

Skolverket (1998a). *Skolan i siffror, 1998). Del 2: Elever och lärare [The school in figures, 1998. Part 2: Pupils and teachers]*. Stockholm: National Agency for Education.

Skolverket (1998b). *Barnomsorg och skola i siffror, 1998). Del 3: Kostnader [Child care and school in figures, 1998. Part 3: Costs]*. Stockholm: National Agency for Education.

Skolverket (1998c). *Skolan. Jämförelsetal för skolans huvudmän: Organisation—Resurser—Resultat, 1998 [The School. Comparative figures for school owners. Organization—resources—results. 1998]*. Stockholm: National Agency for Education.

Skolverket (1999a). *Barnomsorg och skola i siffror, 1999. Del 1: Betyg och utbildningsresultat [Child care and school in figures, 1999. Part 1: Marks and educational results]*. Stockholm: National Agency for Education.

Skolverket (1999b). *Barnomsorg och skola i siffror, 1999. Del 2: Barn, per-*

sonal och lärare [Child care and school in figures, 1999. Part 2: Children, staff, and teachers]. Stockholm: National Agency for Education.

Skolverket (1999c). *Barnomsorg och skola i siffror, 1999. Del 3: Kostnader [Child care and school in figures, 1999. Part 3: Costs]*. Stockholm: National Agency for Education.

Skolverket (1999d). *Nationella kvalitetsgranskningen 1998 [The national quality assessment 1998]*. Stockholm: National Agency for Education.

Skolverket (1999e). *Fristående skolor 1998 [Independent schools 1998]*. Stockholm: National Agency for Education.

Skolverket (1999f). *Fristående skolor. Grundskolor. Särskolor [Independent schools. Comprehensive schools. Special schools]*. Stockholm: National Agency for Education.

Skolverket (1999g). *Fristående skolor. Gymnasieskolor. Gymnasiesärskolor [Independent schools. Upper secondary schools. Upper secondary special schools]*. Stockholm: National Agency for Education.

SMES (1997). *The Swedish education system, August 1997*. Stockholm: Ministry of Education and Science.

Söderqvist, B. (1999). *Market forces in lower secondary education. A case from a Swedish municipality*. Unpublished master's thesis, Institute of International Education, Stockholm.

Sou (1988). *En förändrad ansvarsfördelning och styrning på skolområdet [A changed distribution of responsibility and steering within the area of education]*. Stockholm: Ministry of Education and Science.

Sou (1990). *Långtidsutredningen. Utbildning inför 2000-talet [Investigation of long-term development. Education for the 21st century]*. Stockholm: Ministry of Education and Science.

World Bank (1979). *World development report, 1979*. Washington: World Bank.

World Bank (1986). *World development report, 1986*. Washington: World Bank.

World Bank (1991). *World development report, 1991*. Washington: World Bank.

World Bank (1995). *World development report, 1995*. Washington: World Bank.

CHAPTER 5

School Choice Policies and Their Impact on Public Education in Australia

Max Angus

In Australia, the public policy debate about school choice is focused on access to private schooling. Since the 1970s, state funding of private schools has been a fact of Australian life. How much funding and what conditions should be attached to the funding, nevertheless, remain lively questions, particularly since it appears that the funding has lead to a reversal of the fortunes of the public and private sectors. The private sector has increased its enrollment share every year since 1979. Nearly one in three students now attends a private school. All the major political parties recognize the power of policies that enable parents to choose a private education for their children. There is a mood to extend rather than curtail that option.

Clearly, the steady growth of the private sector has serious consequences for public schooling. To understand why governments have enabled this growth, and to gauge how the enrollment shift is impacting on the public school sector, it is necessary to briefly review the history of state aid for private schools.

HISTORIC COMMITMENT TO PUBLIC SCHOOLING

The Emergence of a Dual System

A dual system of public and private schooling was set in place soon after European settlement in 1788. When the First Fleet arrived at

Botany Bay, there was no plan for schooling in the instructions for the governor of the new colony. In the British tradition, the education of children of the "lower ranks" was not a priority; in the case of the penal colony of New South Wales, it was an afterthought even though the fleet carried children of marines and convicts (Austin, 1972). During these years, colonial governments provided practical forms of support for church schools as a matter of expediency.

By 1840, the colony faced a pivotal decision: Should it set up a system of nondenominational schools or delegate responsibility for schooling to the churches? There was by this time a substantial Irish presence in the colony, and the Catholic clergy were as distrustful of the idea of nondenominational schools as the Protestants. Each denomination preferred to assume pastoral responsibility for the members of its own group; neither believed in the religious neutrality of nondenominational schools. The governors, for their part, consciously resisted delegating the full responsibility to the Church of England, Britain's church of state. The resolution was a compromise. In 1848, the governor of New South Wales appointed the Board of National Education to establish public schools based on the Irish system of nondenominational schools. A denominational school board was also appointed to administer government funds to church schools. From the beginning of European settlement, the differentiation between church and state was blurred, much more so than in the United States.[1]

The commitment to the public maintenance of a dual system of schooling lasted until the latter half of the 19th century, when, in relatively prosperous and optimistic times, colonial governments set out to expand their systems of public schooling. In this context, government subsidies for private schools were abolished. However, a residual system, composed mainly of Catholic parish schools and Protestant grammar schools, endured the hard times. One in five Australians continued to be educated in private schools. In the decades that followed the federation of the colonies at the turn of the century, church leaders campaigned for a restoration of aid, giving rise to acrimonious sectarian disputes.

The Resumption of Government Aid

By the 1950s there was bipartisan political support for a resumption of some form of federal government aid even though, constitutionally, education was a state responsibility. Support initially took the form of modest income tax concessions and special-purpose grants to schools for science laboratories and libraries. Subsequently, relatively small recurrent grants for the operating costs of private schools were introduced separately by federal and state governments.

The big boost in government aid to private schools followed the 1972 federal election. At the time, states were having difficulty funding their public school systems and private schools were in dire financial trouble. Both of the nation's major political parties promised substantial increases in funding for education, including grants for recurrent and capital costs for private schools. The Labor party, however, which assumed government under Prime Minister Gough Whitlam, was committed to providing federal funds to schools on the basis of need rather than by means of flat per-capita grants. It proposed that a statutory body, the Schools Commission, should assess the need for aid and make grants on behalf of the federal government. In its landmark report (Karmel, 1973), the committee established to advise the interim Schools Commission recommended that a huge quantum of needs-based funding be allocated to the public and private school sectors. Needs were to be determined according to a common resource standard. Catholic schools would be the major beneficiaries.

The Institutionalization of "Aid"

The effect of the Whitlam government's intervention was to energize the private sector. It could look forward to unprecedented levels of federal aid. Further, the conditions attached to the aid did not require private schools to modify their enrollment policies. As Marginson (1997) points out, the Whitlam funding, while greatly improving the resource standards in public schools, had the effect of normalizing the principle of government funding for selective private schools with which the public schools would increasingly be required to compete for enrollments.

Since the 1970s, governments, both federal and state, Labor and non-Labor, have continued to support the private school sector. The growth of the sector has been accompanied by a change in public discourse. State ministers of education, once ministers with a primary responsibility for public education, are now bipartisan in their representation of sectoral interests. Progressively, the private sector has established low-fee schools in low-income neighborhoods. This has had the effect of mitigating criticisms of elitism and thereby has weakened the argument by public school advocates against state aid.

Without substantial government funding, the expansion of the private sector would not have been possible. Up until this point, the concept of "choice" meant choice between a public school and a private school. It was provided largely to satisfy the demand of a sector of the community for the education of Catholic children in Catholic schools. By 1996, the beginning of the Howard government's first term of office, support for private schools had been institutionalized. A wider conception of choice, one that implied a diversity of types of schools operating in an education marketplace, was not yet part of the discourse.[2]

FUNDING POLICIES AND ENROLLMENT TRENDS

The Interdependencies Between State and Federal Funding

Although the public face of private school funding belongs to the federal government, the state governments also make crucial contributions. There are complex interdependencies between the two levels of government.

The federal government has no administrative responsibility for schools, public or private. Schools operate under state acts of parliament. Therefore, the federal government needs the cooperation of the states in order to achieve its education policy objectives. However, it does have considerable financial leverage because it is the sole collector of income tax revenue, portions of which it returns to the states through general- and specific-purpose grants. About half of each state's revenue is acquired from this source.[3] The states use federal general-purpose grants to supplement their own revenue sources in order to meet the operating costs of public school systems. The *state* grants for private schools also come out of this revenue pool. *Federal* funding of private schools and some grants to state systems for public schools are drawn from the pool of tax revenue that it retains for federal purposes. Put simply, the larger the number of private schools under its administrative jurisdiction, the less the state has to draw on its own financial resources. From the state point of view, it is cheaper to extend the private sector; whereas from a federal government's viewpoint, its funding of private schools can be seen as a bonus to the states.

As Table 5.1 shows, half of the income of Catholic schools now comes from the federal government and about a fifth from the state government. The Catholic system could no longer function without government funding, particularly federal funding. By way of compari-

Table 5.1. Sources of funding for Catholic and non-Catholic private schools as proportions of total school income.

Year	Catholic			Non-Catholic private schools		
	Federal	State	Private	Federal	State	Private
1974	23.0	16.4	57.6	11.0	9.5	79.5
1977	40.4	22.2	37.4	15.3	15.3	69.4
1981	44.9	24.5	30.6	21.9	18.2	59.9
1988	46.7	22.9	30.4	23.4	14.9	61.7
1991	49.0	22.8	28.2	19.5	13.3	67.2
1994	50.9	21.3	27.8	21.3	12.3	66.4
1997	50.3	21.5	28.2	22.0	12.3	65.7

Sources: Schools Commission (1984), Ministerial Council on Education, Employment, Training and Youth Affairs (MCEETYA), National Report on Schooling in Australia, 1989–1997.

son, the federal government funds only about 10% of the costs of public schools through special-purpose grants. The states are expected to use their share of federal income tax revenue to meet the general running costs of public schools. This is one reason that advocates of public schooling are critical of the federal government. They argue on equity grounds that there should be a pro-rata distribution of federal funding between public and private sectors. The federal government has rejected this criticism, contending that it has separately funded the public school sector through its general-purpose grants to the states.

It is in the fiscal interests of federal and state governments to ensure that private schools maintain their share of income from private sources. The Catholic system has been unable to do this, principally because of the decline of religious orders that supplied teachers to Catholic schools and the consequent need to employ salaried lay staff. As shown in Table 5.1, little more than a quarter of the income of Catholic schools now comes from fees and other private sources, whereas nearly two-thirds of the income of non-Catholic private schools is drawn from private sources.

The state governments are now dependent on federal funding. The funding arrangements have entwined the political fortunes of both levels of government. After nearly three decades of federal funding for private schools, the states would now be unable to meet the shortfall in the unlikely event that the federal government withdrew its support for private schools.

State Financial Support for Private Schools

In most accounts of the growth of private schooling, the role of state governments is underplayed or ignored. There is no national, cohesive account. One reason is that even though all seven states provide aid to private schools, each has pursued a somewhat different course. The federal story is easier to tell. It has suited state governments to ride on the coat tails of the federal government in relation to the expansion of private schooling; the main focus of state governments has been the public school systems for the very practical reason that public school education consumes more than a quarter of each state's budget.

Western Australia was the first state to provide recurrent funding to private schools. In 1965, well before the advent of the Schools Commission, it introduced per-capita grants for students in private high schools. Grants were extended to primary schools in 1967. The grants, at this time, amounted to 6% of the average costs of educating a student in a government school. In 1975, following the establishment of the Schools Commission and its huge injection of federal funds, this figure jumped to 23% of the cost of educating a student in a government school (Madigan, 1989). Federal funding appears to have had a multiplier effect on state funding of private schools.

The provision of low-interest loans for new schools has been an important form of state support. Often combined with capital grants from the federal government, cheap loans have made it possible for communities or private bodies wanting to establish a new school to acquire buildings and grounds of a relatively high standard from the beginning. This has given the schools a sense of permanence and made them attractive alternatives to public schools.

There have been economic as well as political reasons for supporting private schools. State Treasury officials frequently pointed to the lower state costs of educating a student in private schools, since the federal government and the private providers contributed the most (see Table 5.1). The critical comparison was the average cost of schooling in public and Catholic schools. The Catholic schools appeared to be able to provide a comparable quality of education for much less than the running costs of public schools. By 1997, with the increases in state and federal funding, the differential has been reduced; in the case of Catholic schools, the expenditure per student is 7% less than the average expenditure per students in public schools. However, non-Catholic private schools spend on average 45% more on their students than public schools (Ministerial Council on Education, Employment, Training and Youth Affairs [MCEETYA], 1997).

The Growth of Private-Sector Enrollments

There is considerable diversity among schools in the private sector. Although the net enrollment of the public and private sectors is a critical indicator, it is helpful to break the private school component into three parts. Catholic schools controlled by Catholic education authorities in state or regional capitals constitute the largest section, enrolling nearly 20% of Australian students. The schools of the Anglican system constitute a smaller second section. National statistical collections usually group the remainder into another category, referred to as "other private." This category is the most diverse, since it contains high-fee schools (the so-called elite private schools) as well as low-fee, religious, and alternative schools. This has been the major growth area; within it, the growth has been among the low-fee, religious, and alternative schools. The relative growth rates are shown in Figure 5.1.

Although the significant levels of federal funding began in 1974, it was not until 1979 that the effects were felt on enrollments. As shown in Figure 5.1, over the 20 years 1979–1999, the enrollment share of public schools fell 9%. The Catholic system has gained nearly 3%; the larger share—about 5%—has been acquired by the nonsystemic "other" category.

CHANGING FEDERAL POLICIES: STRENGTHENING THE CONDITIONS FOR CHOICE AND COMPETITION

If demonstrating support to the private school sector were a political necessity, then all the Howard government had to do when it took office in 1996 was continue business as usual. However, led by a reformist Minister for Education, the government is assertively attempting to reframe the way in which schools are funded. Choice is being situated within a neo-liberal framework. Federal government statements on education remind readers that the government promotes quality, choice, and equity in education. "The right of parents to choose the most appropriate schooling for their child" is part of Howard government policy refrain. In 1974, in his maiden speech in the federal parliament, the present prime minister, John Howard, stated that his support for private schools was about choice: "They are not privileged people, but they are people who feel they ought to have the right to exercise this freedom of choice" (quoted in McGregor, 1999, p. 5).

Figure 5.1. Share of student enrollment by school sector, 1975–1999.

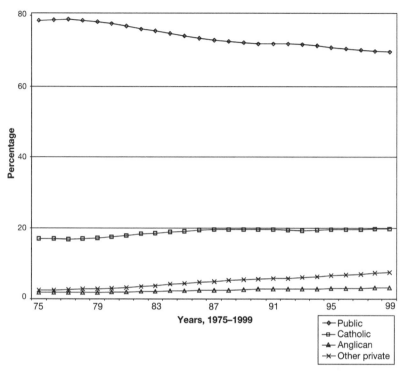

Source: Australian Bureau of Statistics (1975–1999).

The federal government has sought to extend choice of schooling by expanding and diversifying the private school sector. The growth area has been low-fee, nonsystemic private schooling. Increased funding to private schooling is to be partially funded by reductions in federal grants to the states for government schooling. Public education is being represented as the states' responsibility. The four primary instruments have been the following:

- a mechanism that redirects federal funding from public to private systems
- the abolition of federal restrictions on the establishment of new private schools

- the revision of the mechanisms for recurrent private school funding
- public reporting of school performance

Each of these instruments is described with reference to policy antecedents.

The Redirection of Federal Funding from Public to Private Systems

Under the Howard government arrangements, grants to government schools have been indexed to changes in the proportions of students enrolled in public and private schools. If the private school sector increased its proportion in a particular state, then the federal government reclaimed a portion of its funding from the state. Even though absolute enrollments might be increasing, as long as private school enrollments were increasing at a faster rate, then public schools could lose federal funding. This mechanism, highly unpopular among the states, was known as the Enrolment Benchmark Adjustment (EBA). Under considerable political pressure, it was abolished in 2001.

The Abolition of Federal Restrictions on the Establishment of New Private Schools

In 1985, the federal Labor government introduced the New Schools Policy. It maintained that the dual system required the adoption of a planned approach to the establishment of new schools. The unregulated growth of new schools was jeopardizing the viability of existing public and private schools. As shown in Figure 5.2, the policy quickly had an effect.

Later the federal government set a minimum enrollment of 50 in primary schools and 25 per grade in secondary schools. The level of funding for new nonsystemic schools was pegged at the middle of the funding schedule. These measures were disincentives to communities or bodies seeking to establish small private schools (McKinnon, 1995).

In 1996, prior to assuming power, the Howard government abolished the New Schools Policy. An alliance of associations representing Christian non-Catholic schools had campaigned vigorously for the removal of the funding cap for new schools, arguing that there was a need for cheaper private alternatives (Browning, 1998). The new funding arrangements came into operation in 1997.

Since the Howard government took office in 1996, the number of schools in the non-Catholic, non-Anglican sector has grown nearly

Figure 5.2. Number of private non-Catholic, non-Anglican schools, 1975–1999.

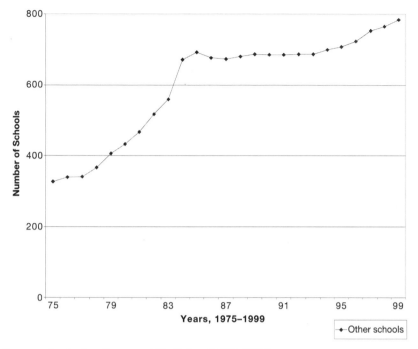

Source: Australian Bureau of Statistics (1975–1999).

10%. To put these numbers in perspective, it should be pointed out that during the term of the Fraser government, 1975–1983, the numbers nearly doubled.[4]

The Revision of the Recurrent Funding Mechanism for Private Schools

Under the system instituted in 1973, private schools were classified according to their capacity to generate income. Government assistance was meant to meet the shortfall between a school's private income and a standard level of resources based on per-student costs in government schools. Later, in 1985, private schools were classified according to a framework consisting of 12 resource levels. The level of government funding was differentiated according to the resource level. This system was known as the Educational Resource Index (ERI).

It was the subject of considerable criticism among schools concerning its fairness and responsiveness to the changing circumstances of schools.

A new method was introduced in 2001. It is based on the socioeconomic status (SES) of the households in which students in a school community reside rather than being a measure of the school's resources. An SES score is calculated for each school by linking home addresses with national census collection districts, units much smaller than postal-code districts (Department of Education, Training and Youth Affairs [DETYA], 1999a). A school's enrollment profile can then be described in terms of the average income, education, and occupation in the immediate areas in which students live.[5]

The SES scheme amounts to more than a redistribution of existing funding for private schools, since no school had its income reduced. Schools that would have received less funding under the SES model have their funding maintained at the year-2000 level, indexed against any rise in the cost of public schooling. It should also be noted that the Catholic systemic schools, comprising two-thirds of the private sector, were exempted. The Catholic systems have been block-funded at one of the highest levels available under the former ERI scheme. Catholic education authorities in each state distribute the funds to their schools, using their own measures of need. The withdrawal of the Catholic sector considerably weakens the legitimacy of the new procedures.

The shift from using an index of school resources to a scale of a school's enrollment profile represents an important change in policy. Schools can attach a financial value to students based on their residential address. School income from federal recurrent grants can be adjusted by changing selection and enrollment criteria. Schools that extend their enrollments to lower-income communities will benefit financially from the government grants. Thus, while the amount of funding to private schools will increase over the next quadrennium as a result of the SES scheme, the opportunity exists for a higher proportion of it to be spent on schooling the children of low-income families.

Public Reporting of School Performance

In addition to its funding measures, the federal government has campaigned assertively for the national assessment of student performance, particularly literacy, and the comparing of school and student performance against national benchmarks. The purposes of this federal initiative are to address the perceived problem of inadequate levels of literacy and to improve the information base according to which parents and students choose their school. According to the federal government, parents have a right—indeed, an obligation—to withdraw their children from a school that fails to provide a satisfactory grounding in literacy skills.

Although literacy has been the primary target of the federal government, it plans to extend the benchmarking to other curriculum areas, including science, civics, and enterprise education. The federal government wants to exercise the political leverage afforded by such performance data. It argues that it operates in the national interest, transcending state and local political agendas. However, because they maintain responsibility for the administration of school systems, the states want to retain control of their own assessment systems and the release of comparative data. This contest is not yet fully played out.

Competition within the Private Sector

Though high-fee private schools are able to wield considerable political influence and although they enjoy tangible resource advantages, they also operate under substantial competitive pressure. The school market is segmented. Those at the high-fee end have to attract parents willing to pay the fees. Government funding provides only a small proportion of their recurrent costs. Some schools, particularly those with boarding facilities that are underutilized as a result of the rural recession in Australia, have turned to the Asian market for fee-paying students.

In recent years, new competitors have entered the market. Private providers have set up schools for overseas students, offering senior high school courses that articulate with university courses. The universities, now operating in heated market conditions, are establishing their own school campuses, either in conjunction with private providers or under special arrangements with public school authorities. The aim is to channel academic local students and full-fee-paying overseas students into their courses. These are relatively new developments that are likely to exacerbate the financial pressures on traditional, high-fee private schools. Just as small enrollment shifts can hurt public school systems, similar shifts can have a dramatic effect on the economics of private schooling.

In addition, low-fee private schools with religious affiliations have been able to imitate many of the features of the more prestigious private schools by adopting strict dress codes, emphasizing academic achievement, and, with government support, providing impressive buildings and grounds. Parents who might have considered paying $10,000 yearly tuition fees to place a child in a high-fee school can get a similar "product" for less than $3,000.

The competition is for academic students who complete the university entrance requirements for year 12. A major scholarship program operates to draw students from public and other private schools.[6] There are several reasons for this preference. First, substantial kudos are acquired by schools that produce above-average results in university entrance exams. Second, these students contribute to a scholarly ethos in which order and effort are valued. The third reason is economic. Schools like to provide an academic program with as much subject choice as possible. The range of choices that the school is able to offer is dependent on the size of enrollments in the year-level cohort. Income from enrollments allows the school to employ staff. Not only do schools need sufficient enrollments to offer an appropriate curriculum, they also need continuity of enrollment to avoid the financial losses associated with honoring commitments to staff and students when a course fails to hold its numbers.

These developments are occurring not only after the federal deregulation of new school conditions but also within the ambit of the federal and state regulatory frameworks favoring competition in business and industry. Schools fall under the aegis of these frameworks. There will inevitably be conflicts of interest when new providers attempt to enter the market but encounter opposition from established interests. Questions will arise as to whether state authorities should reject applications to establish schools: In such instances, the public may wonder whether authorities are acting in the public interest or demonstrating a breach of competition policy.

Seen from this perspective, the policies of the federal government are less partisan toward the private schools, particularly the high-fee schools, than advocates of public schooling purport to be the case. Although there may be unmet demand for places in the private sector, even established private schools cannot afford to be complacent. For nonsystemic schools, a decline in enrollments could require the termination of staff or, in the longer term, the closing of the school.

Effect of the Howard Government Changes

Though it lacks the powers to require competition among public schools, the federal government is creating an environment conducive to it. The policies are serving to institutionalize market relations among both schools and sectors. The abolition of the New Schools

Policy means that in several states new schools do not have to have their proposals considered within the scope of existing school provision. The enrollment benchmark prompted competition between sectors. The new SES system of private school funding is likely to accelerate competition for academic students from poor neighborhoods. The publication of literacy performance will accentuate comparisons and prompt migration across sectors.

CHANGING STATE POLICIES: CHOICE WITHIN THE PUBLIC SCHOOL SECTOR

Thirty years ago state education systems in Australia were characterized by highly centralized and bureaucratic forms of administrative control, uniformity of educational provision, and student intakes determined by residence within enrollment zones. Over the last decade, these features have changed significantly. Local management, flexible enrollment policies, and curriculum specialization are driving contemporary public school reform. All these features are conducive to the extension of parental choice of schooling, though it would be simplistic to attribute their adoption to a rational determination by state governments to promote choice policies.

Flexible Enrollment Zones and Curriculum Specialization

For several decades during the mid-20th century, Australian states provided a comprehensive public education system. In most cities and large towns, a network of primary schools channeled students to local, coeducational high schools offering a comprehensive, statewide curriculum. Though a few states retained selective high schools, these were the exception, and it seemed that eventually state Labor governments would end the selective enrollment.[7] Parents opting for the public sector had few choices, since residential enrollment zones were policed, largely to facilitate the work of the central planners concerned with the efficient utilization of capital and other resources. For their part, given the standardized resource levels and curricula of public schools, central planners saw little purpose in extending parental choice. Uniformity was supposed to extinguish the need for choice. This period represented the zenith of comprehensive public education. The move away from comprehensive schooling was motivated by two considerations—the cost of specialist provision and recognition that private schools had acquired a competitive advantage.

During the 1970s, public schools came under pressure to provide specialist facilities for elective subject areas such as music and art. The government could not afford to locate a highly subsidized orchestra in every high school. Further, the standards and commitment that would draw students to such a music program appeared to require the designated school to draw from a much larger area than one intake zone. These programs initially appeared to constitute only a minor corruption of the principle of comprehensive schooling. Later, state systems developed special programs for "gifted and talented" students. At the time, these programs were supported by parents and teachers on the understanding that they would not have a negative impact on the curriculum of nonspecialist schools. This development was nominally instigated to improve the quality of the public school system; however, an unstated purpose was to stem the loss of potential high achievers to the private sector. This same end was achieved in New South Wales and Victoria with selective high schools.

By the late 1980s, curriculum specialization had become commonplace, not only in academic areas but also in vocational and sporting areas. Although enrollment zones were still in place, schools with authorized special programs were able to enroll their preferred students from out of zone. Some public schools used their own resources to provide scholarships and to advertize in the state media.

In 1997, two out of five students in "specialist high schools" came from outside the neighborhood. The figures are significant not only because of the scale of difference in enrollment patterns—the concept of a neighborhood high school is dubious under these conditions—but also because of the loss of students from the nonspecialist schools. From a systemic point of view, enrollment shifts of this kind may constitute a zero-sum transaction: The strengthening of one school potentially weakens several others.

Local Management

During the 1980s, all state governments sought to modernize their agencies by introducing aspects of corporate management practices. Public school sectors were prime targets because they consumed about a quarter of each state's overall budget. One of the core ideas was that schools should be able to respond to local needs within a statewide framework. This meant that schools should have more latitude to decide on how to spend their budgets, providing there were corresponding mechanisms for demonstrating that the public funds had been expended efficiently and effectively. Although the government wanted to cap spending on education, some of the key principles behind corporate managerialism fitted comfortably with the interests of innovative schools that had chafed against the microcontrols of the state education bureaucracies. The initiative to give schools more local control was known in Australia as "devolution."

In Australia, these ideas have developed furthest in the state of Victoria, which introduced single-line budgets, extended school discretion over staff appointments, devolved powers to local school councils, required schools to adopt public charters, and instituted regular, formal reviews of each school's performance in relation to the charter. The system constructed closely resembled those of New Zealand and England, with which Victorian officials and political leaders maintained close contact (Caldwell & Haywood, 1997). Other states have adopted some of these features but stopped short of the uncompromising commitment to the system made by the Victorian non-Labor government during 1993–1999. In its final year in office, Victoria's Kennett government set in motion an even more radical development—the establishment of self-governing public schools, analogous in many respects to grant-maintained schools in Britain and charter schools in the United States. Special legislation enabled the creation of self-governing schools, able for the most part to operate independently of the public school authorities and thereby functioning more like private than public schools. The initiative was short lived. In 1999, one of the first actions of the incoming state Labor government was to return the 51 self-governing schools to the public school mainstream. In doing so, it adopted the same political course as the Blair government in the United Kingdom, which abolished the special status of grant-maintained schools. It is not clear whether the local management reforms are a spent force in the Australian education sector.

The devolution reforms in state education systems were not explicitly instituted to extend choice of schooling, though they enabled a degree of "customization." Nor was their primary intention to enable the public sector to regain its former enrollment share. At the same time that state governments were implementing the devolution reforms, they were extending financial support to the private schools and in other ways legitimating the private sector.

THE IMPACT OF CHOICE POLICIES

At one level, school choice policies can be deemed an obvious success. It is clear that by subsidizing the provision of student places in the private school sector, the policies have enabled increasing numbers of parents to exercise choice. However, there appear to be important side-effects that are the result of these policies.

Diversification within the Public Sector

Australian public school systems have been noted for the uniformity of their resource standards and curricula and envied for these reasons by visitors from other countries, including the United States. Attitudes among Australian education department officials are changing. Uniformity of educational provision is now less often cited as a virtue. The pressure on state department officials to halt the enrollment decline has been an important contributing factor. For example, in 1999 the Queensland education department launched a review of the status of public education. In its report of the consultations held during the review, concern is expressed at the continuing decline of the public school market share and at the market opportunities that exist for private schools in the state. The report noted that public schools cannot be "all things to all people all of the time."

Attempts to do this lead to schools doing too many things and doing them in a mediocre way. There is a general impression of "sameness" about state (public) schools that teachers, students and parents said meant "blandness" (Education Queensland, 1999, p. 8).

Further school diversification is a logical response. Luke (1999), writing on behalf of the Queensland education department, calls for the end of the "one-size-fits-all" approach to public schooling by diversifying based on sound educational grounds and an analysis of community and student needs. Schools could be distinctive, for example, by selecting their student intake on some systematic basis, providing a specialized curriculum and drawing students from out of zone, becoming centers for teacher professional development, establishing programs of excellence in selected areas, becoming centers for community services, and so on. Luke cautions against the public system going down the market route whereby schools differentiate themselves on superficial grounds, for example, by forming corporate partnerships or by adopting market images. Luke warns that without such interventions, the Queensland public-sector share of enrollments could fall as low as 50% by 2010. The unstated principle behind diversification is that parents can shop around and get what they want at a cheaper price without leaving the public system.

Western Australia is also pursuing a policy of diversification with a view to competing more effectively with the private sector. It has established new schools in strategic areas that will operate on quite different lines from conventional private schools. The intention is to create new public schools that will be larger than private schools, offer more subject choices, enroll students in years 11 and 12 only, provide accredited university and technical courses, and operate on flexible timetables. The younger high school students will attend middle schools, an innovative concept in that state. Generally speaking, the neighboring private schools are likely to be smaller, associated with Christian churches, more academically focused, and more traditional in their curriculum and dress codes. The impact of this differentiation on enrollment share remains to be seen. The developments do illustrate the dilemma of public school officials in addressing the problem of declining enrollments. They can seek to imitate some aspects of private schools, hoping to capture the essence of what prompted families to opt for private schooling, or they can make their schools even more different—less bland—hoping that in acquiring a new "look" they do not alienate those parents who have steadfastly supported them in the past.

Diversification policies are still in their infancy, and it is difficult to assess their long-term impact. The policies could exacerbate existing inequality in systems proud of their egalitarian roots. Whether because of their selective entry policies or because of the location of the schools in middle-class suburbs, a relatively small number of public schools have acquired reputations for academic excellence that match the reputations of the wealthier private schools. These public schools are the front-runners in the competition for prestige and legitimation. The whole system benefits from the kudos derived from their success but at the same time is weakened where their success depends on the concentration of able students from the zones of many schools. The strategic decision facing public school officials is whether to push school diversification to the limit. This could happen if school diversification was left entirely to the hidden hand of the market and local responses to it, but this is unlikely. State governments would be under too much pressure to appear responsive to community complaints about the ad hoc nature of provision. On the other hand, it is unlikely that states will revert to the provision of uniform comprehensive education. It is more likely that public school authorities will adopt basic service provision units several times the size of a high school enrollment zone. Within such a region, the state could provide a comprehensive school, a vocationally oriented school, a K–12 school, a senior campus, and a school for dropouts—in effect, a mix of specialist high schools.

Diversification may turn out to be a two-edged sword. Although diversity may indicate how public schools are responsive to their communities, it is also possible that the more diverse the schools in the public sector, the more difficult it becomes to represent what public schools stand for. Public school teachers already have quite divergent views on the values that they think should underpin public education (Angus & Olney, 1998). There is the danger for the public sector, whether uniform or diverse, that it will position itself such that it stands for nothing in particular.

Social Residualization

Proponents of public education argue that private schools *selectively* draw students from the public sector. Research evidence suggests that parents who actively choose are different from those who do not: The former are more likely to value education and to be supportive of academic norms (Martinez, Godwin, Kemerer, & Perna, 1995). There is also some evidence that the private sector is acquiring a disproportionate number of academic high-fliers because of scholarship programs targeting this group and because of parental preferences. The perception of these differences among the sectors is fueling concerns that the public sector is being "residualized," that is, becoming a provider for those unable to find a place in a private school (Marginson, 1997).

Proponents of government policies supporting private schools counter this argument by pointing out the growth in the number of low-fee private schools that bring a private education within reach of most Australian families. Further, high-fee private schools offer scholarships and denominational schools may waive fees in the case of students from needy families. Private schools, it is therefore argued, cater for the full spectrum of Australian families.

To address this issue, the 1996 national census database was analyzed in terms of the income of households from which children attended public, Catholic, or independent schools. It should be noted that the 1996 census data show school choice patterns for the year in which the Howard government took office. In that year, the private-sector enrollment share was 29.3%. Figure 5.3 shows the relationship in 1996 between household income and the type of schooling received by children within each income category.

It is clear from Figure 5.3 that the higher the income of households, the more likely children from those households will attend private schools. Further, this is the case for Catholic as well as other private schools. The income distribution of households with children

Figure 5.3. School attendance at public, Catholic, and independent schools in 1996 according to household income.

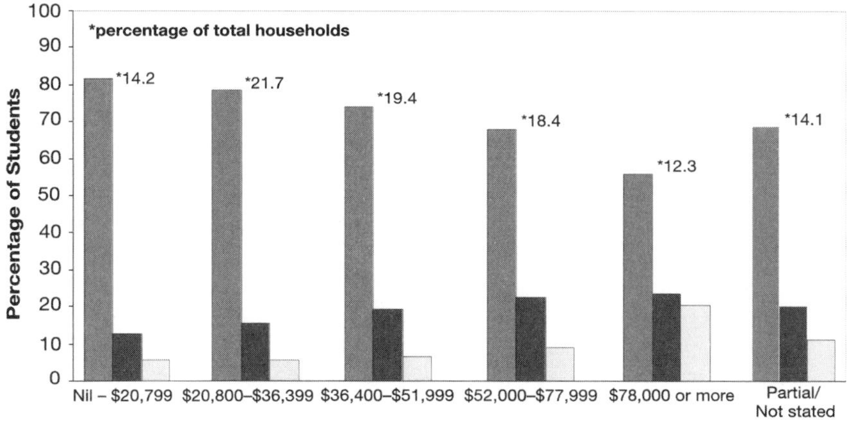

	Nil – $20,799	$20,800–$36,399	$36,400–$51,999	$52,000–$77,999	$78,000 or more	Partial/ Not stated
Public	81.8	78.64	73.97	68.13	56.15	68.76
Catholic	12.59	15.6	19.29	22.69	23.5	20.02
Independent	5.61	5.76	6.74	9.18	20.35	11.22

Household Income

- ■ Public
- ■ Catholic
- □ Independent

Source: Calculated by the author from data provided by the Australian Bureau of Statistics from the census of 1996.

attending Catholic schools corresponds more closely with that of other private schools than with the profile for the public school sector. In the context of the contemporary debate on school funding, this is an important observation because Catholic schools tend to be low-fee schools and their student intakes are likened to those of schools in the public sector.

In the highest income level ($78,000 or more), the non-Catholic-sector enrollment share nearly matches that of the Catholic sector. The school destinations of children from these households are not known. It seems reasonable to assume that many of the children from these households attend high-fee private schools—the so-called elite schools. In total, in the top income level there are nearly as many children attending private schools as public schools.

Evidence similar to that shown in Figure 5.3 has been cited to support each side of the debate on school funding. Advocates arguing for a continued growth of the private sector contend that the data show private schools to be enrolling many low-income children. In other words, private schools are not for the exclusive use of the wealthy and therefore should not be condemned as elitist. On the other hand, critics of current funding policies argue that wealthy parents are more likely to choose a private school than parents with lower incomes and that existing policies are therefore, in effect, subsidizing school fees for parents who can most afford them. Further, the policies are producing a public sector that is primarily for those with low incomes.

These data must be interpreted with some caution. First, 14% of households did not state their income. Second, income is not the same as wealth. It conceivable that some households reporting low income levels actually have considerable assets and the members were not therefore living in poverty. This may account for the somewhat anomalous result for households reporting an income of less than $21,000. Third, household income is not exactly the same as family income. A household is defined as a group of people who usually reside and eat together. Fourth, to simplify the graph, the small numbers of households reporting children in both public and private schools (4.6% of the total) were excluded.

Without comparing changes in enrollment share by income level over time, it is not possible to demonstrate that the public sector is being residualized. The public sector may always have enrolled a higher share of children from lower incomes than the private sector. Nor is it possible to demonstrate that government policies have caused the changes in profiles over the two decades. Had no new places been made available in the private sector, there may still have been a shift in the numbers of middle- and high-income parents finding places for their children in it. Whatever the cause, these data indicate that in 1996, Catholic and other private schools tended to draw more of their enrollments from households with higher income levels than was the case for public schools.

Student Academic Performance

The question of whether the extension of parental choice of schooling leads to higher overall student outcomes is not a question that has engaged federal or state governments, or even the wider Australian public. There are several reasons that this is the case. One reason is that the crisis that led to a restoration of state aid was constructed in terms of a shortage of resources rather than low test scores. Unlike the situation in the United States, choice policy is not being shaped by the flight of students from inner-city public schools. A second reason has to do with federal–state relations. The states have been unable to recognize an advantage in submitting to national testing that would enable comparisons between public and private sectors according to an assessment system controlled, directly or indirectly, by the federal government.

The states have also been wary about undertaking their own comparative examinations of the relative performance of the two sectors, since it is not clear what the consequences would be if one sector performed better than the other. Such an outcome would prompt some intervention that might resurrect the specter of sectarianism. Public school authorities have been lodged on the horns of a dilemma. If the public sector compared unfavorably, it might exacerbate current enrollment trends; on the other hand, it might take the publication of such data to mobilize political support for public schools.

Notwithstanding the disposition of state governments and their officials to downplay comparisons between the performance of students in the two sectors, what evidence exists?

Quantitative comparisons of student performance in the two sectors tend to show higher overall levels in the private sector. Gannicott (1998) reports an analysis of the results in the year-12 end-of-school assessment for students in New South Wales. The results for the 2 years reported, 1994 and 1996, show that students from independent private schools scored nearly 20 percentile points higher than students from Catholic schools and a further 5 points higher than students from public schools. The differences are too large, Gannicott thinks, to be explained by differences in intake. A more recent study by Kelley (1999) also showed non-Catholic private schools outperforming public schools after adjusting for difference in family background.

The validity of this kind of evidence turns on the question of whether researchers have been able to adjust for initial differences in the intakes of the two sectors. It is clear from the evidence presented earlier that there are differences in the socioeconomic backgrounds of the intakes and that the differences are widening. Hence, the better average performance of private school students should be expected, other factors being equal. Whether the statistical adjustments made by researchers can adequately take account of those differences is a matter of academic dispute. The issues are similar to those raised by the claims of Coleman, Hoffer, and Kilgore (1982) in their study of Catholic schools in the United States.

THE FUTURE OF PUBLIC EDUCATION

At the present time, public education is stuck. The Howard government will continue the flow of federal funding to private schools but provide it within a progressively more competitive framework. States will augment this funding while managing a decline in enrollments in their public sector and avoiding, as far as possible, the emergence of political contention about private school funding. Because the major political parties have shared a commitment to private schooling and in practice pursued similar policies when in government, an interruption of state aid or even a major redirection of policy seems improbable. None of the parties can see a political advantage in provoking a debate on this issue. As Hogan (1984) observes, the debates on state aid in the 1960s and 1970s were the most divisive public issue other than Australian participation in the Vietnam War. In these circumstances, school principals in the public sector hold very pessimistic views on the future of public education. The majority expect their sector to continue to lose enrollment share to the private sector. They also expect the divide between rich schools and poor schools to widen (Angus & Olney, 2001).

The ball is in the court of state governments. They are administratively responsible for schooling, public and private. Yet none can explain how public and private school systems can function in a market environment without the private sector succeeding at the expense of the public. In at least some respects, the current position of state public school systems is an accident of state policy. There are three different courses that proactive state governments might consider. These are:

- the restoration of comprehensive public schools
- the introduction of structural and regulatory changes
- the extension of deregulated market conditions

The Restoration of Public Comprehensive Schools

There is a generation of Australians for whom the neighborhood primary and secondary school continues to be an icon of social cohesion. These schools, they argue, have molded the Australian character. Some advocates of public education, therefore, still hope that market forces in education will be reversed or at least blunted, thereby enabling the rebuilding of a public system of comprehensive high schools. Public schooling of this kind is seen as an antidote to the maladies of the market economy.

Such advocates (Boston, 1997; Connors, 1999; Marginson, 1997) construct the debate about school choice in terms of social values: the community versus pluralism, inclusiveness versus exclusivity, altruism versus self-interest, secularism versus sectarianism. The argument parallels the debates on state aid during the 19th century; the issues are basically the same. One difference, however, is that Catholic schools no longer bear the brunt of criticism. The targets are the wealthier private schools and the smaller schools founded on fundamentalist religious or quasi-religious principles that together enroll fewer than 8% of students.[8]

A return to a system of fully comprehensive schooling seems unlikely for three reasons. First, insofar as state aid has been the instrument that has undermined the institution of the neighborhood public school, a cessation of such aid seems highly improbable. As the proportion of enrollments in the private sector has grown, so has its political leverage. Even if a state government wanted to cut private-sector funding, state and federal policies, and their lines of support, are so interwoven that a decisive change would be very difficult to accomplish. There are few signs that governments want to redirect funding from the private to the public sector.[9]

Second, a reason for the decline of comprehensive schooling is that the states could not afford it. Differentiation and specialization are the prevailing concepts, partly because they are cheaper.

Third, restoring comprehensive schooling is unlikely to address the issues that led parents to exercise their choice and withdraw their children from the public schools in the first place. More public funding for public schools may or may not cause them to be more attractive to the parents who are exiting the sector.

Structural and Regulatory Changes

A second option would be to reregulate the conditions under which public and private schools compete for students. Advocates of markets propound the need for a "level playing field." Current regulations structure the market in favor of some providers and disadvantage others. Blackburn (1996) points out that Australia is the only OECD country in which private schools are subsidized unconditionally, other than for financial accountability, from public funds. In all other countries, private schools may be funded from public revenues only by becoming part of the public system, sharing its obligations, and abiding by rules common across it.

To achieve this end, it would be necessary to form a new public system consisting of public schools and those private schools that are recipients of substantial public funding (Angus, 1997; Foggo, 1992). In other words, low-fee private schools, which serve a similar clientele, would be subject to a common regulatory framework. The remaining schools, those opting to remain independent, would constitute a much smaller proportion, comparable to that of private schools in the United States, Britain, and New Zealand. Governments could then adjust the level of funding of private schools that elected to stay out of the system, either freezing the level or phasing it out. New Zealand provided a precedent for such a reform when, in 1975, it passed legislation enabling private schools to integrate with the public system while retaining their "special character."

This option would be difficult to implement in the current political environment. First, the private sector has grown in size and influence in recent times, and there is now less reason for it to seek a settlement of this kind. The public sector is not such an attractive partner. Second, the high-fee schools have flexed their considerable political muscle when confronted with a cut in government support, and on each occasion government has backed down because of the solidarity of the private sector. Third, the idea of subjecting private schools to more regulation is antithetical to the notion of market and unappealing to private school principals. On the other hand, there is a growing awareness among those who work in the private school sector that their schools have become dependent on government funding and that, to varying extents, they are "state-maintained." They expect a quid pro quo.

The Extension of Deregulated Market Conditions

Critics of the Howard government's education policies see them as precursors to the introduction of more fully fledged market conditions. They point to the wider social and economic policies of the government, which reflect its commitment to the principle of "user pays" and the progressive withdrawal of the government as a provider of social services. Though the government may be ahead of public opinion in relation to these reforms, there is at least some support for them.[10] Changing attitudes to privatization of public utilities could lead governments to set even more conducive conditions for further growth of the private school sector.[11] During its consultation with private school interest groups, federal officials reported that there was strong support for an income-tested base grant for all students, even those attending public schools. Proponents of private schooling argued that many relatively wealthy families whose children attend government schools receive virtually full public subsidy for their school education (Department of Employment, Education, Training and Youth Affairs [DEETYA], 1997). In other words, those with sufficient means should pay for their children's education.

This has led critics to forecast a future in which public and private schools are merged into a single, fully market-oriented system. Families would be provided with basic tuition credits and would be able to use them to enroll their children in schools of their choice. Those who wanted to supplement the tuition credit from their own resources and enroll their child in a high-fee school could do so at their own expense. Such a scenario, however, would be very difficult to realize. Although the federal government wants competition among public and private schools, believing that competition would be good for the system, it has never proposed vouchers for schools. Though there has been some canvassing of the idea among academics,[12] in general the Australian public is wary of the concept. In 1999, the federal minister for education was forced to withdraw from a proposal to introduce a voucher system in the higher education sector after a cabinet briefing document was leaked to the press.[13] There would be even greater community opposition to the extension of vouchers to schools.

Like previous governments, the Howard government is aware of the potential divisiveness of the issue of state aid—an issue so far not linked with vouchers. The art of Australian government has been to extend support for private schools without turning state aid into an electoral issue. Though the notion of "market" is the coherent idea upon which the Howard government's education policy platform has been built, it is unclear how it will move its agenda forward. It cannot count on the support of state governments; they would be reluctant to leave the array of issues that arise from policies that support school choice to be solved by the "hidden hand" of the market.

CONCLUSION

Private schooling was "rescued" by state and federal intervention in the 1970s. The problem was defined as a deficiency of resources, a deficiency that reached crisis proportions. Huge amounts of federal and state funding led to all schools, public and private, exceeding the resource-level targets set at that time. As a consequence of that intervention, the stock of the private sector rose considerably, and its enrollments began to rise at a faster rate than enrollments in public schools. Official projections indicate an indefinite continuation of this trend. The most alarming aspect of the enrollment shift is the likelihood that those leaving the public system are the more "educable," so that the two sectors are progressively being polarized in terms of their student intakes. For various reasons, this development is not perceived as a problem by governments.

The market paradigm still has life in it, although it is unclear whether the paradigm will assume a new form. It may take another decade for the effects of further enrollment decline to trigger a political response. In any event, even were there a perceived crisis brought about by a series of events of the kind mentioned above, it begs the question of what kind of relationship Australians want between their public and private school systems and what restrictions they want to impose on school choice. So far there is only the vaguest notion of what might constitute an ideal system of public education a decade from now, one that takes into account the reality of a healthy private school sector.

NOTES

The author wishes to acknowledge the assistance of Harriet Olney, Bronte Parkin, and Helen House in the preparation of this chapter, which draws on work supported by the Australian Research Council.

1. As Smelser (1985) notes, in the United States the conflict over church versus state control of education was centered on how to keep religious bodies out of public education. By way of contrast, in Britain, the political authorities could not intervene in support of education without resorting to the religious bodies.

2. For example, the Schools Commission program, Choice and Diversity in Government Schooling, that ran from 1979 to 1984 received only lukewarm support from the states. The program deliberately skirted the issue of the growing private school sector and eschewed the application of market principles to education (Schools Commission, 1985).

3. Though a national commission advises the federal government on the needs of states, inevitably states want more than the federal government will concede. For a detailed account of the tax-sharing arrangements and how they have applied to education, see Jones (1982). The introduction during 2000 of a new federal consumption tax may alter these arrangements over the next few years.

4. In 1997, 111 applications to establish new schools were approved. Numbers tailed off in 1998 (36 applications approved) and 1999 (21 applications approved). Not all approvals lead to the establishment of schools. There is a large gap between intention and actuality. Also, there is a relatively high

mortality rate among small independent schools. The census data for that period, shown in Figure 5.3, shows that there were 29 new schools established in 1996–1997 and 12 the following year, far fewer than the number of approvals and the 51 new schools established in 1981–1982 during the peak of the Fraser term.

5. The system was simulated in a 1998 project involving 720 nonsystemic private schools and has been validated by comparing the results with other indicators of student socioeconomic status and disadvantage (DETYA, 1999b). The SES scores of schools will be scaled. Schools with SES scores of 130 or above will receive a base entitlement set at 13.7% of the average government schools recurrent costs. The maximum payment will be 70% of these costs—14% higher than the maximum rate available under the ERI scheme.

6. The Australian Council for Educational Research (ACER) conducts the Cooperative Scholarship Testing Program for private schools. The results from a survey of 90 schools using the tests indicate that the scholarship winners identified by the test later achieved a tertiary entrance score that placed them in the top 2% of year-12 students (ACER Assessment Services, 1999).

7. New South Wales retained 23 selective (competitive-entry) high schools. Victoria retained 2. Western Australia, on the other hand, converted its only prestigious selective-entry high school to a neighborhood comprehensive high school in 1959.

8. For example, two schools have been funded that are based on the "learning technologies" of Scientology founder L. Ron Hubbard (Yaman & Healy, 2000).

9. One exception is the decision in 1999 by the New South Wales Labor government not to pass on to private schools the normal increment in state per-capita grants arising from the indexation of the grants to the cost of living. This was a small amount, of more symbolic than practical importance.

10. In the current debate on choice and competition, it is often forgotten that the Labor governments under Hawke and Keating pursued a vigorous program of deregulation and privatization typically associated with governments of the right. During their terms, they implemented competition models for delivering public services (Eardley, 1997), though these models did not extend to school education.

11. There is some evidence that, over time, market-based economic reforms are followed by a shift of public opinion in their favor (Saunders, 1999). Australians appear to have become slightly less egalitarian between 1987 and 1993. The implication is that over time they will become more receptive to the further marketization of schooling than at present.

12. The possibility of vouchers for school education has arisen from time to time. In its 1979 discussion paper, the Schools Commission canvassed the desirability of introducing a system of transportable payments to individuals. Seven different models were considered, including vouchers confined to the private sector. The report noted that the scheme would be dependent on the support of "those who exercise the most immediate control over schools

at present—the professionals (teachers and officials)—who were prepared to countenance a shift in the locus of power" (p. 61). Though there was little debate at the time, the issue continues to surface, particularly in the university sector and in the public and professional media (e.g., Baldwin, 1997; Caldwell & Haywood, 1997; Gannicott, 1997).

    13. See Illing and McGreggor (1999).

REFERENCES

ACER Assessment Services. (1999). *Your views on the CSTP: Some initial findings from the study 'The Evaluation of the Cooperative Scholarship Testing Program'*. Melbourne: Australian Council for Educational Research.

Angus, M. (1997). The integration of the public and private schooling sectors in Australia. In B. Lingard & P. Porter (Eds.), *A national approach to schooling in Australia? Essays on the development of national policies in schools education* (pp. 140–161). Canberra: Australian College of Education.

Angus, M., & Olney, H. (1998). *Extending parental choice of schooling: Non-systemic government schools*. Canberra: Department of Employment, Education, Training and Youth Affairs.

Angus, M., & Olney, H. (2001). *Our future: Report of a survey of Australian government primary school principals*. Sunbury, Victoria: Australian Primary Principals Association.

Austin, A. G. (1972). *Australian education 1788–1990: Church, state and public education in colonial Australia* (3rd ed.). Melbourne: Pitman.

Australian Bureau of Statistics (1975–1981). *Schools, Australia*. Catalogue No. 4202.0. Canberra: Author.

Australian Bureau of Statistics (1981–1983). *National schools collection: Government schools, Australia*. Catalogue No. 4215.0. Canberra: Author.

Australian Bureau of Statistics (1981–1983). *Non-Government schools, Australia*. Catalogue No. 4216.0. Canberra: Author.

Australian Bureau of Statistics (1984–1988). *National schools statistics collection, Australia*. Catalogue No. 4221.0. Canberra: Author.

Australian Bureau of Statistics (1989–2001). *Schools, Australia*. Catalogue No. 4221.0. Canberra: Author.

Baldwin, P. (1997). The lighthouse: Towards a Labor vision of the learning society. <http://education/labor.net.au>.

Blackburn, J. (1996, July 16). A lesson in school funding. The Australian, p. 11.

Boston, K. (1997). *The future of government schooling*. Paper presented to the 1997 conference of the Australasian Association of Educational Administrators, Perth.

Browning, P. (1998). The birth, life and death of a Commonwealth educational funding policy. *Unicorn, 24*(3), 5–14.

Caldwell, B., & Haywood, D. (1997). *The future of schools: Lessons from the reform of public education*. London: Falmer.

Coleman, J. S., Hoffer, T., & Kilgore, S. (1982). *High school achievement: Public, Catholic, and private compared*. New York: Basic Books.

Connors, L. (1999). *Schools in Australia: A hard act to follow*. The Radford Lecture, annual conference of the Australian Association for Research in Education, Melbourne.

Department of Education, Training and Youth Affairs (DETYA). (1999a). *Schools funding: SES Simulation Project Report*. Canberra: Author.

Department of Education, Training and Youth Affairs (DETYA). (1999b). *SES Simulation Project: Validation report*. Canberra: Author.

Department of Employment, Education, Training and Youth Affairs (DEETYA). (1997). *Schools funding: Consultation report*. Canberra: Author.

Eardley, T. (1997). *New relations of welfare in the contracting state: The marketisation of services for the unemployed* (Social Policy Research Centre Discussion Paper No. 79). Sydney: University of New South Wales.

Education Queensland. (1999). *Report on the consultations: 2010 Queensland state education*. Brisbane: Author.

Foggo, D. (1992). *Education: An investment in the future*. Presidential Address to the Australian Teachers Union Annual Conference. Melbourne: Australian Teachers Union.

Gannicott, K. (1997). *Taking education seriously: A reform program for Australia's schools* (Policy Monograph No. 38). Sydney: Centre for Independent Studies.

Gannicott, K. (1998). *School autonomy and academic performance*. Canberra: Department of Employment, Education, Training and Youth Affairs.

Hogan, M. (19984). *Public versus private schools: Funding and directions in Australia*. Ringwood, Victoria: Penguin.

Illing, D., & McGreggor, R. (1999, October 16–17). The blackboard jungle. *The Weekend Australian*, p. 28.

Jones, P. (1982). The Commonwealth Grants Commission and education 1950–1970. In G. Harman & D. Smart (Eds.), *Federal intervention in Australian education* (pp. 53–66). Melbourne: Georgian House.

Karmel, P. H. (1973). *Schools in Australia: Report of the Interim Committee for the Australian Schools Commission*. Canberra: Australian Government Publishing Service.

Kelley, J. (1999). Non-Catholic private schools and educational success. *Australian Social Monitor, 2*(1), 1–4.

Luke, A. (1999). Frameworks project rationale: A modest proposal. <http://education.qld.gov.au/corporate/framework/rationale.htm>.

Madigan, J. (1989). *Historical outline of government funding of non-government schools in Australia: A paper written for the review of non-government education*. Perth: Ministry of Education.

Marginson, S. (1997). *Educating Australia: Government, economy and citizen since 1960*. Cambridge: Cambridge University Press.

Martinez, V., Godwin, R. K., Kemerer, F., & Perna, L. (1995). The consequences of school choice: Who leaves and who stays in the inner city? *Social Science Quarterly, 76*(3), 485–501.

McGregor, R. (1999, May 18). Philosophy stamped in maiden speech. *The Australian*, p. 5.

McKinnon, K. (1995). *Review of the New Schools Policy*. Canberra: Australian Government Publishing Service.

Praetz, H. (1980). *Building a school system: A sociological study*. Melbourne: Melbourne University Press.

Saunders, P. (1999). The perception of equality. *Social Policy Research Centre Newsletter*, No. 75, 1, 4–6.

Schools Commission. (1979). *Some aspects of school finance in Australia: A discussion paper*. Canberra: Author.

Schools Commission. (1984). *Funding policies for Australian schools*. Canberra: Author.

Schools Commission. (1985). *Choice and diversity in government schooling*. Canberra: Author.

Smelser, N. J. (1985). Evaluating the model of structural differentiation in relation to educational change in the nineteenth century. In J. Alexander (Ed.), *Neofunctionalism*. Beverly Hills, CA: Sage.

Yaman, E., & Healy, G. (2000, August 7). Funds for all. *The Australian*, p. 14.

CHAPTER 6

Education Reform and School Choice in South Africa

John Pampallis

Given South Africa's recent history, it is perhaps not surprising that the issue of school choice is inextricably bound up with overcoming the legacy of apartheid and racism. Expanding the choice of South African parents and students with regard to school attendance has been associated mainly with expanding the opportunities available to Black[1] students previously disadvantaged by apartheid. Despite the somewhat unique context provided by South Africa's political realities, though, many of the issues that have shaped school choice debates in other countries have also been important in South Africa.

Areas of discussion in South Africa that resonate with the school choice debates in other countries include parental control and community participation, school fees, marketization and competition between schools, class privilege, resource distribution, decentralization, liberty versus equality, and school admissions policies.

This chapter begins with a short outline of the legacy inherited by the democratically elected government when it took office in 1994. A brief history of desegregation in South African schools up to 1994 precedes an examination of some of the important policy changes from 1994 onward that have affected school choice in South Africa: the constitution, the new schools policy, and issues of school funding. The paper then examines changes in school attendance since 1994 and concludes with a reflection of some of the issues associated with school choice and South African school reform.

THE LEGACY OF APARTHEID

Prior to 1994, the education system in South Africa was extremely complex. There were 15 different education ministries:

- One for each of the 10 *bantustans,* or homelands, the areas officially designated for the various African ethnic groups
- One for each of the four officially recognized racial groups outside of the *bantustans* (African, White, Colored, and Indian)
- One responsible for the Department of National Education, whose task was to set national norms and standards

Despite the existence of central controls, the system was in fact a conglomeration of different subsystems. Each department had its own school models, its own funding formula for schools, its own relationship to individual schools and to parents, and its own arrangements for school governance. School attendance was strictly segregated on the basis of race. A school that belonged to a particular education ministry could admit only members of the ethnic group for whom that particular ministry was established.

The schools of the different racial groups were differentially resourced, with an enormous gap between the relatively abundant resources available to White schools and the meager resources provided for African schools. The level of resourcing for colored and Indian schools was somewhere in between that for White and African schools.[2] Although this gap in expenditure became somewhat narrower in the latter years of apartheid, the fact that Black schools became key sites in the struggle against apartheid resulted in a deterioration in the quality of Black education as school boycotts, strikes, and other forms of resistance took their toll on "normal" schooling processes. This increased the quality gap between the education offered at White and African schools. Under these circumstances, it is not surprising that many Black (especially African) parents and students resented their exclusion from the better schools and that the democratic movement, as part of the broader struggle against apartheid, demanded that schools should be open to all irrespective of race.

SCHOOL DESEGREGATION BEFORE 1994

In the decade and a half preceding the legalization of the Black liberation movements in 1990, a few chinks appeared in the armor of strict school segregation. Yielding to pressure from various opposition group-ings, including the churches, and in an environment of growing Black opposition to apartheid, the South African regime reluctantly allowed the admission of a small but increasing number of Black students to private primary and secondary schools (Pampallis, 1991). By 1988, pri-vate schools registered under the White Department of Education had 107,225 students, of whom 14,543 (13.6%) were Black (5,974 African, 5,620 Colored, and 2,949 Indian). In 1989, 197 out of 233 "White" private schools had admitted students who were not White, although the proportion of such students varied widely from school to school: At a few schools up to half of the students were Black, while at others a token number of Black students were admitted. Although this move-ment did allow a small number of Black students to escape the ravages of the inferior public education available for Blacks, one should keep in mind that less than 0.5% of students in South Africa attended pri-vate schools in the late 1980s (minister of national education, quoted in the *Cape Times*, August 3, 1988).

After the government lifted the ban on the liberation movements in 1990, pressures began to build up for the desegregation of White state schools, which formed approximately 7% of the total number of schools in South Africa (Department of Education, 1995a). In 1990, the minister responsible for White education, Piet Clasé, announced that White state schools would be allowed to change their status from the beginning of 1991 if a large majority of parents voted to do so.[3] Three new models were available:

- Voting for Model A would result in the privatization of the school. The school would then be able to admit Black students, like any other private school.
- Model B would remain a state school but could admit Black students up to a maximum of 50% of its total enrollment.
- A Model C school would receive a state subsidy but would have to raise the balance of its budget through fees and donations. Model C schools could admit Blacks up to 50% of enrollment.

From the beginning of 1992, a fourth option was added; Model D would be a school belonging to the White Department of Education and Culture but would be allowed to recruit an unlimited number of Black students. This option was introduced largely because of declin-ing enrollments of White students in some state schools.

In early 1992, most of the 1,983 White state schools retained their old status (and were thus referred to as "status quo" schools). A little over a third of the schools (692) voted to change to Model B, while only 1 opted for Model A, 51 for Model C, and 6 for Model D. The following year, however, the government announced that all the formerly White schools (except Model D) would become Model C schools unless parents voted by a two-thirds majority to remain status quo or become Model B schools, and that subsidies to all model schools would be cut. As a result, from April 1992, 96% of the former White state schools became Model C schools. (The restriction on the admission of Black students to 50% of the total enrollment remained in place until after the first democratic election in 1994.)

The parent body in each Model C school elected a governing body. Title to the fixed property and equipment of the school was given by the state to the school, to be administered by the governing body. The schools became juristic persons with the right to enter into contracts and to sue and be sued. They gained a high degree of autonomy, including the right to charge compulsory school fees and to determine the admissions policy.

The reasons for this change in the status of the White schools appear to have been twofold. First, the state was increasingly unable to provide the same level of financial support to White schools as previously; this was due both to the slow economic growth of the 1980s and early 1990s, and to the changing political climate, which obliged government to move to greater equality in spending on Black and White education. Thus, the National party government realized that White communities would have to contribute substantially if conditions in their schools were not to deteriorate (Karlsson, Pampallis, & Sithole, 1996). Second, the change to Model C was an attempt to ensure that White communities could continue to control their schools rather than allowing them to fall into the hands of a democratically elected government, which was seen as imminent.

In the schools for Coloreds and Indians, desegregation—that is, the admission of African students—started in 1985 (earlier than in White state schools) and, especially after 1990, was more rapid than in White schools. The opening up of these schools to African students took place outside the framework of the law and was the result of schools responding to pressures from African parents and communities and not, as with the White schools, from legislative changes (Carrim, 1992).

With the election of South Africa's first democratic government in 1994, all legal racial barriers were abolished, and all schools became—de jure—open to all students irrespective of race.

POLICY DEVELOPMENTS AFFECTING
SCHOOL CHOICE SINCE 1994

South Africa's interim constitution of 1993 and the "permanent" one of 1996 have fundamentally shaped the environment in which schools function. In stark contrast to the previous system, they establish a state based on the values of human dignity, nonracialism and nonsexism, the rule of law, and universal adult suffrage. Through the Bill of Rights contained in the 1996 constitution, all South Africans have the right to a basic education, including adult basic education, and the right to receive an education in any of the 11 official languages where it "is reasonably practicable."

The constitution splits control over schooling between the national and provincial levels of government. The national Department of Education is responsible for establishing national norms and standards, and nine provincial departments are responsible for administering the school system and establishing provincial policy within national parameters.

In the period immediately following the 1994 election, the main task facing the provincial departments of education was the creation of a single provincial system out of the former racially and ethnically based departments that had operated in their territories. Some provinces had to integrate bits and pieces of as many as nine of the old departments.

At the same time, new education policies were being elaborated through the first White Paper on Education and Training (Department of Education, 1995b). This document set out the framework for policy and elucidated the main principles on which it was to be based. These included, among other things, increased access to education for all, redress of past inequalities, equity in the deployment of state resources, public schools as partnerships between the state and communities, democratic governance at all levels of the education system, and financial sustainability.

Schools Policy

Basic to the reform of schooling in post-apartheid South Africa, is the South African Schools Act of 1996, which attempts to give shape to the principles of access, redress, equity, and democratic governance that were outlined in the 1995 White Paper. The act replaces the multiple school models of the various apartheid education departments with two legally recognized categories of schools—public schools and independent (private) schools. The act also makes schooling compulsory for all children between the ages of 7 and 15 and bans corporal punishment. Most importantly, it provides for the establishment at all public schools of governing bodies with considerable powers (see below). These governing bodies must be composed of the school principal and elected representatives of parents, teachers, nonteaching staff, and (in secondary schools) learners; governing bodies may also co-opt nonvoting members. Parent representatives must make up the majority of members. Governing bodies are juristic persons.

In order to deal with the heterogeneity of the school system, the act makes it possible for the governing bodies of different schools to have different powers and functions. A basic set of functions are stipulated for *all* school governing bodies. They are required to develop and adopt a constitution and mission statement for the school; to determine the admissions policy of the school, subject to certain restrictions (see below); to administer and control the school's property, buildings, and grounds, including the right to rent them out for fundraising purposes; to recommend to the Department of Education the appointment of teaching and nonteaching staff; and to develop a budget for the school, which could include school fees, for approval at a meeting of the parents.[4] Once approved, school fees become compulsory and all parents, unless specifically granted exemption, are obliged to pay them. Children may not be removed from a school if parents do not pay fees, nor can they be denied access to the school because their parents cannot afford to pay fees. However, the school may sue the parents for fees that are owed. A discussion of the reasons for allowing schools to charge compulsory fees and the government's attempts to compensate the poorer schools for the inequities of the past appears below.

Governing bodies may also apply to their provincial education department to be allocated additional functions consistent with the act and with provincial law. These could include (but are not restricted to) the right to maintain and improve the school's property, buildings, and grounds; to determine extracurricular activities; to choose the subject options offered at the school, within the parameters of provincial curriculum policy; and to purchase textbooks and other materials and equipment. To date, these powers have been given mainly to formerly White schools whose governing bodies usually include skilled professionals and managers; however, it is the aim of the government to eventually grant additional powers to all school governing bodies as they become willing and able to exercise them. In recognition of the fact that many school governing bodies may have difficulty fulfilling their basic functions or qualifying for additional functions, due to the lack of experience or skills, the act obliges provincial governments to provide training for governing bodies.

A 1997 amendment to the act allows all public schools to employ teachers in addition to those allocated and paid for by the provincial departments of education, as long as the funds for these additional teachers are raised by the school.

As mentioned above, the act allows the governing body of a public school to determine the admissions policy of its school. However, this right is subject to many restrictions:

- It is subject to national norms and standards or to any applicable provincial law (e.g., with regard to age of admission or to school feeder zones).
- A school must admit students "without unfairly discriminating in any way."
- Schools may not administer admission tests.
- No student may be refused because his or her parents are unable to pay or have not paid school fees, do not subscribe to the school's mission statement, or refuse to waive their right to claim for damages from the school.
- Parents of students who are not admitted to a school must be informed of the reasons in writing, and the parent or the student may appeal the decision to the member of the (provincial) executive council responsible for the education portfolio.

Although these restrictions give schools little formal control over admissions, in practice schools exercise actual control of the administration of admissions, and this does allow them to discriminate in many ways, both legal and illegal, overt and subtle. In addition, school fees act as a natural barrier to those who cannot afford them, although this has been ameliorated somewhat by the provisions for exemption contained in the new norms and standards for school funding discussed below.

In October 1999, the national minister of education issued a policy statement on public school admissions (Department of Education, 1999a). Among other things, this policy allows heads of provincial education departments to establish feeder zones for public schools "in order to control the learner numbers of schools and co-ordinate parental preferences." These zones need not necessarily be "geographically adjacent to the school or each other." Although students may seek admission to any school they choose, first preference must be given to those who live in the school's feeder zone and second preference to those whose parents work in the zone. How this policy will affect the distribution of students and school choice will depend, among other things, on whether provincial education departments do create feeder zones and, if they do, on the exact delineation of the feeder zones. No province had delineated feeder zones by the beginning of 2000.

School Funding and the Issue of Fees

The development of school funding policy has proved to be particularly difficult and controversial, and is clearly related to the issue of school choice.

The government's policy regarding the funding of public schools was only partially finalized with the adoption of the South African Schools Act in 1996. The issue of funding is probably the most difficult for the new government to come to terms with, largely because of the difficulty in reconciling the aims of equity and quality education with the constraint of insufficient state funding. The relatively small size of the more privileged sectors (mainly the previously White, Colored, and Indian schools) meant that merely equalizing expenditure would not result in any significant improvement in the schools that served the African majority. The options for government were to increase the size of the education budget or to find ways of utilizing nonstate funds for public education.

The first option was not tenable given the government's adoption of economic policies that emphasized the importance of reducing the deficit; government departments were under enormous pressure to cut spending. It was argued by the more privileged social groupings—especially those representing White constituencies—as well as by some within the broad democratic movement that school fees would bring private resources into the school system, thus freeing government to channel state resources to those schools in greatest need. The ruling African National Congress (ANC) and allied educational organizations thus reluctantly accepted the second option.

After a vigorous public debate, the Schools Act—largely on the basis of the recommendations of the international consultants, Colin Colclough and Luis Crouch—adopted a system that allowed governing bodies, with the consent of the majority of parents, to determine school fees that all parents would be compelled to pay (Department of Education, 1995c).

The rationale for this system was as follows. The government could not afford to fund the middle-class (mainly formerly White) schools at the same level as before. If the cut in funding at these schools caused the quality of schooling to fall—as it probably would if no other source of funding were available—then middle-class parents would begin to remove their children from the public school system and place them in independent (private) schools. In time this would deprive public schooling of its most influential advocates as businesspeople, professionals, politicians, senior public servants, and even teachers no longer depended on the public schools for the education of their own children and grandchildren. This would be to the detriment of the *whole* public school system, and the only way to avoid it would be to allow parents to supplement state funding for their own schools. Therefore, parents at all public schools should be allowed (but not compelled) to opt for a school fee and to determine its amount. Consequently, the South African Schools Act allowed for school fees to be charged as outlined above.

The South African Schools Act, while not providing in detail a system for school funding by the state, lays down the principle that the state is obliged to fund public schools on an equitable basis "in order to ensure the proper exercise of the rights of learners to education and the redress of past inequalities in education provision." This is an attempt to ensure some way of overcoming both the inequalities of the past and those inherent in the system of school fees by compelling educational administrators to develop mechanisms that move toward a more equitable funding system.

The result was the National Norms and Standards for School Funding (Department of Education, 1998), issued by the national Department of Education. This document is an attempt to establish funding procedures that promote equity and redress within the context of inadequate government funds and of increasing parental financial support for education. The Norms and Standards deal with public funding of public schools, exemption of parents who are unable to pay school fees, and public subsidies to independent schools.

The Norms and Standards place emphasis on giving the poorest public schools and those in bad physical condition a larger resource allocation than relatively advantaged schools.[5] Capital expenditure on new schools or additional classrooms and facilities must be based on a ranking of geographic areas from the neediest to the least needy, and backlogs must be eliminated by prioritizing the most needy areas.

In addition, provincial education departments are required to direct 60% of their nonpersonnel and noncapital recurrent expenditure to 40% of the poorest schools in their provinces. Provinces must compile a list of schools based on their socioeconomic levels of development and physical resources. This "resource targeting list" must then be used to divide schools into five categories based on needs. Table 6.1 shows the framework that acts as a guideline for the procedure.

The Norms and Standards recognizes that poorer parents who send their children to more advantaged schools may have difficulty in paying the fees agreed to by the majority of parents. It provides for this by exempting certain categories of parents from paying fees. Parents are exempt if their combined annual gross income is less than 10 times the annual fees per learner. If their combined annual gross income is less than 30 times but greater than 10 times the annual school fee per learner, the parents qualify for partial exemption. If their combined annual gross income exceeds 30 times the annual school fee per learner, the parents do not qualify for any exemption. However, the regulations do not provide a blanket exemption for all the poor—parents have to apply to the school governing body for a fee exemption. If parents fail to apply and do not pay the full school fee, the governing body can take legal action to recover the fees from parents.

While the Norms and Standards were originally meant to be implemented in 2000, problems related to both resources and management capacity have meant that they are only likely to be fully implemented by 2001 at the earliest.

Table 6.1. Resource targeting table based on condition of schools and poverty of communities.

School quintiles from poorest to least poor	Expenditure allocation (% of resources)	Cumulative percentage of schools	Cumulative percentage of nonpersonnel and noncapital recurrent expenditure	Per-learner expenditure indexed to average of 100
Poorest 20%	35	20	35	175
Next 20%	25	40	60	125
Next 20%	20	60	80	100
Next 20%	15	80	95	75
Least poor 20%	5	100	100	25

Source: Department of Education (1998), p. 28.

CHANGING PATTERNS OF ATTENDANCE SINCE 1994

Since the 1994 election, there has been an increasing movement of Black students into schools that had legally excluded them before 1990 (Vally & Dalamba, 1999). By 1997 (the latest figures available at the time of writing), approximately 28% of all South African schools were integrated (i.e., they had students from more that one racial group). Of the unintegrated schools, just over 5% had only White, only Colored, or only Indian students[6] (Department of Education, 1999b). The other 95% of unintegrated schools contained African students exclusively. About four-fifths of formerly White, Colored, and Indian schools were integrated in 1997, a proportion that has almost certainly increased since then. Nearly all integrated schools are in cities or towns, rather than in rural areas. Most of the schools that remain uniracial are schools catering to Africans in townships, informal settlements, and former homelands, largely because their paucity of resources makes them unappealing or because their location makes them inaccessible to other groups.

A representative sample of secondary schools surveyed by the South African Human Rights Commission in 1998 found that 27.2% of learners in formerly White schools were Black; of these Black learners, 15.8% were African and the rest were Colored and Indian (Vally & Dalamba, 1999). In Gauteng, the most urban of South Africa's nine provinces, the proportion of African students in White schools in 1998 was 23.8%, while a further 5.9% of students were Colored or Indian. African enrollments in Gauteng's former Indian schools have risen much faster than in White schools, so that by 1998, 52% of students enrolled in these schools were African. This could be due to the fact that the formerly Indian schools are closer to African townships than the formerly White schools, that they tend to charge lower school fees, and, possibly, that they are less resistant to admitting larger numbers of African students. The changing demography of the formerly Indian schools also suggests that Indian students are choosing to move more and more into the formerly White schools or into private schools. In the formerly Colored schools of Gauteng, 34.3% of students were African in 1998.[7]

Most of the integration results in students commuting daily from areas previously exclusively reserved for their own racial group to schools in areas that were reserved for more privileged groups. In addition to this, integration has resulted from the movement of members of the growing Black middle class into the suburbs and from the admission into formerly White schools of children of domestic workers who live on their employers' premises.

The movement of children from Black townships on the periphery of cities to the formerly White, Colored, and Indian schools in relatively more affluent areas is largely the result of the belief of Black parents and their children that those schools offer a better quality of education (Hoadley, 1998; Naidoo, 1996; Tikly & Mabogoane, 1997; Zozi, 2000). In general, it is a fact that those schools achieve better learning outcomes, have a better infrastructure and better learning and teaching resources, have better-qualified teachers and school managers, and have an ethos that is more conducive to learning than that of most township schools. The motivation of township parents to send their children to schools outside their township is bolstered by the appalling state of disorganization in many township schools (especially secondary schools). A significant number of these schools are characterized by tardiness; poor discipline; absenteeism of both students and teachers; poor teaching and learning; poor management; and the prevalence of drugs, gangsterism, and violence.

This helps to explain why children and their parents put up with the considerable difficulties involved in attending schools in distant suburbs: high transport costs, long traveling times, early waking times (in order to get to school punctually), higher schools fees, higher school uniform costs, and other expenses associated with schools in more affluent areas (e.g., stationery, school trips, sports clothing and equipment, etc). It should be noted that while students who commute from townships tend to come from the new (and rapidly growing) Black middle class, a sizable number come from working-class families who often make enormous sacrifices to cover the costs. One report cites the example of a single parent who spent R9910 (59% of his annual earnings) to send his two children to school. Since only R1400 (a little over 14%) of the total amount was for school fees, the partial fee exemption that he received did not make a significant difference (Vally & Dalamba, 1999; see also Hoadley, 1998).

In addition to the problems associated with cost, many of these "migrant" children—particularly those who started their school careers in township primary schools—have difficulty coping with the academic demands and feel a sense of alienation in schools with cultures quite different from those they are accustomed to.

The response of formerly White schools to desegregation has been very mixed. Some schools have welcomed Black pupils, attempting to help them when they need assistance in integrating into their new environments; others have admitted them under duress and made life difficult for them. The South African Human Rights Commission report states that most of the teachers and students in integrated schools do appear to be supportive of Black learners, but also reports many instances of racial discrimination and even abuse at some schools (Vally & Dalamba, 1999). In a few instances, particularly in schools in smaller country towns, blatant and pernicious—and illegal—racial discrimination has been practiced. Examples include Black students being segregated into separate classes, having separate break (recess) times, or even suffering violence from other students while the school authorities ignore the problem (Tolo, 1998; Vally & Dalamba, 1999).

Even among schools that have displayed a more positive attitude toward Black students, most have adopted an assimilationist model, attempting to draw new Black students into the preexisting culture and ethos of the school (Carrim, 1998; Naidoo, 1996; Vally & Dalamba, 1999; Zafar, 1999). This tendency is exacerbated by the fact that there are still very few African teachers in the formerly White, Colored, or Indian schools.

The impact of the migration of students is felt not only in the schools to which they go but also in the schools that they leave behind in the townships. This impact, however, is complex and differs from area to area. For example, in Soweto, South Africa's largest township, many schools have seen dropping enrollments—some by as much as half between 1994 and 1999—as students have left to attend formerly White, Indian, and Colored schools outside the township. This has resulted in some of these schools—previously overcrowded, with high student–teacher ratios—losing teachers in the rationalization and redeployment process that took place in 1999.[8]

Because most of the students who leave the townships to attend school elsewhere come from families who can afford the costs of sending their children to schools in more affluent areas, the schools from which they move are deprived of precisely those parents whose resources could help to boost the schools' resources. Also, since the parents who send their children away are likely to be the more educated parents in township communities or the most motivated to intervene in their children's education, school governing bodies lose some of their best potential members.

Although no studies have been carried out on the matter, declining enrollments are likely to have a negative impact on the morale of teachers, students, and parents who remain in the township schools.

The widespread perception that many teachers also send their own children to school outside of the townships can only depress morale even further.

Schools have not been experiencing decreasing enrollments in all townships, however. In townships such as Alexandra, northeast of Johannesburg, and Vosloorus, on the East Rand, school district officials report that there is pressure on schools to enroll more students than they were designed for despite an exodus by some of their students to the formerly White suburbs. In Alexandra, this appears to be because of the growth in recent years of nearby informal settlements and possibly also because most of the nearby alternatives to township schools are formerly White schools with relatively high fees. In the case of Vosloorus, the presence of new informal settlements, as well as an apparent preference among parents and students in nearby townships for Vosloorus schools, has resulted in the movement of students from those areas to Vosloorus. The reason given for this by the district director of education is the greater levels of violence in neighboring townships a few years ago.[9]

There is as yet little evidence that schools experiencing declining enrollments are improving the quality of education that they offer. While this issue still needs to be studied comprehensively, anecdotal evidence from education officials suggests that quality improvements, if any, are minimal.[10] The apparent lack of improvement could be because their managers and governing bodies are weak and overwhelmed by the deep crises that they face. School principals have mainly been promoted from the ranks of teachers, with no management training, and a significant number of them do not cope well when faced with the challenge of turning around dysfunctional schools. The training programs for school governing bodies that provincial departments of education are obliged to provide have not taken place everywhere, and where they have taken place they have not always been effective.

Despite the general lack of evidence of competitive pressures leading to school improvement, at one Soweto secondary school, the deputy principal reported that the schools gates were now being closed at the beginning of the schoolday to ensure that all students and teachers arrive at school on time and that teachers always prepare their lesson plans before they go to class.[11] This is apparently part of a concerted effort to improve the general functioning of the school. One motivation for these changes is apparently the loss of students over the past few years.[12] Secondary schools with poor pass rates on the matriculation exam have also recently been coming under pressure from politicians and the media to improve their performance. In

1999, for the first time, the matriculation examination results of all schools were published in the country's highest-circulation newspaper—and this may also have contributed to this school's decision to try to improve its effectiveness. It will be interesting to see whether this becomes a trend in other schools experiencing declining enrollments and whether the competition starts to have an impact on more than just the basics of creating a semblance of order in chaotic schools. The evidence so far, however, is too insubstantial for any trends to be discerned.

Intratownship Migration

Even in townships such as Soweto that have been losing students through migration, not all schools are equally affected. Those schools with a good academic reputation (especially those with good matriculation pass rates) have not experienced declining enrollments; indeed, they have experienced a lively demand for admissions, enrolling students from beyond their feeder area.

In a case study of two poorly resourced schools in Khayelitsha, near Cape Town, Ursula Hoadley (1998) shows that working-class parents and children generally seek out schools that they consider to be academically better than others. The "better" school of the two schools studied by Hoadley (it had an 86% matriculation pass rate as opposed the 27% rate of the other school) made efforts to recruit the academically more successful students from the nearby primary schools. Many pupils at the academically poorer school were there because they could not gain admittance to other schools—that is, they had no other choice.

In KwaZulu-Natal province, a handful of "territorial schools" (now called "comprehensive schools") were established by the former KwaZulu homeland. These were elite state schools which were better resourced (both materially and in terms of teaching staff) than others. In the township of Umlazi, south of Durban, for example, the two territorial schools attracted students from all over the township, and they continue to do so. One of them is a boarding school that enrolls students from all over the province.

As mentioned above, where there are informal settlements within or near formal townships, there is often movement of children from the informal settlements into the township schools. Many of the informal settlements are relatively new and do not have any schools or have insufficient school places. The same phenomenon occurs—although its extent is unclear—with poor African students from inner-city areas, who commute to schools in townships because of the shortage of inexpensive public schools nearby.[13]

Private Schooling

South Africa has had private schools since the early days of European colonization, catering to both White colonists and indigenous people. From the 1950s onward, mission schools and others that had catered to Africans had to be registered with the government and follow the notorious Bantu Education syllabi. As a result, most of the mission schools were closed by the churches in protest. Until 1990, private schools catered mainly to the White, English-speaking community and served a range of socioeconomic groups within this community.[14]

In the last years of apartheid and in the post-apartheid era, a new type of private school has developed, located largely in the city centers and catering mainly to African students. While some of these schools are seen as a better alternative to the township schools, many are even more poorly resourced than most township schools, are often staffed by unqualified teachers, and are characterized by instability. They are often referred to disparagingly as "fly-by-nights" because so many have closed down suddenly, abandoning students who have already paid their fees. Many of these schools have not been registered with the education departments as required by law, and the state has so far been unable to enforce the law fully. It is, however, likely to be only a matter of time until this is done. Research needs to be conducted on the motivations of those who attend these schools in order to gain an understanding of why they continue to attract students.

In some informal settlements, where the establishment of public schools has not kept up with the growth of the local population, private schools of variable quality have been established. This has also occurred in some formal townships where parents are dissatisfied with the quality of education offered in public schools (*Financial Mail*, February 14, 2000).

The South African constitution [Section 29(3)] allows every person the right to establish an independent educational institution that does not discriminate on grounds of race, is registered with the state, and maintains standards that are not inferior to standards in comparable public educational institutions.

Independent schools may be subsidised by the provincial departments of education provided that they are registered and meet certain provisions. Independent schools whose fees are higher than 2½ times the provincial average cost per learner in public schools will not receive subsidies. Subsidies to private schools may range from zero to 60% of the provincial average cost per public school learner, depending on the fees the private schools charge (Department of Education, 1998). In order to qualify for a subsidy, an independent school must meet certain criteria, which include being registered with the provincial education department, having been operational for one full school-year, not being operated for profit, meeting certain management standards, not being established in direct competition with a nearby uncrowded public school of equivalent quality, and meeting certain academic criteria with regard to pass rates among its students (Department of Education, 1998).

The number of independent schools grew from 518 in 1994 to 1,557 in 1999. While this is very rapid rate of growth by any standards, independent schools still account for only about 2% of students in South African schools (*Financial Mail*, January 14, 2000). While private schooling is likely to continue to grow, the fact that middle-class parents can still send their children to quality public schools, subsidized by fee income, is likely to limit that growth.

The most rapid growth of independent school enrollment has come from the African communities. In 1988, less than 6% of private school students were African (Pampallis, 1991). While current figures for the whole country are not available since not all provinces keep these statistics, in Gauteng province Africans accounted for 47.15% of independent school students in 1996 and 69.02% in 1998. Whites made up 31.68% of independent school students in 1996 and only 11.79% in 1998; 10.78% of independent school students in 1998 were Indian.[15]

Casual observation indicates that the more expensive independent schools—both new and old—that cater mainly for Whites, as well as the newer Islamic schools, have fairly small proportions of African students. This suggests that the growth of independent schooling is likely to have been greater among Africans from South Africa's poorer communities who either do not have access to public schools or are dissatisfied with them. The future growth of private-sector schooling among these communities is likely to depend on the development of the public school sector. Should the public schools in African areas not improve the quality of education that they offer and should the state not manage to provide public schools in all areas, the independent school sector will certainly continue to grow. However, if the state does manage to improve the quality and quantity of public schooling, there is likely to be a flow of students from the independent schools back to the public schools. At this stage, it remains a matter of speculation whether the competition from the independent schools will add to the state's determination to ensure that the public sector does satisfy the needs of the overwhelming majority of the population.

CONCLUSION

The school reforms of the last decade have certainly made an impact on the degree of school choice and the education opportunities available to many parents and students in South Africa. This has been achieved largely through the dismantling of the racist legislative barriers of the apartheid era, which has been part of the much larger process of post-apartheid transformation. The post-1994 period has seen a significant flow of African students to the schools formerly reserved for Whites, Coloreds, and Indians. Within the African townships, there is also evidence of growing demand for admission to those schools perceived to be academically superior. The increase in the degree of school choice can also be seen in the growth in the number of independent schools, most of which enjoy some level of government subsidy.

However, the reform of schooling, while creating new opportunities—especially for members of the growing Black middle class—has also created a system that favors affluent communities. Because of severe spending constraints and pressing demands on its resources, the government has sought to maximize the means available for development by introducing user fees for schooling—that is, school governing bodies are allowed (and encouraged) to charge school fees and raise other forms of private funding. This has resulted in a tension between, on the one hand, the government's aims of increasing social equity and the steps that it has taken to this end, and, on the other hand, the inevitable effects of markets that "reproduce the inequalities which consumers bring to them, and . . . actively confirm and reinforce the pre-existing social order of wealth and privilege" (Carr & Hartnett, 1996, p. 166). While the fees raised in the more affluent communities have no doubt allowed a greater proportion of state resources to be allocated to the poorer schools, this has not been sufficient to make a significant difference in the resources available to individual schools. While the inequalities may be somewhat ameliorated by the imminent implementation of the Norms and Standards for School Funding, this is unlikely to make a substantial dent in the inequalities until the state—as a result of economic growth—has significantly more funds available to spend on schooling.

It must be kept in mind that the vast majority of South African children are Black and poor; they live in rural or peri-urban areas or in townships, and they have little chance of exercising a right to school choice. The schools they attend cater exclusively to African learners, and although there are exceptions, they are by and large poorly resourced, have larger classes, and are staffed by less-well-educated teachers than the schools that are now in the process of becoming racially integrated. It is the development of these schools that is the major challenge facing the education system. The solution for these children lies not in the opportunity to attend the historically more privileged schools; this would be impossible if only because of the sheer numbers involved. The solution for them lies instead in improving the quality of the schools in the areas where they live.

Whether the increased school choice inherent in the new system can play a significant role in improving the quality of schooling by stimulating competition between schools is still to be established. While there is evidence that some of the poorer schools are being stimulated by declining enrollments to improve their functioning, it remains to be seen whether such competition becomes a real driver of quality improvement in schooling. It must be our hope that a synergy will develop between increased state support—through both the Norms and Standards for School Funding and other quality-improvement interventions—and increased competition fostered by school choice, and that this synergy will contribute to an improvement in the quality of education in the schools of the poorest communities.

NOTES

The author wishes to acknowledge the research assistance of Vuyokazi Zozi of the Centre for Education Policy Development, Evaluation and Management.

1. The term *Black* is used in this chapter to designate the three racial groups oppressed under apartheid: "Africans," "Coloreds," and "Indians." (A "Colored" person in South Africa is an individual who has mixed Black and White ancestry.) This is not universal usage in South Africa, but it corresponds to the usage of the liberation movements that attempted to build a broad unity of those opposed to apartheid and racism.

2. In 1965, per-capita expenditure on education for Africans was R12.70, for Coloreds R71, for Indians R91.50, and for Whites R357. In 1988, the respective figures were R582.93, R1325.64, R1980.41, and R3982.82. (The R represents Rand, the South African currency.)

3. For the status of a school to change, 80% of parents had to vote in an election, with 72% of them voting in favor of a change.

4. All school governing bodies are expected to supplement state funds in order to improve the education that they offer, either through school fees or other forms of fundraising.

5. The Norms and Standards also provide policy for the subsidization of independent schools (see subsection on private schooling, below).

6. Note that these figures do not, of course, tell us anything about the extent of integration within the schools.

7. Calculated on the basis of data supplied to the Centre for Education Policy Development, Evaluation and Management (CEPD) by the Gauteng Department of Education in February 2000.

8. During an interview with the author in October 1999, an official from Lenasia, an Indian township near Soweto, reported that, in an ironic twist, some of the Lenasia schools, which had become overcrowded because of the migration of students from Soweto, had recently received new teachers, redeployed from Soweto schools. They now found themselves teaching some of the very same students whom they had previously been teaching in Soweto, both teachers and students commuting daily to school in Lenasia.

9. Interviews with the district director of education for Gauteng Education Department District C6 (Mr. B. Howarth) on November 11, 1999, and district education coordinator of education for Gauteng Education Department District C5 (Mr. L. Davids) on November 29, 1999. Both interviews conducted by Vuyokazi Zozi and John Pampallis.

10. Ibid.

11. Interview with Mr. A. Kubayi, deputy principal of Orlando High School, conducted by Vuyokazi Zozi of the Centre for Education Policy Development, Evaluation and Management (CEPD), February 3, 2000.

12. The locking of school gates for security reasons is reportedly becoming more and more common in townships, where external thugs and drug dealers often cause disturbances.

13. These inner-city areas, characterized by high-rise apartments, were formerly reserved for Whites, who were generally relatively affluent. However, since the late 1980s major demographic changes have resulted in denser, low-income, mainly Black populations. Although there are some (mainly formerly White) schools in these areas, they are insufficient to accommodate all the children living there.

14. The Afrikaans-speaking White elite generally attended elite state schools, which played a role in producing leaders in the Afrikaner community analogous to that played by the English private schools.

15. Calculated on the basis of data supplied to the Centre for Education Policy Development, Evaluation and Management (CEPD) by the Gauteng Department of Education in February 2000.

REFERENCES

Carr, W., & Hartnett, A. (1996). *Education and the struggle for democracy: The politics of educational ideas.* Buckingham, UK: Open University Press.

Carrim, N. (1992). *Desegregation in Coloured and Indian schooling.* Johannesburg: Education Policy Unit, University of the Witwatersrand.

Carrim, N. (1998). Anti-racism and the "New" South African educational order. *Cambridge Journal of Education, 28*(3), 301–320.

Department of Education. (1995a). *Report of the Committee to Review the Organisation, Governance and Funding of Schools.* Pretoria: Author.

Department of Education. (1995b). The White Paper on Education and Training in a Democratic South Africa: First Steps to Develop a New System. *Government Gazette, 357*(16312).

Department of Education. (1995c). The Organisation, Governance and Funding of Schools: A Draft Policy Document for Discussion. (Draft White Paper 2). *Government Gazette, 365*(16839).

Department of Education. (1998). National Norms and Standards for School Funding. *Government Gazette, 400*(19347).

Department of Education. (1999a). Admission Policy for Ordinary Public Schools. *Government Gazette, 400*(19377).

Department of Education. (1999b). *Education statistics in 1997.* Pretoria: Author.

Hoadley, U.K. (1998, October/November). *For better or worse: School choice in a South African working class context.* Paper presented at Kenton-South African Council of Educators Conference, Kei River Mouth, South Africa.

Karlsson, J., Pampallis, J., & Sithole, S. (1996). *Restructuring educational governance at sub-national levels in South Africa.* Durban: Education Policy Unit, University of Natal.

Naidoo, J. (1996). *Racial integration of public schools in South Africa: A study of practices, attitudes and trends.* Durban: Education Policy Unit, University of Natal.

Pampallis, J. (1991). Private schooling: Problems of elitism and democracy in education. In E. Unterhalter, H. Wolpe, & T. Botha (Eds.), *Education in a future South Africa* (pp. 171–185). Oxford, UK: Heinemann.

Republic of South Africa. South African Schools Act. No 84 of 1996.

Tikly, L., & Mabogoane, T. (1997). Marketising as a strategy for desegregation and redress: The case of historically White schools in South Africa. *International Review of Education, 43,* 159–178.

Tolo, Z. P. (1998). *Report on the situation at Vryburg High School* (prepared for the National Ministry of Education, Pretoria).

Vally, S., & Dalamba, Y. (1999). *Racism, 'racial integration' and desegregation in South African public secondary schools.* [A report on a study by the South African Human Rights Commission (SAHRC)]. Johannesburg: SAHRC.

Zafar, S. (1999). *Desegregation in South African public schools: Emerging patterns and dominant trends.* Unpublished manuscript. Available from CEPD Resource Centre, Johannesburg.

Zozi, V. (2000). *A research study on the migration of learners.* (draft report). Available from the Centre for Education Policy Development Resource Centre, Johannesburg.

CHAPTER 7

School Choice in the People's Republic of China

Mun C. Tsang

This chapter addresses recent developments in parental choice in basic education[1] in the People's Republic of China (China). It has two major objectives. First, it attempts to explain the origin and inherent tension in school choice by relating the recent development to historical changes and the larger societal contexts in post-1949 China. Second, based on studies in both Chinese and English sources, it identifies emerging changes in basic education related to increased school choice. Particular attention is given to the unique characteristics of interventions in school choice in China, the development of different types of nongovernment schools as alternatives to government education, the effort to introduce innovation in school governance and school curriculum, and increased parental and community voice in schooling.

The chapter is organized in five sections. The first section is an introduction to the subject; it explains what school choice means in China today. The second section explains why school choice has become an issue in urban China since the early 1990s. It highlights socioeconomic development in Chinese society since 1978 and conflicting policies within the party-controlled state in post-1949 China. The discussion of the development of school choice and its impact is divided into two sections: (1) a general overview of development in the country and (2) case studies in two major urban centers in China—Tianjin and Beijing. The last section is a summary; it also explores future development in school choice in China.

NATURE OF THE SCHOOL CHOICE PHENOMENON

The effort to accommodate parental choice in schooling is a rather recent phenomenon in education in China. In urban areas, schools are divided into districts or zones, and the government's general policy on school assignment is that students go to the government school in their district of residence. In a few cases, parents can petition to have their child go to school in the district where they work. Parental choice of school is a departure from this general policy, and it can take one of the following forms:

1. Allowing students to go to a government school in another district. The destination school is allowed to charge a relatively high school fee for such students.
2. Allowing students with a lower examination score to enroll in a government school, which requires a certain threshold score for admission. The student has to pay an admissions fee to the school.
3. Allowing students to enroll in a "people-run" school (known as *minban* school), which usually charges a much higher school fee than government schools.
4. Allowing students to enroll in a traditional private school, which usually charges the highest school fee.

Government schools refer to schools sponsored by government agencies, funded by the state, and managed by government agencies at various levels.[2] Traditional private schools and people-run schools are nongovernment schools. Traditional private schools are schools sponsored and managed by a private individual or group and funded by student tuition and other private sources. People-run schools are schools sponsored and managed by a community of people or a collective organization and funded by resources from the community or collective organization and from a variety of sources (student tuition, financial assistance from the state, etc.). There are nongovernment and nonprivate schools that lie somewhere between government schools and traditional private schools. There is a range of people-run schools, some of which are more like government schools while others are more like traditional private schools.

There are several reasons that parents choose to pay a high school fee to send their children to another school. First, parents want their children to study in a higher-quality school[3] so that they have a better chance of eventually going to college. The destination government school is usually a "key" government school, a "demonstration" government school, or an "experimental" government school that has a high rate of educational transition. Key schools are located throughout the country, are designated by the government as elite government schools, and admit the top-achieving students. Demonstration and experimental schools are special government schools located in selected areas for certain educational purposes and are often affiliated with a university. Such schools often have a high-quality teaching staff, an effective principal, better facilities, and more government investment. Some parents send their children to people-run and traditional private schools so that they do not get stuck in a low-quality neighborhood government school. Second, access to schooling is still an issue in many parts of China. By paying a school fee, parents can buy a place for children who do not have the required examination scores. Third, some parents send their children to the traditional private schools because of a variety of taste-related or personal reasons. Some traditional private schools attract students by offering specialty programs (such as in the English language, computer studies, and music or the arts). Some are boarding schools that appeal to parents with a busy work schedule, especially when both parents work and are often away from home. So far, the school choice phenomenon is confined primarily to urban areas, where families have much higher incomes and can afford the high school fees.[4]

School choice has become a major issue in urban China and has attracted the attention of various stakeholders in education. Educational quality has become a focus of government educational policy, and the large quality gap among government schools is an underlying contributing factor of parental demand for choice. In a society that is becoming relatively more open, government educational decision makers have begun to pay some attention to parents' demand for school choice. Principals of government schools are interested in raising additional revenue from choice students and are at the same time concerned about competition from nongovernment schools. Teachers in government schools derive more income from choice students; they can also seek employment in nongovernment schools. Increased school choice is a controversial issue that reflects divergent views on the purposes of schooling.

UNDERSTANDING SCHOOL CHOICE:
ORIGIN AND NATIONAL CONTEXTS

Historically and culturally, Chinese society places a high value on education. Being educated is a source of esteemed social status. There is a Chinese saying: "Everything else is inferior; only education is of superior status." In imperial China, individuals spent years studying for the government's civil examination so as to become a government official. Parents are willing to incur significant sacrifice in order to improve educational opportunities for their children.

Throughout their long history, Chinese people have acquired learning through both officially run schools and traditional private schools (Qu, 1993; Sun, 1992). More than 2,000 years ago, prominent educators such as Confucius and Lao Tzu established private schools for the common people, which broke the monopoly of officially run schools. Private schools and officially run schools have coexisted for 2000 years.

In the early 1900s and during the era of the Republic of China (1911–1949), private education received two new sources of sponsorship. First, some private schools were founded by Chinese educators who had received their education overseas; prominently among them were Tao Xingzhi and Yan Yangchuen (Deng, 1997). These educators were motivated by a strong desire to spread learning among the masses; much of their effort was directed at the *rural* population. Second, in the wake of Western imperialism, missionaries came to China to spread the gospel and establish schools. Some of the more reputable educational institutions in China today were originally established at that time (Fairbank, 1987). Some well-known overseas educators, such as John Dewey, also came to China to promote Western philosophy and educational ideas. Again, parental choice in schooling was not restricted to government educational institutions only. The education system during the era of the Republic of China tended to be fragmented and highly differentiated, with limited access that favored students from privileged backgrounds. Families from well-to-do backgrounds undoubtedly had more schooling options for their children.

Education has experienced a radical transformation since 1949, with the founding of the People's Republic of China. Traditional private education institutions at all levels were promptly converted to government institutions by the new government. Between 1949 and the early 1990s, traditional private education vanished in the Chinese education system. The dismantling of private education was consistent with the heavy emphasis on the role of the state in a socialist country; it was also motivated by the government's attempt to rid the country of Western influences and to remove educational differences due to school type, which were thought to be related to the socioeconomic background of parents. The egalitarian ideal was strong, both in society and in school. School choice was not made available to parents. Between 1949 and the early 1980s, the collective or nationalist ideology was dominant, and individual goals were submerged in favor of social ones. During the post-1949 period, expanding educational access was consistently a focus of educational policy. Over time, the government managed to essentially achieve universal primary education; by 1985 the major educational goal was universal compulsory education by around 2000 (*Documents on the Reform*, 1985). Access to higher levels of schooling was purportedly based on merit, particularly on performance on examinations. However, government spending on education was persistently low, in terms of both national-effort and fiscal-effort indicators.[5] This low spending level imposed a serious constraint on educational development in China and contributed partly to the school choice problem in the 1990s.

While only government schools were found in urban areas during much of the post-1949 period, many of the *primary* schools in villages in the rural areas were not government schools in the traditional sense. They were people-run (*minban*) schools that received government assistance. These schools were sponsored and managed by the community of people in the village and were financed primarily from resources of the village community. The teachers were known as *minban* teachers; they were hired and financially supported by the village community, not the government. The majority of rural primary teachers were *minban* teachers. Initially, many of the schools were constructed from contributions, in kind and in cash, from the village community. The term *people-run* has a mass or community connotation to it and has a distinctively different meaning from private individuals or groups. People-run primary schools in rural China were an invention of the Chinese Communist party (CCP) to promote basic literacy among the rural masses, based on the approach of "people's education to be run by the people" (Lai, 1994). Since the early 1980s, the Chinese government has taken a more active role in the support of rural people-run schools. Initially, the government provided a monthly stipend to *minban* teachers in order to improve their living conditions; it subsequently implemented a plan to convert *minban* teachers into *gongban* teachers (teachers hired by the government) over a number of years (World Bank, 1991). Also, both the village community and the government shared in the major repair of schools and in the construction of new schools. Thus, people-run primary schools are moving toward becoming government schools in rural China. Secondary schools in rural China are generally government schools; they used to have a small percentage of *minban* teachers who were later converted into *gongban* teachers. In much of the post-1949 period in rural China, parents were eager to have a school in their community for their children; having a choice of school was a luxury.

In recent years, the government's willingness to allow more parental school choice through the development of people-run schools and traditional private schools in urban areas has represented a clear break with past educational policy and ideology. The government encouraged the establishment of nongovernment schools in its *Outline of Chinese Education Reform and Development* in 1993 (State Council, 1993). Article 16 of this *Outline* states that "the State adopts a policy of active encouragement, vigorous support, correct guidelines, and enhanced management toward the lawful establishment of schools by social groups and individual citizens" (p. 3). Obviously, having schools run by social groups and individuals is not a new idea. Traditional private schools existed before the founding of the People's Republic and people-run schools were common in rural China. What was new in 1993 was the decision to break the monopoly of government schools in urban areas. The government's decision reflected the fundamental changes in Chinese society and in the policy of the CCP since 1978.

Observers of post-1949 China point out that the CCP, which controls the Chinese state, is not monolithic; instead, it has two competing factions, labeled as the radicals and the moderates, which differ fundamentally in their policies for national development and for education (Montaperto & Henderson, 1979; Townsend, 1980; Tsang, 1991). Briefly, the radicals argue that socialist national development is to be achieved through continuing class struggle and revolution to transform the social relations of production, with the objective of maintaining the uncontested dictatorship of the state by the proletariat class. The process of socialist national development is characterized by the active grassroots participation of the masses in all aspects of social life and by constant consciousness raising of the masses in communist ideals through political campaigns and educational means. Politics and ideology are at the core of social life. Schools are an important instrument in political and ideological education. The education system should promote social equality and ideological "redness," not reproduce socioeconomic inequality and encourage individualistic goals. The ideological content of the curriculum needs to be tightly controlled, and teachers should have the appropriate political credentials. The radicals oppose stratification in schools and the national university entrance examination. They had complete control of the state (and the education system within it) during the period of the Cultural Revolution (1966–1976).

The moderates, on the other hand, believe that the first key step in socialist national development is the transformation of the forces of production, with the ultimate goal of achieving material (and moral) improvement of people's lives. The process is mostly economic and technical, and much less political and ideological. The development and application of science and technology, as well as the employment of a skilled labor force, are important strategies in economic transformation. The education system has an important role to play in developing and nurturing the "expertise" required in economic production. The moderates favor the establishment of key schools and universities for high-achieving students, the use of competitive examinations for educational selection, and the use of general and vocational schools for socioeconomic streaming. They have been in power in China since 1978.[6]

Deng Xiaoping was the supreme leader of the CCP and the Chinese state from 1978 until his death in 1997. He and his followers reversed the national and educational policies of the radical faction. Through successful implementation of the twin policies of reform and opening up to the outside world, the Chinese economy grew rapidly and the average living standard of the Chinese people has improved substantially (Dernberger, 1999). In 1992, Deng toured southern China and reaffirmed the twin policies and the market-oriented economic experimentation in the special economic zone of Shenzhen. His tour subsequently unleashed additional momentum for reform in the economy and in other sectors. His remarks also provided the foundation for a national policy of increasing the role of nongovernment initiatives in different sectors. The 1993 *Outline of Chinese Education Reform and Development* presented the official policy for encouraging nongovernment education in China. The central government first announced a temporary regulation in 1987 permitting the establishment of schools by "social forces." But the 1993 *Outline* was the definitive government policy for encouraging nongovernment educational institutions as part of the education system.

A number of changes in Chinese society since 1978 have contributed to the parental demand for school choice and the development of nongovernment schools in the 1990s to accommodate such parental choice. First, the twin policies of reform and opening up have contributed not only to rapid growth of the national economy but also to a relatively more tolerant political environment in which citizens can begin to speak their mind. Chinese citizens are now less likely to blindly believe in their political leaders. Corruption and conflicts within the CCP over the years have weakened the legitimacy of party leadership. Many political leaders and citizens alike recognize the important but daunting task of moving Chinese governance from "rule of people" to "rule of law." And government officials, including those in educational bureaucracies, are relatively more willing to hear what the common people have to say. For example, both the National People's Congress (NPC) and the National People's Consultative Congress (NPCC) use survey and study teams to sample public opinion and parents' desires. Parents can voice their preference for school choice through the education subcommittees of the NPC and NPCC.

Second, with economic progress and improved material resources, families want more and better education for their children. Chinese families have a high savings rate, and they are willing to increase their consumption of education and restrict their spending on other goods and services. The high cultural value that families place on education is an important source of social support for education. A significant number of families in urban areas can *afford* the high costs of people-run and traditional private schooling. Parental interest in education is also intensified by the government's one-child policy in urban areas. The only child in urban families is often treated like a prince or princess by parents and grandparents.

Third, reform policies since 1978 have also contributed to substantial and even widening economic disparities across areas and regions of the country (Li & Zhao, 1999; World Bank, 1998) and to disparities within education (Jiang, Zhang, & Wang, 2000; Tsang 1994). There are large differences in quality (and in transition rates) between key schools and regular schools. Quality differences between schools are more pronounced at the secondary level than at the primary level. Parents not only want their child to get into a school; they also want their child to get into a key school. Educational competition begins early in life, in preschool and in early primary grades. Parents with children stuck in a low-quality school are eager to seek a way out. The high cultural value placed on education and the large gap in quality among schools constitute the driving force for school choice.

Fourth, the reform in educational financing since the mid-1980s has been a contributing factor to educational disparities and to the urge to seek alternative resources for the education sector. The reform was based on two financing strategies: financial decentralization, whereby financing responsibility is delegated to local governments, and resource diversification, whereby both government and nongovernment resources are mobilized for education (Tsang, 1996).[7] However, with little fiscal equalization through intergovernmental education grants, the reform leads to the expected result of substantial financial inequality among areas and regions in the country. Not only is the distribution of educational resources uneven; the total amount of national spending on education has been consistently low. School principals in China have the important task of raising additional revenue, for example, to augment the meager income of teachers and to improve the physical conditions of their school. Charging school fees is an attractive way to raise school income. People-run schools and traditional private schools can charge high fees and are subject to less regulation than government schools.

Fifth, economic reform in China since 1978 has led to a diminished role of the state in economic production and to an increased reliance on market forces. Some policy makers see breaking the monopolistic role of the state in education as an extension of what is happening in the economic sector. People-run schools in urban areas are an extension of people-run schools in rural areas, and traditional private schools have a long history in Chinese education. There has been an increasing interaction between China and the outside world since 1978. One may legitimately speculate that external exposure has some impact on educational thinking in China, including the interest in school choice.

Taken together, these several changes combined to spark the development of nongovernment schools in urban areas to accommodate parental demand for school choice in the early 1990s, despite a negative attitude toward individualistic goals and traditional private schools in the four decades after the founding of the People's Republic of China.[8] The rapid development of nongovernment schools in the urban areas since 1993 has its unique features, and increasing parental choice in school has been a subject of intense debate among key stakeholders of education in China. To get a better understanding of these features and tensions, one must recognize the Chinese contexts and the focus of educational policies in the 1990s.

China is a huge country with immense diversities and disparities in terms of its peoples, geographic areas, cultural practices, religious beliefs, and socioeconomic development. Educational development is likely to be different in different parts of the country. A uniform educational policy is often not applicable across the country; local adaptation and modification are necessary.

Politics and decision making regarding major policies have so far been largely confined to the state and party hierarchies (Pye, 1999), even though there is now some initial experimentation to allow local election of government officials by the people and to allow nonthreatening nonstate social and political groups (Burns, 1999). People's input to policy has to go through government-controlled people's congresses at various levels. Despite the loss of some popular legitimacy, the CCP has so far demonstrated its ability to adapt to changes and maintain its grip on power (Schoenhals, 1999). These features of Chinese politics have several implications for educational policy. The state and party hierarchies still maintain unchallenged power in setting education policy. Conflicts and power struggle within the state and party hierarchies often lead to abrupt changes and even reversals in educational policies. Popular pressure for educational change has some possibility of being accommodated as long as it is not a threat to political stability and the party's power.

By the early 1990s, universal 9-year compulsory education was accomplished in most of the urban areas in China. The focus of educational policy in urban China shifted toward the expansion of upper-secondary education and the improvement of "all-around" educational quality at various levels. "All-around" quality encompasses academic, moral, and physical development. A student has to achieve both expertise and redness (Li, 1997). The low quality of some government schools, especially at the lower-secondary level, is of particular concern both to educational policy makers and to parents. Educational policy makers and parents both seek expanded opportunities for access to upper-secondary education. There is thus motivation to link efforts to improve quality and expand access to efforts to expand school choice.

There have been two persistent tensions in the goals of educational development in post-1949 China. The first is the tension between education for promoting social equality and education for economic efficiency; and the second is between education for inculcating socialist ideals and education for developing talents ("redness" vs. "expertise"). With its support for key educational institutions, the use of the national examination for educational selection, and the emphasis on science, technology, and productive skills, the current government's policy tends to favor education for economic efficiency and for developing talents. However, there is still a strong national ideology supporting social equality and the achievement of social goals through education.[9]

Problems in educational financing, particularly low educational spending and substantial disparity in financial health among schools and localities, remain a key issue in Chinese education today. Educational policy makers see school choice as an opportunity to mobilize additional resources for education and to use part of the additional resources for assisting low-quality government schools.

OVERVIEW OF DEVELOPMENT OF NONGOVERNMENT
SCHOOLS AND AVAILABILITY OF SCHOOL CHOICE

Nongovernment schools in urban China were basically nonexistent in the four decades after the founding of the People's Republic of China. The 1993 *Outline* has really sparked the rapid growth of such schools in the past few years. In 1994, there were an estimated 500 registered nongovernment schools in urban areas (Wu, 1994), and the number rose to about 4,000 by the end of 1997, according to the Ministry of Education.[10] However, the pace of development of nongovernment schools varies across different urban areas in the country.

Table 7.1 presents the number of nongovernment schools (consisting of both people-run schools and traditional private schools[11]) and students by level in the four centrally administered metropolitan areas in China. It shows that there was substantial variation in nongovernment enrollment by area and by education level. At both the primary and secondary levels, Tianjin was the highest among the four urban areas in terms of the proportion of nongovernment enrollment. In fact, since the national policy to encourage nongovernmental education was promulgated in 1993, the pace of development of nongovernment schools in Tianjin has been quite remarkable; alternatives to government schools are definitely present and in fact are available to about 10% of families with children in secondary schools. Although the proportion of nongovernment students is quite small in Beijing, Shanghai, and Chongqing, the absolute number of nongovernment students is not small. In these three areas, school choice is still available to families with sufficient financial means.

For all four areas, the proportion of nongovernment enrollment at the secondary level was clearly higher than that at the primary level. This is consistent with the common observation that the quality gap among schools is relatively smaller at the primary level than at the secondary level. In addition, the proportion of nongovernment schools seems to be related to the intensity of the parental pressure for school choice. Information from Tianjin (Chen, Ye, Zeng, & Wang, 1998) indicates that lower-secondary education, which has the most intense demand for parental choice, also has the highest proportion of nongovernment enrollment; for example, in 1997, the proportion was at 2.2% for primary education, 12.9% for lower-secondary education, and about 8.0% for upper-secondary education.

Not only do different urban areas vary in the pace of the development of choice schools, they also differ in the mix of choice schools available (Chen et al., 1998; Hu, 1997; Kwong, 1997; Lin, 2000; Qu,

Table 7.1. Government and nongovernment schools in metropolitan areas, 1997.

Area/School level	Government Schools		Nongovernment Schools		% enrollment non-government
	Number of schools	Enrollment	Number of schools	Enrollment	
Beijing					
Elementary	2,696	977,323	4	3,129	0.32
General secondary	735	626,208	41	16,410	2.55
Vocational secondary	174	108,308	9	1,425	1.30
Shanghai					
Elementary	1,533	1,024,402	20	14,409	1.39
General secondary	825	744,337	78	24,338	3.17
Vocational secondary	75	102,852	2	1,078	1.04
Chongqing					
Elementary	16,261	2,854,307	125	19,694	0.69
General secondary	1,606	1,002,915	47	8,544	0.84
Vocational secondary	206	79,507	36	7,702	8.83
Tianjin					
Elementary	860,800		19,000		2.16
Secondary (general & vocational)	540,100		63,700		11.79

Note: Beijing, Shanghai, Chongqing, and Tianjin are the four metropolitan areas in China reporting directly to the central government; they are at the level of a province in China's administrative structure.

Sources: Computed from information from Ministry of Education and Chen et al. (1998).

1993). In Tianjin, the majority of nongovernment students are found in people-run schools, not in traditional private schools. But in some of the southern cities, such as Guangzhou and Shenzhen, the traditional private schools thrive and have grown rapidly in number. There is actually a range of people-run schools; some of them are more like government schools and others more than traditional private schools. But a popular type of nongovernment school consists of those people-run schools that are affiliated with key government schools (more details are presented in the case study of Tianjin later in this chapter). These affiliated schools are attractive because they draw upon the established reputation, management, teaching, and facility resources of the parent government key schools. Parents' reactions to traditional private schools have been mixed. In some urban areas (especially economically very advanced areas), traditional private schools are able to charge very high fees (e.g., a one-time admissions fee of 30,000 yuan or more plus annual tuition fee at 15,000 yuan and more), so that they can pay high salaries to attract good teachers and to provide attractive facilities. Traditional private schools in other urban areas that do not have such income from school fees have more difficulty in recruiting good teachers and providing attractive facilities; in fact, some of these schools were forced to close because of financial difficulty. Even though China is in a transition from public ownership to more nongovernment ownership of the means of production, some members of society are still wary of the pursuit of private profit by some traditional private schools.

School choice has hastened the change in school governance in China. Even before the onset of the push for school choice in the early 1990s, China had started to experiment with a "principals' responsibility scheme" in school governance (China Education Yearbook Editorial Board, 1990). According to this scheme, principals of government schools have more say in the use of the school budget. For example, a principal could choose to use a smaller teaching staff so as to raise the average teacher salary or could hire "contract" teachers instead of regular teachers to enhance flexibility in the employment of school staff. The scheme was intended to increase decision-making power at the school level so that available resources would be more efficiently utilized. However, such discretionary power in government schools is quite limited. The school curriculum is still set by government educational bureaucracies and driven by competitive examinations; and it is difficult to fire underperforming regular teachers. The school principal is held accountable to the education bureaucracy. Nevertheless, this is an important change because, in Chinese education, effective leadership of the principal is considered a key element of an effective school.

Principals of nongovernment schools have more power than their government counterparts. They can make decisions regarding the admission of students, the hiring of teachers, and the choosing of teaching materials without getting prior approval from the concerned education bureaucracy. In particular, they can more easily dismiss school personnel and can pay school personnel according to performance. In fact, nongovernment schools often rely on higher salaries to compete with key government schools for good teachers (Qu, 1993). However, additional decision-making power is accompanied by increasing responsibility for generating revenue for the school. In fact, revenue generation is an important task for principals of government and nongovernment schools alike. And principals often find it stressful to handle both academic and revenue-generation responsibilities.

In addition, nongovernment schools have more flexibility in their operation, including course offerings. Because they do not have to obtain permission from the concerned education bureaucracy, these schools can make changes to their courses so as to respond to parental preferences and changing market conditions. Furthermore, principals of nongovernment schools generally report to a school board, not to government education officials. The school board often consists of members from different backgrounds in the local community. It is thus not surprising to find that many government school principals want similar power so that they can compete on more equal ground with nongovernment schools (see the case of Beijing later in this chapter). Thus, indirectly through the development of nongovernment schools, parents and other members of society can exercise some degree of influence on government schools and the government education bureaucracy. It is hard to quantify such influences, but a new channel for "voice" in basic education is present.

While further research on the impact of school choice on the school curriculum is desirable, no published studies have indicated that school choice has so far had any significant impact on innovation in school curriculum or pedagogy. This situation is not difficult to understand. Schools in China, both government and nongovernment ones, are driven by the same competitive examination system. To most parents, a good school is one that has high student academic achievement and high transition rates with respect to the next schooling level. Secondary school principals, for example, are careful not to depart too much from the prescribed curriculum of selected subjects in the national examination for admissions to postsecondary education. So far, Chinese educators have encountered a stiff challenge in promoting an "all-around" education within the confine of an examination-oriented system. Of course, both educational tradition and limited resources have limited the adoption of more student-centered pedagogy (instead of a teacher-centered pedagogy) in the classroom. Innovations in instruction must be in line with reform in educational assessment. As pointed out previously, some of the most popular nongovernment schools are those people-run schools that are affiliated with key government schools and with government demonstration schools. These schools want to duplicate the instructional model of their parent schools; educational innovation is not the major marketing point for them.

This is not to say that there is no attempt to alter the curriculum and experiment with alternative pedagogy. For example, some traditional private schools offer *additional* courses or classes that are not available in government schools.[12] A small number of traditional private schools use educational models (such as the Montessori model in the United States) from overseas and have students from both expatriate and domestic backgrounds. These features are attractive to some parents, but they are not pervasive. Actually, in recent years, Chinese educational leaders (and teachers, too) have begun to recognize the need to promote critical thinking and problem-solving skills so that graduates of the education system can more effectively participate in an increasingly global and competitive economy. There is experimentation in government schools to alter classroom instruction from an overwhelmingly teacher-centered approach to one in which learning perspectives are incorporated. But such a shift in educational thinking is probably due more to the educational leaders' understanding of the Chinese situation and their exposure to external ideas, and less to the impact of increased school choice.

Although increased school choice gathered some momentum in the 1990s, it has not been smooth sailing and the development of nongovernment schools has been a subject of intense debate. Many parents and educators are seriously concerned about increased educational inequity arising from income-based school choice; they still favor educational selection through a merit-based examination system. While not espousing absolute social equality, many members of Chinese society see school choice as contributing to increased stratification and inequality in education within the larger context of an increasingly unequal society.[13] There is still a clash between education for social equality and education for economic efficiency. School choice may add to the focus on transition rates as the primary yardstick for measuring school success and may make it more difficult for schools to achieve all-around quality. While traditional private schools are thriving in some urban areas, there is still a negative societal attitude toward them because of the concern for private profit and the history of these schools. Some people see the conversion of some government schools into people-run schools in some urban areas as a form of corruption in that public assets may eventually be passed into the hands of individuals.[14] In a society that is not yet democratic, the development of nongovernment schools is an opportunity both for popular input to educational policy and for reduced public accountability.

So far, the government is still supporting increased school choice and the development of nongovernment schools (Zhang & Li, 2000). In particular, it sees increased school choice through nongovernment education as a way of mobilizing additional private resources for educational development. In China, parents do not get a voucher from the government to go to a nongovernment school; rather, they pay a high school fee to enroll their children in such schools. Nongovernment schools are often required to transfer part of their tuition revenue to the concerned government bureaucracy that uses such money to assist low-quality government schools.

Information from the Ministry of Education shows that nongovernment schooling continued to expand rapidly in urban China between 1998 and 2000 (Chinese Education Society, 2001; Wang, 2000). For example, at the primary level, there were 727,645 students in 2,504 nongovernment schools in 1998, and 1.308 million students in 4,341 nongovernment schools in 2000. In general secondary education, there were 768,605 students in 2,146 schools in 1998, and 1.495 million students in 3,316 schools in 2000. Nevertheless, nongovernment urban schools still constitute a small part of all schools dispensing basic education. For example, in 1998, nongovernment schooling accounted for 0.52% of all students and 0.41% of all schools at the primary level, and 1.2% of all students and 2.8% of all schools in general secondary education.

SCHOOL CHOICE IN TIANJIN AND BEIJING

Tianjin is one of the four metropolitan areas in China directly administered by the central government.[15] In 1997, it had a total population of 9.5 million, and its urban residents had an average per-capita disposable income of 6,608 yuan, which was 28% above the national average (at 5,160 yuan). It is one of the special economic zones established along coastal China to experiment with market-oriented economic reform. Economically and educationally, it is among the most advanced areas in the country (State Statistical Bureau, 1998).[16] As an important industrial center in north-central China and in close proximity to Bohai Bay, it had frequent interaction with the outside world in the postimperial era and its residents have a relatively more open mind and are probably more receptive to change.

Tianjin is a leader among urban areas in its expansion of school choice and the development of nongovernment schools. The government in Tianjin has devised and implemented a four-pronged policy to accommodate parental demand for school choice and to regulate the development of nongovernment schools. First, the government strictly limits the number of choice students in government schools. In fact, government schools are forbidden to have choice students in compulsory education (primary and lower-secondary levels). The government assumes the responsibility of providing access to compulsory education in government schools for all children. At the upper-secondary level, the government sets the rules for admission of choice students in government schools. For example, it specifies which government schools can admit choice students, the number of choice students, the test score for admissions, and the amount of the school fee for choice students.

Second, the government accommodates school choice through its encouragement of the establishment of different types of nongovernment schools. The important point here is that the government made an early decision to *allow* school choice instead of actively fighting parental demand for school choice. With governmental encouragement, nongovernment enrollment reached 12.9% in lower-secondary education and about 8.0% in upper-secondary education by 1997. With the peak of the student population moving into upper-secondary education, the focus of school choice is shifting from lower-secondary education to upper-secondary education. And the government expects that nongovernment enrollment will reach about 10% at that level in the next few years.

Third, there is a strong government effort to regularize nongovernment schools to ensure adequate quality and proper operation. Through its issuing of more than 10 regulation documents, the Tianjin government specifies the rules and procedure for nongovernment schools in such areas as school management, finance and accounting, basic educational standards, and student management. Since many people-run schools are initially affiliated with a government school, the government requires that such schools achieve independence in four areas: school buildings, financial management, instructional management, and legal identity as an educational institution.

Fourth, the government requires all nongovernment schools to have a tuition fee of less than 10,000 yuan per academic year. The purpose of this requirement is to make nongovernment schools accessible to more families. These schools are also required to collect school fees on an annual or semester basis; they cannot have a one-time collection at the beginning of the schoolyear unless they receive special permission from the government to address an unusual situation. In addition, nongovernment schools are required to give 10% to 15% of their tuition revenue to the district education bureaucracy to be used to improve and reform low-quality government schools in the same district.

According to the government of Tianjin, school choice in the 1990s took place within a larger context of the reform of the structure of basic education in the city. The development of nongovernment schools has been promoted to achieve several educational objectives: achieving the streaming of peak student population into schools at the lower-secondary level, moderating parental pressure for school choice, developing supplemental resources for basic education, and increasing school autonomy and more flexible use of educational resources.

Nongovernment schools in Tianjin are mostly of the people-run type. Many of them have gone through a process of incubation and development in association with a government school. A popular model is given in Table 7.2. A people-run school starts as people-run classes or as a people-run minischool *within* a well-regarded government school (usually a key/demonstration/experimental government school). After getting permission to establish people-run classes or a people-run school, the government school can recruit choice students and charge a tuition fee.[17] Choice students receive instruction in the parent government school from teachers from the same school. Initially the "two" schools have the same legal identity, the same financial and accounting books, and the same campus. Over time, the "inside" school will "move out" of the parent school and become an affiliated school. The principal of this affiliated people-run school is usually a retired principal from another government school, but administratively this principal is often subject to the influence of the principal in the parent school. The affiliated people-run school is required by the education bureaucracy to achieve independence from the parent school in the four areas of school building, financial management, instructional management, and legal identity. Some teachers from the parent school work as contract teachers in the affiliated school, and students from the affiliated school often continue to use the facilities of the parent school. In return, the affiliated school often pays up to about 30% of its tuition income to the parent school. In addition, the affiliated school is required to pay 10% to 15% of its tuition income to the education bureaucracy of the district in which it is located; this money is designated for assistance to low-quality government schools in the same district.

The key selling point of this type of people-run school is its connection to the well-regarded parent school. Choice parents hope that their children will receive a quality education because of the close association of the two schools. In fact, the affiliated people-run school often does not want to be too separate from the parent government school.[18] Additional income is the primary incentive for the parent government school. Both schools want to maintain their relationship. One way to do this is for the two schools to form a school group, governed by the same school board, with a different principal responsible for the educational affairs of each school. Thus, initially this type of school is a "government-run people-assisted" school. Later, it is transformed into a "people-run government assisted" school. Parents

Table 7.2. Different types of schools in China.

Financing	Provision of schooling		
	Government	People-run	Private
Government	Traditional government school*	People-run government-assisted school People-run school affiliated with government school People-run school owned by government (converted school)	
People (community)	Government-run people-assisted school	Stand-alone people-run school Rural people-run school	
Private (individual/ group)	Government-run privately assisted school		Traditional private schools

Note: * In China, traditional government schools (government run and government financed) often receive financial support from community groups and from individuals.

in Tianjin tend to favor this type of school over the traditional private schools. In addition to the negative societal view, traditional private schools have to deal with the problems of constructing or finding a school building, hiring competent teachers, and paying competitive salaries and social insurance. In fact, because of the financial difficulty faced by traditional private schools,[19] the Tianjin government does not require these schools to pay part of the tuition income to the government. There are other variations in nongovernment schools, too. For example, the district education bureaucracy may convert a highly dysfunctional government school into a people-run school and choose a retired principal to be the new principal of the new stand-alone people-run school.

Beijing is the capital of China and has been the cultural and political center of the country for many centuries. In 1997, it had a total population of 12.4 million, and its urban residents had an average per-capita disposable income of 7,813 yuan, which was 51% above the national average (State Statistical Bureau, 1998). Like Tianjin, Beijing is one of the most advanced areas in the country in economic and educational terms, and its residents are exposed to new ideas through interaction with the outside world and with other parts of the country. But compared to Tianjin, Beijing is much closer to the center of political power and has been at the very center of political upheavals in post-1949 China.

Compared to Tianjin, the development of nongovernment schools has been much slower. In 1997, for example, at the primary level, only 4 of the 2,700 schools were nongovernment schools and the proportion of choice students was negligible. While relatively more nongovernment schools were found at the secondary level, nongovernment enrollment accounted for only 2.6% in secondary general schools and 1.3% in secondary vocational schools. Nevertheless, the total number of registered nongovernment schools did increase two and a half times from 21 in 1994 to 54 in 1997 (Lai, 1994, Table 1). According to the Beijing Municipal Education Commission, the quality gap among government schools is not large at the primary level; differences in facilities and teaching staff are relatively larger at the lower-secondary level. The government's basic policy is not to allow choice in government schools at the compulsory level (China Education Yearbook Editorial Board, 1998). In fact, the two areas differ sharply in the extent of nongovernment education at the lower-secondary level.

A variety of nongovernment schools exist in Beijing. For example, there are stand-alone people-run schools that were converted from dysfunctional government schools. In these "government-owned people-run" schools, the school assets belong to the government but the school enjoys the added autonomy of a people-run school.[20] The students from poor backgrounds originally in the government school are transferred to other government schools. The new people-run school is then allowed to charge high tuition fees. In addition, there are government schools that run people-run schools (similar to those shown in Table 7.2), people-run schools sponsored and managed by companies, traditional private schools, and nongovernment schools run by other members of "social forces."[21] Interestingly, nongovernment schools in Beijing do not hesitate to use the word *sili* (private) in the school name. For example, among the 21 registered nongovernment schools in 1994, 11 had the word *sili* in their name, two had *people-run* in their name, and the rest did not use *sili* or *people-run* (Lai, 1994).

Educators in Beijing point out that the best schools in Beijing now are still government schools. Most nongovernment schools are around the middle of all schools in terms of quality. The highest-achieving students are assigned to the top government schools, and choice students (though generally from relatively well-to-do families) are not necessarily the most talented ones. However, despite the relatively small size of the nongovernment sector, principals from government schools, including those from the reputable ones, are concerned about competition with nongovernment schools. These government school principals feel that they do not compete with their nongovernment counterparts on a level playing field. They point out that nongovernment schools can charge high tuition fees and have more decision-making power. They are particularly concerned about the loss of competent teachers to nongovernment schools. They would not fear competition with nongovernment schools if there were a level playing field. With their advantages, some nongovernment schools may become the top schools in the future.

A recent study of 35 people-run government-assisted schools and 50 traditional government schools (mostly in general secondary education) demonstrates the significant differences in financial conditions of these types of schools in Beijing (Wen & Liu, 2001). In this study, people-run government-assisted schools consist of the following types of nongovernment schools: schools affiliated with existing key government schools, people-run schools converted from dysfunctional government schools, schools formerly run by enterprises, new pilot schools in small residential districts, and people-run schools converted from traditional private schools. In 1999, the Beijing municipal government set the annual school fee at 320 yuan in lower-secondary traditional government schools, 640 yuan in upper-secondary traditional government schools, 5,000 yuan in lower-secondary people-run government-assisted schools, and 6,000 yuan in upper-secondary people-run government-assisted schools (note that, in contrast, people-run schools not receiving any government assistance could charge between 8,000 and 15,000 yuan in school fees at the secondary level). The study found that people-run government-assisted schools had much higher per-student expenditures than their counterparts. For example, in 1999, people-run government-assisted schools had a recurrent expenditure of 4,129 yuan per student and a capital expenditure of 2,371 yuan per student; the corresponding figures were 2,797 yuan per student and 460 yuan per student for traditional government schools. The average annual salary of regular teachers in people-run government-assisted schools was 35% higher than that in traditional government schools. The two types of schools also differ sharply in their revenue sources. In 1999, people-run government-assisted schools received 59.9% of their revenue from school fees, 11.5% from government allocations, and 28.6% from other sources. Traditional government schools received 15.5% of their revenue from school fees, 64.8% from government allocations, and 19.7% from other sources.

There are some strong similarities in school choice policies between Tianjin and Beijing. For example, people-run schools in both areas are required to transfer a portion of their tuition income to the district educational bureaucracy, which is used for assisting low-quality government schools (15% in Beijing, and 10% to 15% in Tianjin). Both areas have very strict limits on school choice in government schools in compulsory education; school choice is largely effected through nongovernment schools. This is consistent with the national policy that compulsory education should be made accessible to all and should be primarily government education. Nongovernment schools have more autonomy and decision-making powers than their government counterparts.

There are several possible explanations for the different rates of development of nongovernment education in Tianjin and Beijing. First, being in the national capital, educational decision makers in the municipal government of Beijing are more cautious about change in educational policy and about large-scale and rapid educational experimentation. Some observers point out that decision makers in metropolitan Beijing, compared to those in other coastal and particularly southern urban areas, are more conservative in their policies and are not the first to experiment with radical change because of the location of central power there.

Second, educational decision makers in the two areas appear to have a major difference in their focus in the reform in basic education. Educational decision makers in Tianjin decided early that they would accommodate parental demand for school choice through their more active encouragement of the establishment of nongovernment schools. At the same time, the Tianjin government uses tuition income (plus government resources) from nongovernment schools to assist low-quality government schools. In Beijing, a major focus in basic education is the improvement of the quality of low-quality government schools. The mayor and leaders from the Beijing's People's Congress, the Beijing Education Commission, and the Beijing Finance Bureau all place a high priority on the improvement and reform of low-quality government schools, and additional resources from both government and nongovernment sources are mobilized to support such an effort. For example, between 1996 and 1998, 300 million yuan were used on such an effort. By 1998, 80% of government schools previously in the low-quality category achieved the teaching and facility standards set by the government. And, according to the municipal government, the quality gap among schools has decreased since 1998, and students are allocated to neighborhood schools based on examination results. Revenue from nongovernment schools was a funding source for the effort to improve the quality of low-achieving government schools.

Third, one may speculate that the wider access to upper-secondary and university education through government educational institutions in Beijing may have maintained the people's belief in the effectiveness of government education. For example, the enrollment ratio in upper-secondary education for urban residents in the Beijing metropolitan area is estimated to have been 95% in 2000. With a relatively large number of universities located in Beijing, the gross enrollment ratio for Beijing residents is about 30%[22] at the university level.

SUMMARY AND DISCUSSION

Increased school choice is a rather recent development in education in the People's Republic of China. It represents a clear departure from official education policy for the four decades after 1949. However, the accommodation of parental choice through the development of nongovernment schools since the early 1990s has not been undertaken in isolation from other educational issues. Rather, it has been incorporated into the larger effort to address key concerns in basic education, such as the improvement of the quality of low-quality government

schools and the mobilization of additional resources for the education sector. Since it is a national policy that the state has the primary responsibility for the universalization of compulsory education, particularly through government-funded and -operated schools, school choice has been severely restricted in government schools at this level. The state does allow school choice in nongovernment schools in both compulsory education and postcompulsory education. School choice and the development of nongovernment schools have proceeded at widely different paces and forms in different areas in China. Local education policy and disparities in socioeconomic conditions as well as in cultural and political tradition are important explanatory factors. Table 7.2 summarizes the different kinds of schools in China today. School choice has so far been mainly an urban phenomenon. While different types of nongovernment schools can be found in a given urban area, the traditional elitist private schools tend to be more common in the economically most advanced areas in China.

The development of nongovernment schools has been credited with providing school choice for some parents and with generating additional resources for basic education, particularly for assisting low-quality government schools. But it has also been criticized for increasing differentiation in education, introducing additional inequity in access to knowledge, and reinforcing the tendency towards "expertise." The controversy reflects the enduring tension between equality and efficiency, and between redness and expertise in education in post-1949 China.

The development of nongovernment schools does lead to more schooling alternatives for parents. School choice is available only to the most well-to-do families in some urban areas but to relatively more families in other areas. Some local governments close the most dysfunctional government schools and convert them to nongovernment schools, while others make the improvement of low-quality government schools the focus of their effort in basic education. As part of the state's policy of increasing autonomy and decision making at the school level, nongovernment schools actually provide a place for testing some of the ideas in the reform of school governance. In fact, principals from government schools want to have the same additional power given to principals of nongovernment schools. School choice probably hastens the pace of the reform of school governance that will eventually alter the role of the state in education. While there are efforts to introduce innovative instructional strategies and additional curricular features in some nongovernment schools, their overall impact is probably very small because of the strong influence of the examination system. School choice does give some voice to parents and community groups, though there should be no illusion as to who ultimately makes the decisions. In China today, it is not a meaningful exercise to compare the cost-effectiveness of government and nongovernment schools because of the way that students are allocated to schools and the different regulations and practices governing schools.

Predicting what will happen in education in China is more an art than a science, and many experts or observers have been proven wrong in their past predictions. If the government maintains its twin policies of reform and opening up to the outside world, and if the country continues to make economic progress and Chinese society continues to become more open, the demand for school choice will intensify. In urban areas, the focus of school choice is shifting (or will be in some areas) from lower-secondary to upper-secondary education. And school choice will become an issue in some *rural* areas in the near future. It is not a matter of whether or not to allow school choice, but of how to manage school choice throughout the country.

Recognizing the difficult historical circumstances before 1949, the low level of economic development, and the diversities and tensions within the country, one may say that the People's Republic of China has made substantial and significant achievement in the education of its people since 1949 (World Bank, 1999). Despite some weaknesses, the education system, which has been mainly government education, has been functional so far. The issue is not replacing government education with nongovernment education, but how to enrich the education system and address some of its weakness with nongovernment education. A differentiation of educational policy by educational level is useful.

There is common consensus on the role of compulsory education in the socioeconomic, cultural, and political development of a nation and its people (Inter-Agency Commission, 1990), and access to quality compulsory education is often considered to be a basic human right. Thus, assuring access for children from all backgrounds and promoting equality in access to knowledge are fundamental goals in compulsory education. The government should have strong involvement at this level. In present-day China, government education at the compulsory level is functional. On both efficiency and equality grounds, the focus of policy at this level should be the expansion of access to quality government compulsory education in rural areas and the improvement of the quality of low-quality government schools in all areas.

The state has to ensure that adequate resources from various sources are available to support compulsory educational development. A recent study has documented the low public spending on education and the highly uneven distribution of educational resources in China (World Bank, 1999). It suggests that the government should substantially increase its spending on education over time and that an intergovernmental scheme in education should be developed to both target resources for poor areas and to reduce financial disparities among areas. There is ample room for raising additional government revenue because the "public finance rate" (total government revenue from tax and nontax sources as a percentage of gross domestic product) is relatively low for China and the efficiency in tax collection can be improved over time. Strengthening government financing of compulsory education will enhance efficiency and equality and reduce inequality due to school choice.

In postcompulsory education, families have a larger responsibility in sharing the costs of education. Nongovernment educational institutions can have an important role to play in expanding access to postcompulsory education and providing educational alternatives to accommodate the diverse preferences of parents.[23] In addition to running educational institutions, the state can modify its role with respect to nongovernment education, for example, by providing and enforcing a legal framework; defining, monitoring, and enforcing minimally adequate quality standards; facilitating access to information about school; defining management and governance structures; and facilitating an adequate supply of qualified teachers. Given the large differences across the country, state policies should allow for local adaptation and variation.

NOTES

The author would like to acknowledge the helpful comments provided by Halsey Beemer and Christopher Wheeler on an earlier draft of the paper.

1. Basic education in China covers primary and secondary education. Primary education generally lasts 6 years; secondary education consists of 3 years of lower-secondary education and 3 years of upper-secondary education. Compulsory education generally consists of 6 years of primary education and 3 years of lower-secondary education.

2. In general, in rural areas, primary schools are currently administered and financed by government at the village level, lower-secondary schools by government at the township level, and upper-secondary schools by govern-

ment at the county level (see Tsang, 1996). Administratively, cities are also divided into smaller units of districts and neighborhoods.

3. In China, parents often associate school quality with educational input (students, quality of teaching staff, school facilities), process (such as principal leadership and school management), and output (test scores and transition rates). A good teacher is one who has "heart" and dedication, in addition to having good subject-matter knowledge and pedagogical skills.

4. The admission fee to a good school is often 10,000 yuan (about $1,200) or more; and the *annual* tuition fee of a secondary school for "choice" students is several thousand yuan or more. Government primary and lower-secondary schools charge no tuition. Government upper-secondary schools may charge tuition, which can be up to 200 yuan per year. Government schools do charge a number of school fees (e.g., sports fees, examination fees, etc.) that total about 100 to 200 yuan across education levels and across areas (Tsang, 1995, 2000). In 1997, the annual per-capita disposable income of urban residents was 5,160 yuan and the per-capita net income of rural residents was 2,090 (State Statistical Bureau, 1998: 324). Compared to many other countries, China is still a very poor country.

5. *National-effort indicator* is defined as government spending on education as a percentage of gross national product (GNP) or gross domestic product (GDP). During much of the post-1949 period, China's national-effort indicator was between 2.0% and 2.5%, compared to an average of about 4% for developing countries. *Fiscal-effort indicator* is defined as government spending on education as a percentage of total government spending. China's fiscal-effort indicators was between 6% and 10%, compared to an average of 16% for developing countries. See Tsang (1988, 1994).

6. The moderates have not been completely in power since 1978; radical or "conservative" forces can still be found inside the CCP. For example, within the leadership in the central education bureaucracy (known as the State Education Commission or the Ministry of Education at various times), there has been a changing balance between the radicals and the moderates over time.

7. In China, resources for education are put under budgetary resources and out-of-budget categories. Budgetary resources come from government allocation. Out-of-budget resources consist of education levies and surcharges, school fees, work–study, social (domestic) contributions, and overseas contributions. Nongovernment resources fall under the out-of-budget category. Different localities differ significantly in their capacity to raise out-of-budget resources for education.

8. The development of nongovernment education since 1978 can be roughly divided into three stages (Hu, 1999): an initial exploratory stage during 1978–1987 to gain acceptance of the concept of nongovernment initiatives in education, a slow development stage during 1987–1991 to actually experiment with nongovernment schools, and a rapid development stage since 1992 in which nongovernment schools have increased significantly and are more widely accepted as supplemental to government schools.

9. Reducing excessive social inequality is seen by the CCP not only as a desirable social goal but also as being essential for maintaining social stability. In recent years, the government has paid more attention to economic development in western China ("Not Missing the Opportunity," 2000) and to the achievement of universal compulsory education in poor rural areas (World Bank, 1999).

10. According to the government, nongovernment educational institutions *at all levels* enrolled a total of 10.66 million students and had a total teaching and nonteaching staff of 520,000 by the end of 1997 ("The Rapid Development," 1998).

11. Information on separate types of nongovernment schools is not available, partly because it is sometimes difficult to distinguish between people-run schools and traditional private schools.

12. For example, a secondary school in Shanghai offers a second-language course in eleventh grade, and a private primary school in Shanghai offers foreign language and computer classes starting in first grade. Some educators point out that the study loads for students in these schools are excessively heavy and may have a negative impact on students' health (Qu, 1993).

13. For example, some Chinese are alarmed at the substantial and widening socioeconomic and educational disparities between the eastern coastal region and the western region, and between urban areas and rural areas. The widening disparities may eventually be politically destabilizing. It is apparent that there is more school choice in the more developed coastal region and in urban China.

14. Well-connected individuals (including party members with power) are able to convert their political capital into physical capital. There is justified concerned that, as the government tries to reform state enterprises, some public productive assets have ended up in the hands of influential members of society (Li, 1996; Liu, 1996). The conversion of some government schools into people-run schools is the educational equivalent of the process going on in the economic sector.

15. The discussion on Tianjin is based on the findings of a recent study by Chen and colleagues (1998). The information on Beijing is based on an inquiry conducted by this author in 1998; the author had discussions with officials from the Ministry of Education and from the Beijing municipal government, school principals, teachers, and parents.

16. In terms of per-capita disposable income of urban residents, Tianjin was fifth among 30 regions in the country in 1997, after Guangdong, Shanghai, Zhejiang, and Beijing. It had achieved universal 9-year compulsory education a few years ago and is moving toward universal 12-year basic education.

17. In China, compulsory education in government schools requires no tuition fee. But compulsory education is by no means "free" for parents. Parents have to spend money on textbooks and workbooks, writing supplies, school uniforms, various school fees (examination fees, sports fee, etc.), and other items (e.g., boarding costs for some students). The total cost of such private educational spending can be a heavy burden for Chinese families, especially those from poor or rural backgrounds (Tsang, 1995, 2000). Govern-

ment upper-secondary schools can charge relatively low tuition fees that are set by the government.

18. Having a separate campus can be a challenge for the affiliated people-run school because of the relatively high cost of school construction. It is easier for the people-run school to have separate financial and accounting books, a separate legal identity, and some instructional autonomy from the parent government school.

19. Part of the financial difficulty of the traditional private schools in Tianjin is the strict government regulation on tuition fee. The tuition policy is much more lax in Guangdong province. Traditional private schools are allowed to charge a high one-time admission fee and high annual tuition fee. Guangdong province has the country's highest per-capita disposable income among its urban residents; some families in areas such as Shenzhen, Guangzhou, and the Pearl Delta area are very rich and can afford the expensive private schools.

20. For example, in 1997, the municipal government of Beijing converted nine government schools into people-run schools (China Education Yearbook Editorial Board, 1998). The new principals will have a school budget based on the government-school norm. But they have more autonomy in school management, as indicated earlier in the chapter. In a sense, the district education bureaucracy is *contracting* the running of the school to an individual or community group.

21. In the Chinese context, "social forces" refer to various elements of the nonstate sector; they include individuals, private groups, community groups, large social groups, and other nonstate organizations (e.g., nonstate enterprises). It may be noted here that schools run by community groups and by companies are not a new phenomenon. As pointed out earlier, many rural schools have been run by the village community since 1949. In urban areas, during various times since 1949, the government did encourage some companies to run their own schools, generally as a way of expanding access to schooling and occasionally as a strategy to relate schooling to work. But in earlier times, students were not charged high school fees.

22. The national average is around 9%. In 1997, Beijing had 65 regular higher educational institutions and 196,082 undergraduate students, while Tianjian had 20 institutions and 73,830 undergraduate students (Ministry of Education, 1998). The gross enrollment ratio is much less than 30% in Tianjian.

23. The case for nongovernment education is particularly strong in college and university education. In fact, the Chinese government has started to expand higher education at a much faster rate than before, particularly through the expansion of nongovernment colleges and universities.

REFERENCES

Burns, J. (1999). The People's Republic of China at 50: National political reform. *The China Quarterly, 159,* 580–594.

Chen, D., Ye, Z., Zeng, T.,& Wang, M. (1998). Guanyu Tianjinshi jieje zexiao wenti de diaocha jianjie [A survey study of Tianjin City's solution to the school choice problem]. *Jiaoyu Yanjiu [Educational Research]*, 222, 37–41.

China Education Yearbook Editorial Board. (1990). *China education yearbook 1990*. Beijing, China: People's Education Press.

China Education Yearbook Editorial Board. (1998). *China education yearbook 1998*. Beijing, China: People's Education Press.

Chinese Education Society. (2001). Quanguo minban jiaoyu chengguo zhanshi hui [Pamphlet on the exhibition of outcome of non-government education]. Beijing, China: Beijing Normal University Press.

Deng, P. (1997). *Private education in modern China*. Westport, CT: Praeger.

Dernberger, R. (1999). The People's Republic of China at 50: The economy. *The China Quarterly, 159*, 606–615.

Documents on the reform of the educational system. (1985). Beijing, China: People's Press.

Fairbank, J. (1987). *The great Chinese revolution: 1800–1985*. New York: Harper & Row.

Hu, R. (Ed.). (1997). *Zhongguo jichu jiaoju fajan jianjiu [Research on basic-education development in China]*. Beijing, China: People's Education Press.

Hu, W. (1999, May). Zhongguo minban jiaoyu fajan xiangzhuang ji chele xujia [Present situation of people-run education in China and its developmental strategies]. *Jianyu Yanjiu [Educational Research]*, pp. 68–74.

Inter-Agency Commission. (1990). *Meeting basic learning needs: A new vision for the 1990s*. New York: Author.

Jiang, M., Zhang, H., & Wang, L. (2000). Disparities in compulsory education among counties in China. In M. Tsang, X. Wei, & J. Xiao (Eds.), *Economic analysis of educational policy*. Beijing, China: Educational Science Press.

Kwong, J. (1997). The reemergence of private schools in socialist China. *Comparative Education Review, 41*(3), 244–259.

Lai, J. (1994). Guanyu sili xuexiaode gainian ji chengwei. [The concept of private schools and their proper appellation]. *Jiaoyu Yanjiu [Educational Research]*, 3, 25–29.

Li, H. (1996, September). Economic analysis and policy choice of the corruption based on pubic granted power. *Economic Research Journal*, pp. 75–80.

Li, N. (1997). Orientating to the 21st century and striving to create a new situation in basic education. In China Education Yearbook Editorial Board, *China Education Yearbook 1998* (pp. 13–19). Beijing, China: People's Education Press.

Li, S.,& Zhao, R. (1999, April). A restudy of income distribution among Chinese inhabitants. Economic Research Journal, 3–17.

Lin, J. (2000). *Social transformation and private education in China*. Westport, CT: Praeger.

Liu, S. (1996, December). Some issues on deepening reform of state enterprises. *Economic Research Journal*, pp. 3–7.

Ministry of Education. (1998). *Educational statistics yearbook of China 1997.* Beijing, China: People's Education Press.

Montaperto, N., & Henderson, J. (Eds.). (1979). *China schools influx.* White Plains, NY: Sharpe.

Not missing the opportunity to promote big development in the western region. (2000, January 24). *People's Daily*, p. 1.

Pye, L. (1999). An overview of 50 years of the People's Republic of China: Some progress, but big problems remain. *The China Quarterly, 159,* 569–579.

Qu, T. (1993). Danqian wuoguo sili xuexiao fazhan jianshu. Dongbei shida xuebao: zesheban [A brief description of current private school development in China]. *Northeastern Teachers' University Bulletin: Philosophy and Sociology Edition, 6,* 88–91.

Wuoguo minban jiaoyu xuanxu fajan [The rapid development of nongovernment education in our country]. (1998, September 7). *People's Daily*.

Schoenhals, M. (1999). Political movements, change and stability: The Chinese Communist party in power. *The China Quarterly, 159,* 595–605.

State Council. (1993). *Outline of Chinese education reform and development.* State Council, Beijing, China.

State Statistical Bureau. (1998). *China statistical yearbook 1998.* Beijing, China: China Statistical Publishing House.

Sun, P. (Ed.). (1992). *Zhongguo jiaoyushi [History of Chinese education].* Shanghai, China: Huadong Teachers' University Press.

Townsend, J. (1980). *Politics in China* (2nd ed.). Boston: Little, Brown.

Tsang, M. (1988). Cost analysis for educational policy making: A review of cost studies in education in developing countries. *Review of Educational Research, 58*(2), 181–230.

Tsang, M. (1991). The structural reform of secondary education in China. *Journal of Educational Administration, 29*(4), 65–83.

Tsang, M. (1994). Costs of education in China: Issues of resource mobilization, equality, equity, and efficiency. *Education Economics, 2*(3), 287–312.

Tsang, M. (1995). Public and private costs of schooling in developing countries. In M. Carnoy (Ed.), *International encyclopedia of education* (2nd ed., pp. 393–398). Pergamon.

Tsang, M. (1996). The financial reform of basic education in China. *Economics of Education Review, 15*(4), 423–444.

Tsang, M. (2000). Household educational spending in rural China. In M. Tsang, X. Wei, & J. Xiao (Eds.), *Economic analysis of educational policy* (pp. 1–20). Beijing, China: People's Education Press.

Wang, W. (2000). Jiaoyu gaige yu fazhan zhong de jichu jiaoyu minban xuexiao [Nongovernment schools in the reform and development of basic education]. In Z. Zhang & J. Li (Eds), *Minban jiaoyu de yanjiu yu tansuo [Research and exploration of non–government education]* (pp. 48–53). Beijing, China: Beijing Normal University Press.

Wen, D., & Liu, D. (2001). *Cong jingfei shouzhi zhuangfong kan "minban gong zu" xuexiao de fazhan [Based on condition of revenue and spending to examine the development of people-run government assisted school].* School of Education, Peking University, China (mimeo).

World Bank. (1991). *China: Provincial education sector study.* Washington, DC: Author.

World Bank. (1998). *Regional disparities in China.* Washington, DC: Author.

World Bank. (1999). *Strategic goals for Chinese education in the 21st century.* Washington, DC: Author.

Wu, Z. (1994). Zhongguo sili xuexiao xianzhuang shuyao [Overview of current Chinese private schools]. *Zhongguo jiaoyu xuekan [Chinese Education Journal], 3,* 53–55.

Zhang, Z., & Li, J. (2000). (Eds). *Minban jiaoyu de yanjiu yu tansuo [Research and exploration of non-government education].* Beijing, China: Beijing Normal University Press.

CHAPTER 8

Public Support for Private Schools in Post-Communist Central Europe: Czech and Hungarian Experiences

Randall K. Filer
Daniel Munich

Some of the most profound changes following the collapse of communism in Central and Eastern Europe occurred in educational systems. For generations, schools had served not only as a means of training workers but also as a vehicle of indoctrination designed to create a "new socialist man." Education was, by law, a state monopoly designed to respond to the dictates of the plan rather than the signals of the market. Very detailed curricula were prescribed by central authorities (Micklewright, 1999). Parental and student preferences played little, if any, role in determining how much or what type of training was provided. Entry into coveted disciplines, while certainly influenced by ability, was also heavily determined by political or other considerations. There are numerous examples of students with an interest in and aptitude for study in particular subjects being forced into entirely unrelated fields because they or their parents were considered politically unreliable.[1]

In such an environment, it is not surprising that one of the first reforms of the transition process was to overhaul the educational system to provide greater flexibility and give far more substantial decision-making power to students and parents. One key reform involved allowing nonstate[2] schools to challenge the state education monopoly. In most countries in the region, nonstate education has achieved only

limited market share. In the Czech Republic, Slovakia, and Hungary, however, the share of students in nonstate schools, at around 5%, approaches that in closely related EU countries such as Germany and Austria.[3] It is not a coincidence that these three countries provide the most generous level of state funding for private and religious schools. In each, funding may be as much as 100% of that provided to government schools. Poland provides a subsidy to nonstate schools of approximately 50% of the funding given to state schools and has approximately 2% of students enrolled in such schools. In most of the other countries of the region, there is little or no public support for nonstate schools and there are even lower enrollment rates.

Since our task is to learn what we can about the impact of voucher-like schemes from the experience of Central Europe, we will limit the discussion to those countries where there is extensive public support for nonstate schools. In addition, to keep the analysis tractable, we will ignore Slovakia, which has a similar history to that of the Czech Republic, and focus almost exclusively on the Czech Republic and Hungary. This chapter traces the development of nonstate schools[4] as well as other education reforms in these two countries since 1989. It provides preliminary evidence regarding the role of such schools in expanding the range of opportunities for parents and students and in bringing pressure for reform to bear on the state school system.

INITIAL CONDITIONS

The Czech Republic has a population of about 10.3 million people and an area of just over 30,000 squares miles. In area it is almost exactly the same size as South Carolina, while the population is close to that of Michigan. Overall, in terms of area, population, and density, one would do well to think of the Czech Republic as a close mirror of Ohio. Administratively, prior to 2000, government functions were divided between the national government and 77 district or local governments.[5] (Recently regional governments have been introduced between the national and district governments, but these did not exist during the period under study here.) Czech districts should be thought of as analogous to U.S. counties in area, population, and responsibilities. Studies of labor markets have found that there is surprisingly little commuting for employment across district boundaries, especially given the relatively small size of districts and the large differences in job opportunities (Erbenová, 1997). Mobility for employment was low even during communism and has declined further since 1990

(Andrle, 1998). Whether this is due to intense localism or poor transportation infrastructure, it suggests that there is also likely to be little commuting to attend schools that are in some way more attractive than those found nearby.

Hungary has a population of about 10.2 million in an area of slightly less than 36,000 square miles. Administratively, the country is divided into 19 counties and 8 cities of county status, including Budapest. These administrative areas are on average, therefore, about three times the size of those in the Czech Republic.

Both educational systems provide several paths that students can follow. In 1989 10 years of schooling was compulsory. Primary or basic education in the Czech Republic lasted for either 8 or 9 years. Talented students were allowed to apply for secondary education after 8 years of primary school, while others, particularly those who did not obtain their desired placement, remained for a ninth year. Then, as now, students applied for various types of secondary school depending on their future career plans, with admission to oversubscribed programs rationed on the basis of exam performance and other considerations. In Hungary primary education ended after 8 years.

The lowest level of additional education available involves 2 years of vocational training.[6] High school education is divided into three types: vocational education leading to a certification exam, specialized secondary (technical) education in professional fields such as nursing and engineering, and general secondary education in academic high schools known as *gymnázia*. Students from all types of secondary education may continue on to university, although it is rare for those from vocational school to do so and the majority of university students come from academic high schools.[7] As elsewhere in the region, university education typically involves the study of a single field and lasts 5 years.[8] Students desiring the most advanced degree typically continue for another 3 years of postgraduate study.

Although educational levels were on average relatively high, the structure of education was highly skewed toward vocational and away from general academic training. In 1989–1990, fewer than one-quarter of secondary students were enrolled in an academic, as opposed to technical, program in both the Czech Republic and Hungary. This percentage contrasts with slightly less than half of secondary-level students being in general academic programs in the average OECD (Organisation for Economic Cooperation and Development) country. In fact, in 1995 the Czech Republic had the lowest proportion of secondary school students in general academic programs of any OECD country (OECD, 1997). Furthermore, the vocational education system is very specialized. There are more than 300 separate "tracks" in the Czech Republic, compared with 16 in Germany, a nearby country with heavy emphasis on vocational training (Laporte & Schweitzer, 1994).

The legacy of the allocation system imposed by the planning authorities has resulted in substantial excess demand for various types of education (Centre for Economic Policy Research [CEPR]). In 1989 only 52% of those seeking university admission in the Czech Republic were offered at least one place. It is not possible to reconstruct from official data the success rate of students seeking admission to academic high schools.[9] It is widely understood, however, that more students seek admission to these schools than there are places available. Similarly, places in popular fields in technical and vocational high schools, especially those required for the expanding service sector, are severely rationed. Thus, there should be market niches that could be filled by entrepreneurial educational providers.

In addition, school systems in the Czech Republic and Hungary, as elsewhere in the region, have substantial weaknesses that may encourage parents to seek alternatives to public schools. In particular, the public school systems are overly focused on memorization rather than creative thinking (Tomášek, Straková, & Palečková, 1997). Finally, some parents regard public schools with distrust, given their role in indoctrination under communism, a situation paralleling the attitudes of groups such as fundamentalist Christians in the United States. Despite these weaknesses, overall the school systems provided strong educational results, especially in scientific and mathematical fields, where Czech and Hungarian graduates consistently tested among the best in the world.

Development of regional educational systems during the 1990s was driven by demographic trends as well as educational reforms. Table 8.1 shows the population at various ages in 1991 and 1999. It is clear that in both the Czech Republic and Hungary there were massive declines in birth rates during the final years of communism. Thus, at the start of the transition educational planners could foresee that the number of students of both primary and secondary school age would fall considerably over the decade. The number of children of high school age (between 14 and 17) fell by more than 25% between 1991 and 1999 in the Czech Republic and by more than 30% in Hungary.[10] This demographic trend should have resulted in increased access to education over the decade even if there were no increase in educational spending or no new schools entering the market.

Table 8.1. Age structure of the school-age population (thousands).

	7	8	9	10	11	12	13	14	15	16	17
Czech Republic											
Number of Children 1991	133.9	134.5	138.6	141.1	150.4	168.0	174.0	177.2	182.0	187.0	188.6
Number of Children 1999	120.8	128.5	127.7	125.9	129.8	128.2	130.6	133.4	134.0	134.5	138.7
Hungary											
Number of Children 1991	123.0	129.3	138.1	143.7	154.6	162.9	170.0	178.0	189.4	181.1	150.7
Number of Children 1999	124.9	123.4	120.7	121.5	122.9	124.2	126.1	120.8	122.9	129.1	137.9
Poland											
Number of Children 1991	679.5	696.6	680.0	651.3	665.7	656.2	644.6	631.2	638.8	623.1	599.6
Number of Children 1999	505.2	536.4	535.3	551.6	574.9	590.3	617.7	657.8	679.5	696.6	680.0

Source: National Statistical Yearbooks, various years.

EDUCATIONAL REFORMS SINCE 1989

In addition to the possibility of nonstate schools, there have been several major education reforms in the Czech Republic and Hungary since the start of the transition that may have played a role in the rise of such schools.

In each country individual schools were given legal status and decision-making authority over enrollment and curricula. The setting of the number of students allowed to enter various disciplines by centralized state planning commissions was abolished. Schools and teachers were given substantially greater freedom to chose teaching methods and textbooks. Even though there are school-leaving exams for most programs, the form and content of these exams were left to the discretion of individual schools. These reforms provided all schools, both public and private, with substantially increased ability to compete for students.

Prior to approximately 1992, all academic high schools were 4-year programs. With the freedom allowed after 1989, a number of *gymnázia* began admitting students after the fourth or fifth or sixth year of primary school and revised their programs so that they lasted between 6 and 8 years. By the 1997–1998 schoolyear, these "extended *gymnázia*" accounted for more than 40% of *gymnázia* students in the secondary school years in the Czech Republic and about half that fraction in Hungary. There has been considerable discussion about the impact of this reform on primary schools. It is generally assumed that the more talented and academically motivated students leave basic school for the extended *gymnázia*, resulting in less classroom stimulation and lower probability of academic success for those left behind. If this is true, then the trend will be self-reinforcing and the share of extended *gymnázia* should continue to grow over time. It should be noted, however, that this reform was independent of the rise of non-state schools. Indeed, the division between extended and conventional *gymnázia* is approximately the same in the state and nonstate sectors in the Czech Republic, although in Hungary extended academic high schools form a greater fraction of nonstate than state schools.

In addition to these common reforms, there have been major educational reforms that were specific to the Czech Republic since 1989 and need to be taken into account when studying the development of the educational sector since the transition. In particular, one reform adopted in 1995 to take effect in the 1996–1997 schoolyear profoundly affected enrollment trends in various types of schools. As discussed above, prior to this time, the ninth year of primary school was optional, with most students opting to enter secondary school after the eighth grade. The main purpose of the ninth grade in primary school was to give students a chance to delay decisions about their educational future (especially if they wished to reapply to secondary schools to which they had been denied admission after the eighth grade) or to provide a stop-gap for students who did not wish to continue their education but completed the eighth grade below the statutory minimum age for employment. By the 1995–1996 schoolyear, fewer than 5% of students completing the eighth grade continued on to a ninth grade in primary school, down from a high of almost 20% a few years earlier. This decline was due in part to shrinking overall numbers of students resulting from the demographic trends seen in Table 8.1, combined with increased opportunities provided by the rise of non-state secondary schools, reducing the fraction of eighth-grade students who were not able to secure admission to their desired type of secondary school. Education law amendments in 1995 rationalized the system by lowering the required years of schooling from 10 to 9 while making the ninth year of primary school mandatory for all students, increasing the normal age of admission to secondary school by 1 year.

Because of this change in the length of primary school, the number of students entering secondary school during the 1996–1997 schoolyear dropped drastically. Admissions to the high school grades in *gymnázia* fell from 26,800 in 1995–1996 to 15,700 in 1996–1997, before rising again to 26,700 in 1997–1998. The decline for other types of schools was even greater. Admissions to technical schools fell from 56,400 in 1995–1996 to 6,700 in 1996–1997, rising back to 56,400 in 1997–1998. For vocational schools, the figures were 67,900 in 1995–1996, 8,100 in 1996–1997, and 53,800 in 1997–1998. *Gymnázia* were able to more successfully maintain enrollment due to the backlog of unsuccessful applicants from previous years, although there has been no investigation of the long-term prospects of this single class of presumably lower-than-average quality. Given that secondary school is typically a 4-year program, this reduced cohort reached the university admission age in the fall of 2000, with the same impact on enrollments, although, here again, the small cohort represented an opportunity to reduce the backlog of excess demand created by rationing in previous years.[11]

Finally, in the Czech Republic, there were traditionally a limited number of post-*maturita* secondary technical schools that typically provided job-specific training to students such as *gymnázia* graduates who did not seek university entrance but, instead, desired to be prepared for the labor force. Such schools enrolled only about 2,000 new students per year at the start of the 1990s but had increased enrollment to around 10,000 new entrants per year by the middle of the decade. These programs (typically associated with existing secondary technical schools) were eliminated in the educational reforms of 1995 and replaced by a new type of institution known as a "higher professional school" as well as by a provision allowing students previously served by such post-*maturita* programs to simply join the third and fourth years of the conventional technical secondary school curricula.[12] Higher professional schools also offered a technical way around the Czech ban on private universities by offering tertiary education under a different name.

The key reform of interest to us remains the rise of private and church schools. Such schools were first legalized in the Czech Republic in 1990. At first they were funded at a level equal to that provided state schools of the same type in the same area. Under pressure from education authorities, the principle of "equal treatment" for nonstate schools was abandoned in 1995, and the level of support for nonstate schools was set equal to 60% to 90% of the subsidy provided to state schools, with the exact amount being set by the Ministry of Education and regional school authorities on the basis of unspecified performance criteria. Dissatisfaction with the arbitrariness of decisions regarding funding levels to nonstate schools resulted in the law being amended again in 1999. Currently, public support for schools is based on a two-part formula. Base support is given according to the type of school and is independent of quality or ownership. There is then a supplement that varies according to quality as evaluated by local school offices (with final determination approved by a board at the Ministry of Education). Nonstate schools can obtain maximum supplements equal to 90% of those available to state schools. In addition, the law now limits the discretion of the ministry and school offices when evaluating quality according to an explicit set of criteria. This policy was adopted to protect nonstate schools from arbitrarily being denied funds by public officials.[13]

In Hungary, reflecting the looser form of communism that prevailed during the 1980s, there were actually a limited number of religious-affiliated academic high schools by 1989. In particular, eight Catholic, one Protestant, and one Jewish school enrolled more than 3,600 students (about 3% of those in academic high schools at the time), with full funding from the state. In general these schools served young men who were interested in eventual religious vocations. After the start of the transition, the scope of activity of nonstate schools was expanded and codified. Amendments to the education law in 1990 provided that "a religious legal entity can provide for any educational activity which is not exclusively reserved for the state." Finally, the 1994 primary education law and later rulings by the constitutional court established that the basic per-student grant (the so-called normative grant) plus other subsidies for "public duties" fulfilled by non-state schools must be provided on the same basis as to state schools.

Currently, therefore, educational spending in both countries is a function both of the formulae adopted for aid to schools and the total number of students enrolled. The authorities presumably could respond to changes in demand by changing the funding formula in order to keep total spending constant. Table 8.2 shows the development of public spending over the decade. During the 1990s there were significant variations in public spending on education both in amount per student and share of the gross domestic product (GDP) in both the Czech Republic and Hungary. In the Czech Republic spending rose both in constant dollars and as a share of GDP until the last years of the decade, when it fell somewhat due to reduced cohort sizes and pressure on the state budget when economic growth slowed after 1997. Between 1991 and its peak in 1996, real spending per student increased by at least 37%. At the end of the decade, it remained 16% higher than at the start of transition. Analysis in Hungary is complicated by its significantly greater rate of inflation (635% between 1990 and 1999 as opposed to 290% in the Czech Republic). Filer and Hanousek (2000) have argued that inflation measures in transition economies contain substantial upward biases. If this is true, then real expenditures were substantially greater at the end of the decade than indicated in Table 8.2 and increased on a per-student basis in both countries.

In addition to public spending, those running schools may be able to top up resources from their own funds. In Hungary and church-run schools in the Czech Republic, such fees can be used only for value-added services; tuition for fundamental education services is not allowed, although schools typically do invent a legal mechanism to collect money from parents (Aradi, Halász, & Nagy, 1998). Czech private schools generally can and do charge tuition fees,[14] while church-sponsored schools are provided additional funds from congregational or diocesan resources for capital expenditures.

CHANGING MARKET INCENTIVES

One of the most profound changes during the transition from communism has been a rapid and sustained increase in the value of education.

Table 8.2. Public expenditures on education.

	1989	1990	1991	1992	1993	1994	1995	1996	1997	1998
Czech Republic										
Billions of 1989 crowns *	21.7	21.4	18.1	20.1	23.3	24.9	26.0	27.2	24.2	22.2
1989 crowns per student	8,870	9,050	7,960	8,990	10,490	11,100	11,590	12,190	10,970	10,260
As share of GDP	4.0%	4.1%	4.1%	4.5%	5.3%	5.3%	5.2%	5.2%	4.7%	4.4%
Hungary										
Billions of 1989 florints *	86.9	94.8	82.4	91.6	88.4	89.4	77.4	69.1	73.0	74.0
1989 florints per student	39,600	44,100	38,700	43,500	42,500	43,400	37,400	33,400	35,500	36,100
As share of GDP	5.0	5.9%	5.7%	6.7%	6.5%	6.4%	5.5%	4.9%	5.0%	4.9%

Source: Authors' calculations based on *National Statistical Yearbooks*, various years.
Note: * The exchange rate has varied between 25 and 35 crowns to the dollar over the decade of the 1990s. Hungary has had a much higher inflation rate and several devaluations of the florint. In 1989 the exchange rate was approximately 63 florints to the dollar.

Filer, Jurajda, and Plánovsk (1998, 1999) and Munich, Svejnar, and Terrell (1999) provide discussions of trends in returns to education in the Czech Republic, while Svejnar (1999) contains a summary of research in other countries. Table 8.3 shows how much more workers who hold various degrees earn than primary school graduates for the entire Czech work force in various years between 1984 and 1997.[15] Clearly the value of all types of education has been increasing, with the greatest increase occurring for workers with general academic or specialized technical education. The figures in Table 8.3 are for workers of all ages combined. Results presented in Filer and colleagues (1998) show that both levels of additional earnings and the increase in these levels associated with various degrees are greater for younger workers, even though many of them were trained under the communist regime. Presumably, the value of education provided after 1989, when curricula were free to adjust to the requirements of the market economy, would be even greater. There is not such exhaustive work on the pattern of wages in Hungary, but findings of existing studies are consistent with the Czech pattern shown in Table 8.3 (see Paihle [1998] and Varga [1995]).

There is one area in which economic conditions differed between the Czech Republic and Hungary during the 1990s that may have played a role in the development of the educational systems. For most of the decade, unemployment in the Czech Republic was less than 4%, rising to a high of between 8% and 9% only in 1998 and 1999. In Hungary, by way of contrast, unemployment quickly shot up to almost 14%, falling to around 9% only at the end of the decade. Since unemployment in both countries was greater among the less educated and the young,[16] there should have been a strong economic incentive

Table 8.3. Increased earnings compared to primary school graduates over time in the Czech Republic.

Level of Education	1984	1993	1995	1997
Academic HS	15%	27%	35%	52%
Technical HS	20%	28%	45%	57%
Vocational HS	n.a.	n.a.	31%	37%
University	40%	60%	92%	125%

Source: Figures for 1984 and 1993 calculated from Chase (1998).
Figures for 1995 and 1997 from Filer, Jurajda, and Plánovsk (1999).

to remain in school during the decade. Based on the lack of employment opportunities, we might expect that the pressure to remain in school would have been greater in Hungary than in the Czech Republic, at least during the first years of the transition.

It would be surprising if individuals did not respond to such massive changes in private pecuniary returns. Indeed, Figure 8.1 shows that enrollment in secondary school as a fraction of the appropriate age cohort increased throughout the decade in both countries such that by 1998 enrollment was close to 100% among 14- to 17-year-old young men and women.[17] In addition, as can be seen in Figure 8.1, the increase in enrollments was greater in those types of schools where the increase in returns was greatest.

A similar pattern can be seen in the demand for university education. Figure 8.2 shows the fraction of each cohort applying to and enrolling in university, where the cohort is defined as those who turn 18 in a given year. Given the high rejection rate among applicants[18] and the tendency for rejected applicants to reapply for several years, it is not appropriate, however, to infer that between 60% and 75% of 18-year-olds actually sought to go to university. It is also the case that the mean number of applications per applicant has been rising over time. In the Czech Republic the average number of applications per applicant increased from 1 (the limit allowed by the communists) in 1989 to 2.2 in 1992, after which it remained roughly constant at 2.45 or less for the remainder of the decade.

GROWTH OF PRIVATE SCHOOLS

Immediately after the collapse of communism, nonstate schools became legal at the primary and secondary level. (Private universities, although allowed from the beginning of the transition in Hungary, were only allowed in the Czech Republic following amendments to the university education law in 1998.) Hungary and the Czech Republic differed in where nonstate schools arose. Despite their legality, there has been very little growth of nonstate primary (basic) schools in the Czech Republic. By the 1998–1999 schoolyear, there were only 33 private and 20 church-related primary schools (1.3% of the total of 4,093 primary schools in the country), enrolling approximately 0.6% of all primary school pupils. Their role has been limited, frequently specializing in marginal students such as those needing special education or not able to adapt to normal school conditions. In Hungary, by way of contrast, in 1999 177 church-affiliated and 87 other primary

Figure 8.1. Share of age cohort in various types of secondary schools.

A. Czech Republic

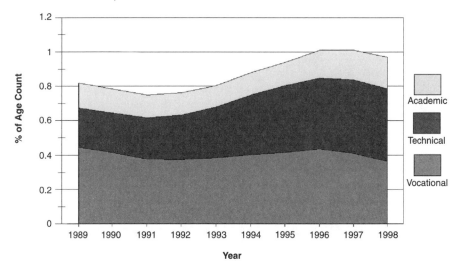

B. Hungary

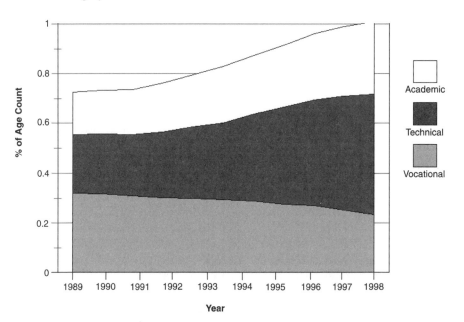

Figure 8.2. Applications and admissions to University.

A. Czech Republic

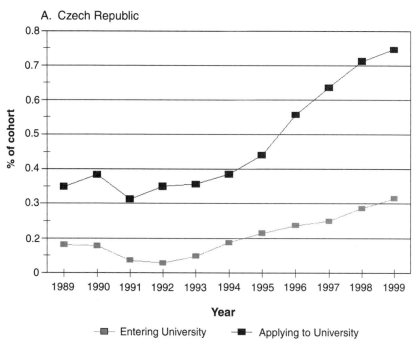

B. Hungary

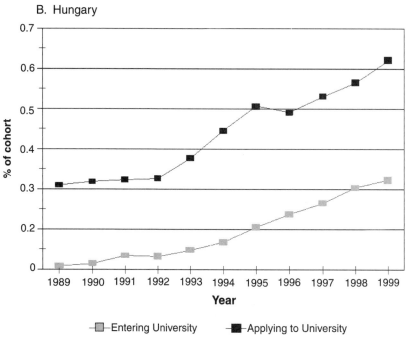

schools (7.1% of the 3,696 primary schools in the country) enrolled 5.3% of primary school pupils.

At the secondary school level the story is very different, with non-state education playing a more important role in the Czech Republic. From a base of zero in 1990, nonstate secondary schools grew to approximately 25% of Czech institutions by the middle of the 1990s. Since the average private or church-related school was significantly smaller than the average public school, however, around 13% of students were enrolled in nonstate secondary schools by the middle of the decade. Both the number of schools and the share of students enrolled in them appear to have leveled off by about the 1995–1996 academic year, and there has been little change since then. In Hungary, the share of nonstate schools and enrollment rose throughout the decade but by its end had reached only 15% of institutions enrolling 8% of students.

Despite declines in the number of students in the relevant age range, there has not been a commensurate decrease in the number of secondary schools since educational reform began in 1990. Indeed, in the Czech Republic the total number of secondary schools increased by 49% from 1,246 in 1989–1990 to 1,859 in 1998–1999, down from a peak of 2,116 in the 1995–1996 schoolyear.[19] Two-thirds of this increase was accounted for by private schools, which grew from none to 448 institutions by the end of the decade (again, down from a peak of 544 institutions 2 years earlier). Similarly, in Hungary, the total number of institutions increased from 1,066 in 1989–1990 to 1,545 in 1998–1999, with nonstate secondary schools increasing from 10 to 238 over the course of the decade. One implication of this increase, combined with the decline in the number of students in the relevant age range seen in Table 8.1, is that the average school size fell precipitously over the decade. Even allowing for the fact that a greater share of secondary students enroll in academic high schools than in the past, the average state academic high school in the Czech Republic in 1999 was 12% smaller than a decade earlier. Enrollment in the average technical or vocational school shrank by more than 40% during this same period.[20] Because institutions tended to retain staff, the falling school size has meant that class sizes have also decreased steadily.

Tables 8.4 and 8.5 show the total number of students in various types of schools over the decade, while Figure 8.3 shows the share of the secondary school–age cohort in state and nonstate schools. It is clear that both the fraction of teenagers enrolled in school and the share of secondary school students in nonstate schools increased dramatically over the decade. From Figure 8.3 it is obvious that in the

Table 8.4. Enrollment in secondary schools by type, 1989–1998—Czech Republic (thousands).

	1989–1990	1990–1991	1991–1992	1992–1993	1993–1994	1994–1995	1995–1996	1996–1997	1997–1998	1998–1999
Academic										
State	100.7	101.8	95.9	89.9	80.5	76.6	77.1	66.8	66.3	68.4
Nonstate	0	0.1.	0.9	3.5	5.8	8.4	9.2	8.3	7.9	7.4
Technical										
State	158.7	166.6	170.4	171.7	176.5	188.8	195.3	151.4	152.7	149.7
Nonstate	0	0.2	4.6	15.5	30.4	44.7	50.5	37.7	31.8	25.5
Vocational										
State	310.2	301.8	278.6	250.8	241.2	242.6	234.7	178.6	156.8	132.9
Nonstate	0	0	0	17.4	27.5	26.0	27.3	21.5	19.3	17.5
Total										
State	569.8	570.2	544.9	510.4	498.2	508.0	507.1	396.8	375.8	350.9
Nonstate	0	0.3	5.5	36.4	63.7	79.1	87.0	67.5	59.0	50.4
% Nonstate	0	1.0	6.7	11.3	13.5	14.6	14.5	13.6	12.6	

Source: Author's calculations based on *National Statistical Yearbooks*, various years.

Table 8.5. Enrollment in secondary schools by type, 1989–1998—Hungary (thousands).

	1989–1990	1990–1991	1992–1993	1993–1994	1994–1995	1995–1996	1996–1997	1997–1998	1998–1999
Academic									
State	112.7	118.3	127.8	127.2	127.1	124.8	123.1	121.9	121.6
Nonstate	3.6	5.1	10.0	12.5	15.4	16.1	17.8	19.4	20.6
Technical									
State	157.2	168.4	182.9	186.8	188.6	198.7	208.7	213.4	217.4
Nonstate	0	0	2.2	4.0	6.3	9.7	11.8	13.8	17.0
Vocational + 2 year									
State	222.2	222.2	209.6	196.2	181.9	168.5	151.1	138.1	121.5
Nonstate	0	0	2.2	2.6	3.8	4.1	4.9	5.8	6.7
Total									
State	492.1	514.0	520.3	510.2	497.6	492.0	482.9	473.4	460.5
Nonstate	3.6	5.1	14.4	19.1	25.5	29.9	34.5	39.0	44.3
% Nonstate	0.7%	1.0%	2.7%	3.6%	4.9%	5.7%	6.7%	7.6%	8.8%

Source: Author's calculations based on *National Statistical Yearbooks*, various years.

Figure 8.3. Fraction of cohort enrolled in secondary school.

A. Czech Republic

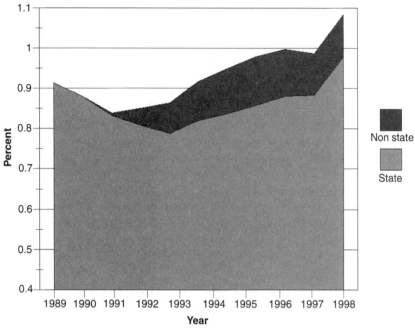

B. Hungary

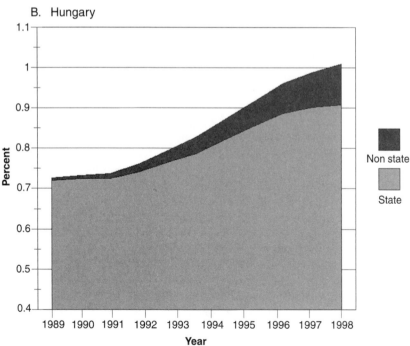

Czech Republic the share of the cohort in state schools was approximately the same at the end of the decade as at its start. Thus, the increase in overall enrollment probability over the decade was almost entirely due to the rise of nonstate schools. In Hungary, by way of contrast, enrollment in state schools increased throughout the decade, while nonstate schools played a relatively smaller role in enhancing educational opportunities.

As can be seen in Tables 8.4 and 8.5, there have been similar shifts in both the Czech Republic and Hungary away from vocational and toward technical and academic high schools. Again, this is in line with the shifting relative wages and unemployment probabilities discussed earlier. What does differ between the Czech Republic and Hungary is the relative importance of nonstate schools of various types. In the Czech Republic nonstate schools have attracted a smaller share of students in academic high schools (9.8%) than in technical schools (14.5%) or vocational schools (11.9%). In Hungary this pattern is reversed, with nonstate schools having the largest share in academic high schools (14.5%) followed by technical high schools (7.3%) and vocation schools (5.2%).

FACTORS INFLUENCING THE ESTABLISHMENT OF NONSTATE SCHOOLS

It is clear that nonstate schools have increased in importance in both the Czech Republic and Hungary since parents sending their children to such schools became eligible for state support. Perhaps more interesting questions arise with respect to whether the creation of nonstate schools has responded to market incentives, including the perceived lack of quality of public schools, and how the public schools have responded when confronted with competition. These are key issues in the debate over the role of vouchers in the United States from which we may obtain insight from the Central European reforms. A number of results, reported in more detail in Filer and Munich (2002), suggest that market forces have worked, both in determining where nonstate schools have arisen and in the responses of state schools to competition. These results are limited to the Czech Republic because the larger number of Czech districts makes econometric work more practical.

Several factors appear to be associated with whether a nonstate *gymnázium* was established by 1995 in one of the 77 Czech districts studied. Among these factors were the education level of the population, the population density, and the relative size of the secondary school–age population. The critical finding, however, was that non-state academic high schools were significantly more likely to have been established where the public schools were doing a worse job in meeting their primary mission. Recall that the primary purpose of *gymnázia* is to prepare students for university admission. The success of a public school in meeting this mission can be measured by whether students from that school do better or worse in obtaining admission to university than would be expected based on the characteristics of the students and the area in which a school is located.[21] Districts where the public schools do worse than they should are significantly more likely to see private academic high schools established in competition with these poorly performing public schools.

There is also strong evidence that nonstate technical high schools in the Czech Republic arise when public schools are not fulfilling their mission. In particular, the proportion of students receiving private schooling in particular subjects is greater in regions where workers with training in these subjects are scarcer.[22] Private schooling is also more common in regions where there is significant unemployment, thereby indicating that current schools are not providing appropriate training. In contrast, there is absolutely no relationship between these two indicators of labor market demand and the provision of appropriate public school technical training. In short, nonstate schools have created opportunities for training in areas and fields where wages have been growing most rapidly, indicating increasing demand, and where unemployment rates are highest, indicating greater regional mismatch of workers and jobs. Public technical schools, on the other hand, exhibit no such market response. These results are consistent with recent reports that the unemployment rate of graduates from nonstate secondary schools is lower than that of graduates from public schools (Institute for Information on Education, 2000).

Finally, there is evidence that public schools respond when confronted by competition. Although the size of the cohort decline between 1992 and 1999 was similar across districts with differing degrees of nonstate competition, total enrollment in *gymnásia* remained almost constant when competition was extensive (more than 20% of local students entering academic high schools enrolling in nonstate alternatives) but declined by more than 20% when there was no competition. More critically, public *gymnásia* in districts where there was significant competition increased the number of classroom teachers by 22% and saw average class sizes fall by almost a third, a 50% greater drop than for public *gymnásia* that did not face extensive competition. The marked reduction in class size suggests that schools facing competition must be reallocating resources away from administrative and other noninstructional personnel toward classroom teachers—real differences in behavior designed to make the public *gymnázia* more attractive.

Perhaps the greatest difference can be seen in the true test of the performance of *gymnázia*: the success of graduates in gaining university admission. If districts are ranked according to the success of graduates from their state *gymnázia* in obtaining university admission, public *gymnázia* facing significant competition by 1995 improved their relative rank by 4.5 positions between 1996 and 1998, while those facing moderate competition improved their ranking by an average of 0.6 positions. Given that there are a fixed number of districts, these improvements came at the expense of state *gymnázia* in districts where there was no competition from nonstate alternatives, which saw their relative position deteriorate by an average of 1.4 positions. This result is not a statistical artifact created by selection effects, with the worst students leaving public *gymnázia* for private ones. Including admissions for *all* graduates in a district, whether from state or nonstate schools, makes the improvement in a district's performance when there is competition even stronger.

Unfortunately, there is also evidence of efforts on the part of state schools to capture the funding mechanism and reestablish their favored position. The fate of private schools in the Czech Republic underlines how critical it is in ensuring effective competition for funding of nonstate schools to be automatic and subject to the lowest possible level of interference from those with a vested interest in seeing alternatives to current arrangements fail.

The growth of nonstate schools came to an abrupt halt around 1996, with their share of schools and of students actually shrinking in the past few years. In large part this can be attributed to roadblocks created by administrators in the Czech Ministry of Education under the influence of lobbying from state schools. As discussed above, pressure from education authorities resulted in the principle of "equal treatment" for nonstate schools being abandoned in 1995, with the level of support for nonstate schools being reduced to 60% to 90% of the subsidy provided to state schools.

SUMMARY AND CONCLUSIONS

Post-communist Central Europe provides an interesting laboratory in which to investigate possible responses were a relatively large U.S.

state to adopt universal education vouchers. Although public schools were initially relatively good by objective standards, there was an initial surge in demand for private alternatives that eventually reached between 10% and 15% of the secondary school population. Private schools appear to have arisen in response to distinct market incentives. They are more common in areas where public school inertia has resulted in an undersupply of available slots. They are also more common where the public schools appear to be doing a worse job in their primary educational mission, as seen by the success rate of academic high schools in obtaining admission to the top universities for their graduates or of technical high schools in obtaining employment and high wages for their graduates. There is also preliminary evidence that public schools facing private competition improve their performance.

Of course, these results are at best preliminary and generalizations must be made with caution. Private schools arose in the Czech Republic and Hungary at a time of great turmoil in the educational system and the society in general. There has been a limited time over which to observe the responses of public schools. In summary, however, the preliminary evidence from the adoption of a nationwide voucher scheme in Central Europe, especially the Czech Republic, supports the claims of advocates for such systems. Private schools supported by vouchers seem to increase educational opportunity and spur public schools to improved performance.

NOTES

This research was supported in part by grant #98-1-152 from the Social Consequences of Economic Transformation in East Central Europe (SOCO) program of the Institut für die Wissenschaften vom Menschen, Vienna. The authors would like to thank Miroslav Prochazka and Michaela Islenhova and the Institute for Information in Education for information and expert assistance. Address correspondence to Randall K. Filer, Department of Economics, Hunter College, 695 Park Avenue, New York, NY 10021; e-mail *rfiler@ hunter.cuny.edu.* Address correspondence to Daniel Munich, CERGE-EI, P.O. Box 882, Politickych veznu 7, 111 21 Prague, Czech Republic; e-mail: munich@cesnet.cz.

1. One common technique was to offer university admission to the children of those in disfavor, but only in highly technical fields unrelated to their background or interests. Thus, a student who desired to study literature might be offered admission only to the faculty of mathematics. When the student was unable to pass, the authorities could say with a straight face that the student had not been denied access to education because of political consider-

ations, while ensuring that the student did not receive the benefits education conferred.

2. We will use the term *nonstate* to refer to all types of education that is administered by nongovernment entities such as churches, foundations, profit-making corporations, and individuals. Schools operated by these entities may or may not receive funding from the state according to local laws and policies.

3. It lags considerably behind the EU average of almost 16%. This average is heavily influenced by very high nonstate enrollments in countries such as France, Belgium, and the Netherlands where the tradition is for each of several antagonistic linguistic or religious groups to operate independent school systems with state funding.

4. Nonstate schools in the Czech Republic can be divided into two types—private and church sponsored. Among academic high schools, about 20% of nonstate schools are church related. The church-related share of other types of schools is much lower. In Hungary church-affiliated schools comprise two-thirds of nonstate academic high schools but 7% of technical high schools and 15% of vocational (apprentice) schools.

5. There are actually a larger number of districts, but we combine educational data for all jurisdictions in Prague into a single metropolitan area. Thus, we have data for greater Prague plus 76 additional districts.

6. Czech students sometimes studied only for 1 additional year if they remained in primary schools for the full 9 years possible.

7. In order to enroll in university, students must leave secondary school with an exam credential known as a *maturita*. Whether or not students receive this credential, and can therefore continue on to university studies, depends on their program or course of study. In the Czech Republic, all *gymnázia* and 96% of technical school programs, but only 14% of vocational school programs, lead to a *maturita* and the possibility of university admission. In fact, many vocation schools are 3 years or less in length and cannot provide the *maturita* required for university admission. There has arisen a market niche for schools providing what are known as "addendum" programs to allow such students to qualify for university.

8. In addition to university, there are so-called "higher professional schools" in some specialized fields that form an intermediate level of education between secondary and true tertiary education. These were legally established as secondary schools in the Czech Republic because the law on higher education did not allow for nonstate tertiary institutions before 1998.

9. Data are reported on the number of applications and the number of acceptances but not on the number of applicants.

10. Although beyond the scope of this chapter, we also note in Table 8.1 that the decline in Poland did not occur until several years after that in the Czech Republic and Hungary. Given this greater potential demand and the country's strong Catholic tradition, it is interesting to speculate as to why nonstate schools are less common in Poland than in nearby countries. One obvious answer involves the lower support provided to such schools in Po-

land, but this begs the question of why elected officials in Poland did not find it necessary to support nonstate education as extensively as did their neighbors.

11. Indeed, press reports indicate that applications for university enrollment to begin in the fall of 2000 were not substantially fewer than in normal years. Given that the number of secondary school graduates in June of 2000 was significantly reduced, this suggests that many applicants denied admission in previous years took advantage of the one-time opportunity to seek entry into highly demanded (and usually oversubscribed) programs. Impacts on the average quality of this class of "rejects" remain to be seen.

12. By 1996 there were 165 of the newly formed higher professional schools enrolling between 6,000 and 8,000 new students per year. These schools represent a move towards what in other European countries is known as "nonuniversity higher education." Since these schools are still marginal and serve a different role from the core types of secondary schools, we ignore them in the following discussion.

13. The difference in support is somewhat larger than these formulae would suggest, since public schools are also eligible for capital funds for construction and maintenance from state sources. During the past decade such investment funds added about 10% to the level of support for state schools that was not available to nonstate institutions.

14. In 1998 the mean annual tuition charged by nonstate *gymnázia* was approximately 15,000 Czech crowns ($450), with a range of from 1,500 to 29,000 crowns. By way of reference, the mean annual wage during this year was approximately 150,000 crowns per worker and most households had at least two workers.

15. Although often called such in the literature, the results presented are not technically "returns to education" since they show only the private benefit of a given degree and ignore both social returns and the costs associated with that degree. Munich and colleagues (1999) show that these adjustments do not have a substantial impact in the Czech Republic.

16. By way of illustration, in 1996, when the overall unemployment rate in Hungary was about 10%, the rate for youths 19 or younger was more than 25%. Those with only a primary school education had a rate of about 15%, while the rate for secondary school graduates was about half as large (Keune, 1998). Czech unemployment did not increase substantially until the end of the 1990s. In 1999 approximately 8% of university graduates were unemployed directly after leaving school, compared with around 13% of academic high school graduates, 15% of technical school graduates, and 20% of vocational school graduates (Institute for Information on Education, 2000).

17. Determination of the enrollment rates for the Czech Republic is complicated by the extension of basic school that occurred in 1996. We have omitted 14-year-olds from the relevant population in 1996 and later. The fact that there is no discontinuity in the trend line in Figure 8.1 at this point suggests that this is approximately the correct adjustment. This may account for the apparent abnormality of enrollment rates reaching over 100% in 1996

and 1997, although, as discussed above, there may also have been some students who remained in secondary school beyond normal ages to acquire additional vocational training.

18. In the mid-1990s, roughly 80% of Czech *gymnázium* graduates, 37% of technical secondary school graduates, and 22% of eligible vocational school graduates (i.e., the 8% to 10% of vocational school graduates who were enrolled in courses leading to the *maturita*) were successful in enrolling in university within 2 years of their graduation from secondary school. Obviously some graduates elect not to apply to university, but, overall, places are still severely rationed.

19. These figures exclude a small number of highly specialized schools such as dance and music academies.

20. This obviously raises questions of overcapacity and excess spending on fixed plant. Although there have been attempts to close unneeded public schools, these attempts—given entrenched bureaucracies and reluctance to commute long distances—have met with only limited success. Excess capacity in public school buildings has, however, facilitated the rise of nonstate schools, many of which have rented unused classrooms from state schools.

21. Although these results were derived independently, the methodology used to assess school quality is similar to that devised by National Opinion Research Center (NORC) at the University of Chicago for a recent survey of high school quality in the United States ("Outstanding High Schools," 1999).

22. Where labor scarcity is measured by the extent to which workers in a given region and occupation have had wage increases since the start of transition beyond what would be predicted based on their age, sex, and so on.

REFERENCES

Andrle, A. (1998). Economic transformation and job-related migration in the Czech Republic during 1992–1996. *Statistika, 5*. Prague: Czech Statistical Office.

Aradi, Z., Halász, G., & Nagy, J. D. (1998). Reforms in education financing. In L. Bokros & J. Dethier (Eds.), *Public finance reform during the transition: The experience of Hungary* (pp. 255–286). Washington, DC: World Bank.

Centre for Economic Policy Research [CEPR]. (1998). *Mediating the transition: Labour markets in Central and Eastern Europe* (Forum Report of the Economic Policy Initiative). London: Centre for Economic Policy Research.

Chase, R. S. (1998). Markets for communist human capital: Returns to education and experience in post-communist Czech Republic and Slovakia. *Industrial and Labor Relations Review, 51*(3), 401–423.

Erbenová, M. (1997). *Essays on disequilibria in early transition.* Unpublished Ph.D. dissertation, Center for Economics Research and Graduate Education–Economics Institute, Prague.

Filer, R. K., & Hanousek, J. (2000). *Output changes and inflationary bias in transition* (Discussion Paper No. 14/98). Center for Economics Research and Graduate Education–Economics Institute, Prague.

Filer, R. K., Jurajda, J., & Plánovsk, J. (1998). *Returns to the market: Valuing human capital in the post-transition Czech and Slovak Republics* (Working Paper No. 125). CERGE-EI, Prague.

Filer, R. K, Jurajda, J., & Plánovsk, J. (1999). Education and wages in the Czech and Slovak Republics during transition. *Labour Economics, 6*(4), 581–593.

Filer, R. K., & Munich, D. (2002). *Responses of private and public schools to voucher funding* (Working Paper No. 160). CERGE-EI, Prague.

Institute for Information on Education (UIV), Ministry of Education, Youth and Sport in the Czech Republic. (1999). *Vývojová ročenka: školství v České republice 1989/90–1998/99* [*Annual trends: The school system in the Czech Republic 1989/90–1998/99*]. Prague: Author.

Institute for Information on Education (UIV), Ministry of Education, Youth and Sport in the Czech Republic. (2000). *Co potrebuji absolventi pro uplatneni na trhu prace* [What Do School Graduates Need to Succeed in the Labor Market?]. Prague: Institute for Information on Education (UIV).

Keune, M. (1998). *Youth unemployment in Hungary and Poland* (Employment and Training Paper No. 20). Geneva: International Labour Organization.

Laporte, B., & Ringold, D. (1997). *Trends in education access and financing during the transition in Central and Eastern Europe* (Technical Paper No. 361). Washington, DC: World Bank.

Laporte, B., & Schweitzer, J. (1994). Education and training. In N. Barr (Ed.), *Labor markets and social policy in Central and Eastern Europe: The transition and beyond.* Oxford: Oxford University Press.

Micklewright, J. (1999). Education, inequality and transition. *Economics of Transition, 7*(4), 343–376.

Munich, D., Svejnar, J., & Terrell, K. (1999). *Returns to human capital under the Communist wage grid and during the transition to a market economy* (Discussion Paper No. 29/99). CERGE-EI, Prague.

Organisation for Economic Cooperation and Development (OECD). (1997). *Education at a glance.* Paris: Author.

Outstanding high schools. (1999, January 18). *U.S. News and World Report.* pp 46–51.

Paihle, A. (1998). La hausse des inégalités salariales en Europe centrale au cours de la transition. [The extent of salary inequality in Central Europe during the transition.] *Economie Internationale 75*(3), 105–133.

Svejnar, J. (1999). Labor markets in the transitional economies of Central and Eastern Europe. In O. Ashenfelter and R. Layard (Eds.), *Handbook of labor economics* (Vol 3B) (pp. 2809–2853). Amsterdam: North Holland.

Tomášek, V., Straková, J., & Palečková, J. (1997). *Třeti mezinárodni výzkum matematického a přiřodovědného vzdeláváni*, [TIMSS international rankings of education in mathematics and the natural sciences]. Prague: Institute for Information on Education (UIV).

Varga, J. (1995). Returns to education in Hungary. *Acta Oeconomica, 47*(1–2), 203–215.

About the Contributors

Max Angus is Professor of Education and Head of the School of Education at Edith Cowan University in Western Australia. He has had extensive policy making experience at state education while serving as Executive Director of Schools in the Western Australian Ministry of Education. In these capacities he has been actively involved in state and national programs of school reform.

Martin Carnoy is a labor economist with a special interest in the relation between the economy and the educational system. To this end, he studies historical and comparative international educational systems. With the recent globalization of the labor force and unprecedented shifts in U.S. domestic demand for cognitive skills, Dr. Carnoy is evaluating the possibility of rapid educational reform and its effect on the labor force.

Holger Daun is Professor in International and Comparative Education at the Institute of International Education, Stockholm University, Sweden. He is involved in different tasks in many countries in the world (including training of researchers and his own research and evaluations) for Sida, Sweden, UNDP, Unesco and others. His most recent books are *Educational Restructuring in the Context of Globalization and National Policy* and *Democracy in Textbooks and Student Minds*. Currently he is conducting research on educational restructuring in several countries, among them his native Sweden.

Randall K. Filer is Professor of Economics at Hunter College and the Graduate Center, City University of New York and CERGE-EI, Prague (a joint workplace of Charles University and the Academy of Sciences of the Czech Republic). Dr. Filer is also a Research Associate of the William Davidson Institute of the University of Michigan.

Edward B. Fiske, formerly the Education Editor of *The New York Times*, is an education writer and editor who has written extensively on school reform in the United States and other countries. He is the author of *Smart Schools, Smart Kids* and co-author (with Helen F.

Ladd) of *When Schools Compete: A Cautionary Tale.* He is currently working on a study with Helen Ladd of South Africa's efforts to construct an equitable and democratic state education system since the end of apartheid in 1994. He is also author of *The Fiske Guide to Colleges,* an annual publication.

Helen F. Ladd is Professor of Public Policy Studies and Associate Director of the Sanford Institute of Public Policy at Duke University. An expert on education policy, she has written extensively on school choice, education finance, and educational accountability. She is the co-author (with Edward B. Fiske) of *When Schools Compete: A Cautionary Tale* and editor of *Holding Schools Accountable: Performance-Based Reform in Education.* She is currently writing a book with Edward Fiske on education reform in South Africa.

Patrick J. McEwan is Assistant Professor in the Department of Economics at Wellesley College. Previously he taught in the Department of Educational Policy Studies at the University of Illinois at Urbana-Champaign. He completed his Ph.D. in education at Stanford University, in addition to master's degrees in economics and international development. His published books (with Henry Levin) include *Cost-Effectiveness Analysis: Methods and Applications* and *Cost-Effectiveness and Educational Policy: 2002 Yearbook of the American Education Finance Association.* He is the author of numerous journal articles, book chapters, and reports, and he has consulted on education policy and evaluation at the Inter-American Development Bank, RAND, UNESCO, and the ministries of education of several countries.

Daniel Munich is Assistant Professor of Economics at CERGE-EI and Research Associate of the William Davidson Institute of the University of Michigan.

John Pampallis has been the Director of the Centre for Education Policy Development, Evaluation and Management (CEPD) since November 1996. Prior to his joining the CEPD, he was Director of the Education Policy Unit at the University of Natal. He has taught at schools in South Africa, Botswana, Canada, and Tanzania. In Tanzania, he spent 8 years as a teacher and deputy vice principal at the Solomon Mahlangu Freedom College, a school for young South African exiles during the apartheid period. He has acquired extensive experience in the field of education policy since returning to South Africa in 1991. In 1995, he was appointed by the Minister of Education to the Committee to Review School Organisation, Governance, and Funding (the "Hunter Committee"). He has worked with the national and provincial departments of education in South Africa in developing policies and building management capacity; he has conducted and overseen numerous research and capacity building projects in the area of education. His recent publications include *The State, Education and Equity in Post Apartheid South Africa: The Impact of State Policies*, which he co-edited with Enver Motala.

David N. Plank is Director of the Education Policy Center at Michigan State University, and Professor in the College of Education. He is a specialist in the areas of educational policy and education finance. He received his Ph.D. in the Economics of Education from the University of Chicago in 1983. He has worked as a consultant in education policy development for the World Bank, USAID, the United Nations Development Program, the Ford Foundation, and Ministries of Education in several countries in Africa and Latin America. He has published four books and numerous articles and chapters in a variety of fields, including the history of education and the economics of education. His current research focuses on issues related to charter schools and school choice, and on the development of effective accountability systems in education.

Gary Sykes is Professor in the Departments of Educational Administration and Teacher Education, College of Education, Michigan State University. He specializes in educational policy, leadership, and teaching. Recent research interests include school choice, teacher leadership, and school improvement processes. His most recent book is *Teaching as the Learning Profession*, with Linda Darling-Hammond.

Mun C. Tsang is Professor of Economics and Education and Director of the Center on Chinese Education, Teachers College, Columbia University. His scholarly interests include costs and financing of education, economic effects of education, and education policy and development in China.

Geoffrey Walford is Professor of Education Policy at the University of Oxford. He has published more than 30 books and over 150 academic articles and book chapters on such areas as school choice, private education, ethnography, and research methods. He is Editor of *The British Educational Reseach Journal* and is Series Editor for Studies in Educational Ethography. His most recent book is *Doing Qualitative Educational Research*.

Index